The Food You **Crave**

Luscious Recipes for a **Healthy Life**

Ellie Krieger

The Taunton Press

For Thom and Bella

 The Taunton Press

The Taunton Press, Inc., 63 South Main Street, PO Box 5506, Newtown, CT 06470-5506
e-mail: tp@taunton.com

Editor: Pamela Hoenig
Copy editor: Karen Fraley
Proofreader: Li Agen
Indexer: Heidi Blough
Jacket/cover design: Stark Design
Interior design: Stark Design
Layout: Cathy Cassidy
Photographer: Christopher Hirsheimer
Food and prop stylist: Melissa Hamilton

Library of Congress Cataloging-in-Publication Data
Krieger, Ellie.
 The food you crave : luscious recipes for a healthy life / Ellie Krieger.
     p. cm.
 Includes bibliographical references and index.
 ISBN 978-1-60085-021-9 (alk. paper)
 1. Cookery. 2. Nutrition. I. Title.

TX714.K75 2008
641.5--dc22
                            2007037528

Printed in the United States of America
10 9 8 7 6 5 4 3 2

The following manufacturers/names appearing in *The Food You Crave* are trademarks:
Corn Chex®, Vespa®

Acknowledgments

This book is a culmination of the work and dedication of so many talented people.
It could not have been accomplished without them and the loving support of my family.
I am honored to have the opportunity to express my gratitude to them here.

First and foremost, thank you, Thom, my incredible husband and best friend, for taking
care of the home front, enabling me to dedicate myself to this book and *Healthy Appetite.*
You are my dream man, the best possible teammate, and a darn good taste tester. Thanks to
my daughter, Bella, for giving everything I do a deeper meaning and for being my sunshine.
And thank you, Mom and Dad, for making me believe I could accomplish anything and giving
me the tools to do it.

Thanks to my managers and agents, Robert Flutie, Hilary Polk Williams, Jane Dystel,
and Miriam Goderich, for keeping the ship moving on course, even through choppy water.
And thank you, Marc Szafran, for your wisdom and guidance and for genuinely being my
advocate. Thank you, chefs Jacqueline Torren and Adeena Sussman, for your culinary expertise,
talent, and friendship, and Elisabeth D'Alto, RD, for helping me pull it all together and for your
skill and dedication. You all helped me meet some intense deadlines without compromising
top-quality work. Thanks for coming through.

I am especially grateful to work with so many wonderful people at Food Network and
I am thrilled to be part of their family. Thank you, Bob Tuschman, for your vision for me
and *Healthy Appetite.* I am honored to work with someone I respect so wholeheartedly.
Brooke Johnson, thank you for all the opportunities and for your great leadership.
Thanks to Roni Weinstock for believing in me and helping elevate the show to where it is.

Thank you, Susan Stockton and everyone in the culinary department, for all your valued
support. And thanks to Lisa DelColle and the public relations team and Susie Fogelson and
the marketing team for your well-coordinated work spreading the word. Thanks to you also,
Irene Wong, for bringing me to the table.

I am lucky enough to work with the most creative, energetic, talented production team
imaginable—Rachel Purnell, Olivia Ball, and everyone at Pacific Productions. You continually

amaze and inspire me. Thanks for making me look good, for producing a fantastic television show, and managing to keep it all fun, even when we are working 14-hour days. And thank you, Suzanne Katz, for your makeup artistry and good company.

Last but definitely not least, thanks to everyone at Taunton Press who literally helped create this book and connect me with the readers. Pam Hoenig, my editor, you pushed me in the best possible way to take this book to a higher level and make it truly excellent. Somehow we managed to be a fine-tuned machine in a matter of months. Thanks for all of your insights and hard work. Thanks also to art director Alison Wilkes for overseeing the beautiful design and photography of this book, to marketing director Melissa Possick and publicists Carrie Bachman and Pamela Duevel for getting the word out on the book, to sales director Kevin Hamric and his team at Taunton and Random House for getting the book into the stores, and to everyone else at Taunton who helped make this book happen. And a big thank you to photographer Christopher Hirsheimer and food stylist Melissa Hamilton for making me and my food look their best.

Contents

The Food You Crave—In a Healthier Way!

This book is much more than a collection of recipes, it is a new way of looking at food—a fresh approach to eating that, just like my Food Network show *Healthy Appetite* is about having the food you crave in a healthier way, using real ingredients prepared simply enough for every day but special and inspired enough to wow you.

Most people think the words luscious and healthy can't be used in the same sentence. I can hardly blame them since many foods billed as "good-for-you" are either boring—dry broiled fish and plain steamed vegetables—or a lame replica of what we really want. If you have ever had a fat-free muffin, you know what I mean; it is certainly not crave-able.

Like you, I crave food that is bursting with flavor and aroma. Food that draws you in and leaves you satisfied. Guess what? That kind of food can be healthy. Take a perfectly ripe peach, for example. Nothing smells better. And what could be more scrumptious and sensuous than taking a juicy bite and having the nectar drip down your chin? You don't need a recipe for a piece of fruit, but the recipes in this book are based on the same peachy idea. You can have food that is enticingly delicious as well as good for you.

Let me ask you this: Are you 100% satisfied with the way you eat? Chances are your relationship with food is a mixed bag. Food gives you pleasure, it helps you unwind, it brings you together with friends and family, and it is one of life's great joys. But it can also provoke feelings of guilt, stress, and frustration and leaves an aftertaste of knowing you don't feel or look as good as you could because of your eating habits. I'll bet sometimes you find that even though your belly is full, you are still somehow unsatisfied.

That struggle is not surprising since the same-old-same-old way of eating often means quantity over quality and makes us a slave to our taste buds at the expense of our bodies. When we try to be "virtuous," we are so dissatisfied and deprived that we are bound to burst into overindulgence. Maybe worst of all, we often eat so mindlessly that even our taste buds don't have their moment, so we leave the table stuffed but not content.

This book can help you turn that all around and change the way you think (or don't think!) about food. Here you will discover a refreshing, completely positive way of eating—one that pleases your taste buds and your body, helps you feel and look better, takes the stress out of food, eliminates guilt, and maximizes satisfaction. This is your tool kit for a relationship with food that is pleasurable and fortifying, physically and emotionally. It's a kit that can help you get there even if you are crunched for time and can't spend a fortune on ingredients. Once you start and see how do-able and rewarding it is, you are going to want to eat like this for the rest of your life.

Filling your kitchen with beautiful, fresh, real ingredients is the starting point and a joy in itself. Your senses will be fulfilled before you even take a bite, with the aroma of fresh herbs, the color and snap of fresh vegetables, the sizzle of grilled meats and fish. You'll use unctuous oils, fragrant vinegars, nutty grains, toothsome breads and pastas, hearty beans, the refreshing zest of citrus, ripe red berries, tangy buttermilk, creamy yogurt, and heady

spices, just to name a few. You will have the highest quality convenience food at your fingertips so you can whip up a delightful meal even on the busiest days.

Besides more than 200 recipes, you will find loads of tips and ideas for getting the most out of your food, from grab-and-go eating to the best lunch options for staying energized. I have also included a New Way Pantry list so you can start fresh with the best ingredients.

As a true food lover and a dietitian, I have always said, to get people to eat well, don't say a word about health, just cook fantastic food for them. This book is my way of bringing delicious food to your table. You will love it because it tastes incredible. But it just happens to be good for you, too. So if you are ready to enjoy food in a whole new way, this is the place to be.

a healthier way to eat (& cook)

In my food world, there is no fear or guilt, only joy and balance. So no ingredient is ever off-limits. Rather, all of the recipes here follow my Usually-Sometimes-Rarely philosophy. Notice there is no Never.

The Usually foods are the backbone of each recipe and the cornerstone of a healthy diet—colorful vegetables and fruit, whole grains, lean meats and fish, beans, nuts, lowfat dairy, and healthful oils. People who focus on these foods tend to be leaner, have better skin, retain youthfulness, and are able to get more out of life instead of being laid up with illness. Most importantly, these foods are delicious. They are Mother Nature's best work, a full spectrum of irresistible flavors and textures—sweet, savory, tart, crunchy, tender, juicy, crisp, chewy.

Sometimes I make the Usually foods the dominant flavor force in a recipe, like in Tomatoes with Green Goddess Dressing (page 123). Other times I sneak them into a seemingly sinful food so you don't even know they are there, as in my Macaroni and Four Cheeses (page 168).

Sometimes foods are somewhat more refined, like regular pasta, white flour, and sugar, or a little higher in saturated fat, like chicken thighs and some cuts of red meat. They aren't on the A list when it comes to health, but they can enhance a recipe and make a food more decadent and crave-able, so I sprinkle them in here and there. Sometimes foods help make it possible to have just about any food you want in a healthier way. For example, I make my Jambalaya on page 236 with white rice because you really need good old Southern-style rice to get that great classic texture. But I power-up that Sometimes base with lots of shrimp and vegetables, making it a good-for-you and satisfying dish.

Rarely foods are those many nutritionists say are off-limits and most chefs use with a heavy hand: butter, full-fat cheese, bacon, cream, and the like. As a foodie and dietitian, I have found a way to use these ingredients strategically in small amounts for maximum impact, so they add loads of flavor and appeal without upsetting the healthful balance.

My Parmesan Mashed Potatoes on page 262 is a perfect example. I start with naturally creamy Yukon Gold potatoes and use lowfat milk and lowfat buttermilk, instead of butter and cream. Then

CRISPIN
a.k.a.
MUTSU
$1.25/

I stir in a little freshly grated Parmesan cheese and top the mound of potatoes with a pat of real butter. We eat with our eyes, so by putting the butter front-and-center, the perception of buttery-ness affects every bite. And the rich cheese adds unmistakable depth and flavor. The end result is the creamy, flavor-packed, comforting mashed potatoes you yearn for, only better for you.

Keeping It FRESH

It's no accident that most of the foods on my Usually list are fresh foods. Sure I use some convenience foods, like unsweetened frozen fruit and canned tomatoes, but my rule of thumb is to buy ingredients as close to their original state as possible. That means buying the freshest available ingredients and preparing them in a way that is simple yet inspired, allowing them to shine.

Cooking this way is so easy to do and so much better for you. For example, it takes about the same amount of time to prepare frozen vegetables prepacked in lemon sauce (frighteningly, containing no actual lemon) as it does to whip up my fresh and fragrant Asparagus with Lemon and Tarragon (page 252), which is so much tastier and is better for you. To me, it's no contest. Knowing exactly what is in your food and being able to relish the experience of preparing it is invaluable.

Cooking from scratch (or close to it) sounds like a romantic notion of the past, something that went the way of frilly aprons and *Leave It to Beaver*. But as a busy working mom, I assure you (and I'll show you) that you don't need to be June Cleaver to make fabulous food. You just don't need to use a lot of processed packaged products to get dinner on the table fast and stress free.

Keeping It REAL

As I just mentioned, I steer clear of foods that have artificial additives or a list of ingredients that reads more like a chemistry experiment than something you want to eat, even if they are lower in fat or sugar than the original. Foods with a lot of chemical ingredients tend to taste like they do, and no one really understands the long-term cumulative health effects of eating them. So, with just a few exceptions, I prefer to go for the real deal. For example, I'm fine with nonfat yogurt because its ingredients are the same as regular, just minus the fat. But I'll take a little bit of real whipped cream over chemical-laden nonfat whipped topping any day.

A Pinch of Salt

One of the additives I try to minimize is sodium. Don't get me wrong. I am not against salt—it is an essential flavor enhancer I use in nearly all my recipes. But I add it sparingly, and I make a point of cooking with no-salt-added or low-sodium canned ingredients whenever possible so that I can better control the saltiness of the recipe.

Knowledge Is Power

I am not a big numbers person. People shouldn't come to dinner with a calculator in hand, just a good appetite. But I believe that information about food can help us understand it and make better choices. That's why I have included nutrition facts for each recipe with the amount of calories, fat, protein, carbohydrate, fiber, cholesterol, and sodium in each serving. Since some fats are beneficial and others detrimental, I further break down fat into saturated (bad fat), and monounsaturated and polyunsaturated (good fats). Note that the information provided for each recipe is per serving and excludes optional ingredients or anything added to taste.

To help put the nutrition breakdown in perspective, here are some daily total numbers to shoot for based on a 2,000-calorie diet (the calorie level for most moderately active women):

Total fat: 65g (Saturated fat, 20g or less; Monounsaturated fat, 25g; Polyunsaturated fat, 20g)
Protein: 90g
Carbohydrate: 275g
Fiber: 28g or more
Cholesterol: 300mg or less
Sodium: 2,300mg or less

Real Power Food

One thing that amazes me about these recipes is that they are absolutely brimming with essential vitamins and minerals. It is great to know the food you are enjoying is truly nourishing your body. To share that feel-good factor with you and help you identify sources of nutrients you may be trying to focus on, I have listed good and excellent sources of nutrients in each recipe. To qualify as a good source, a serving must contain at least 10% of the Daily Value (the standard daily recommended intake); to be called an excellent source, it needs to provide at least 20% of the Daily Value.

Essential Nutrients for Your Good Health

NUTRIENT	DAILY VALUE*	FUNCTIONS
BIOTIN	0.3mg	Helps break down fat, protein, and carbohydrates into energy.
CALCIUM	1,000mg	Plays an important role in developing and maintaining healthy bones and teeth. It also helps to maintain normal blood pressure.
CHLORIDE	3,400mg	Aids in the digestion of foods.
CHROMIUM	120mcg	Works with insulin to utilize sugar from food.
COPPER	2mg	Helps to develop and maintain red blood cells, healthy hair, and skin color.
FIBER	25mg	Helps regulate the digestive system and may help protect against heart disease.
FOLATE	0.4mg	Helps produce and maintain new cells. It's also involved in making neurotransmitters, like serotonin, which regulate mood, sleep, and appetite.
IODINE	150mcg	Necessary for normal thyroid function.
IRON	18mg	Essential for healthy blood cells, which carry oxygen throughout the body.
MAGNESIUM	400mg	Functions in muscle relaxation and contraction. It also helps convert food into energy, support the immune system, and promote normal blood pressure.
MANGANESE	2mg	Plays an important role in the digestion of protein and carbohydrates.

NUTRIENT	DAILY VALUE*	FUNCTIONS
MOLYBDENUM	75mcg	Essential for normal growth and development. It's important in releasing iron from storage in the body.
NIACIN	20mg	Required to help release energy from carbohydrates.
PANTOTHENIC ACID	10mg	Helps break down fat, protein, and carbohydrates into energy.
PHOSPHORUS	1,000mg	Aids in the formation of healthy bones and teeth. It also plays a role in many different body functions, such as converting food into energy.
POTASSIUM	3,500mg	Helps maintain fluid balance, and regulates heartbeat and blood pressure.
RIBOFLAVIN	1.7mg	Important for normal growth and development, producing red blood cells, and releasing energy from carbohydrates.
SELENIUM	70mcg	Works with antioxidants in the body to help prevent diseases like cancer and heart disease.
THIAMIN	1.5mg	Helps the body convert carbohydrates into energy. Essential for the function of the heart, muscles, and nervous system.
VITAMIN A	5,000 IU	Helps promote good vision and build and maintain healthy teeth, bones, and skin.
VITAMIN B_6	2mg	Important in building proteins like hormones and red blood cells. It also regulates your nervous system.
VITAMIN B_{12}	6mcg	Necessary for the building and maintaining of nerve cells and red blood cells in the body.
VITAMIN C	60mg	A powerful antioxidant, it helps boost the immune system, promotes skin repair, and may help protect against cancer.
VITAMIN D	400 IU	Helps form and maintain healthy bones and teeth. It may also have a role in cancer prevention.
VITAMIN E	30 IU	Functions as an antioxidant in the body to help protect it from diseases like heart disease and cancer.
VITAMIN K	80mcg	Helps to regulate normal blood clotting.
ZINC	15mg	Promotes normal growth and development and helps the immune system. It also helps aid in the digestion of protein and detoxifying alcohol in the liver.

*measured in grams (g), international units (IU), micromilligrams (mcg), or milligrams (mg)

The New Way Pantry

Eating and cooking well starts with having the right foods at your fingertips. Use this pantry list as your starting point. If you keep them on hand, you'll be able to whip up a great meal anytime. Whenever you can, purchase organic—besides minimizing your exposure to pesticides and being better for the environment, organic products tend to contain less sodium and additives.

OILS & VINEGARS
Canola oil
Extra-virgin olive oil
Toasted sesame oil
Nonstick cooking spray
Balsamic vinegar
Cider vinegar
Red wine vinegar
Rice vinegar
White wine vinegar

CONDIMENTS AND OTHER FLAVOR BOOSTERS
Asian fish sauce
Calamata olives
Canola mayonnaise
Capers
Chipotle chiles in adobo sauce
Dijon mustard
Hot pepper sauce
Roasted red peppers, packed in water
Soy sauce, low-sodium
Sun-dried tomatoes, not oil-packed
Thai red curry paste

ON THE SHELF
Beans, preferably no-salt-added (black, cannellini, pinto, and garbanzo beans)
Broth, low-sodium (chicken, beef, vegetable)
Mandarin oranges, packed in natural juice or light syrup
Pineapple, packed in natural juice
Solid-pack pumpkin
Tomatoes, preferably no-salt-added (diced, whole, tomato sauce, tomato paste)
Silken tofu (in the shelf-stable box)
Chunk light tuna, packed in water
Canned salmon

SWEETENERS
Brown sugar (light and dark)
Dark chocolate (60–70% cocoa solids, bittersweet)
Granulated sugar
Honey
Maple syrup
Unsulfured molasses
Unsweetened cocoa powder (natural and Dutch processed)

NUTS, SEEDS & DRIED FRUITS
An assortment of shelled, unsalted nuts and seeds (almonds, walnuts, peanuts, pecans, pistachios, pine nuts, pumpkin seeds, sunflower seeds, sesame seeds)
Creamy natural peanut butter
Tahini (sesame paste)
Dried fruit (apricots, cherries, cranberries, dates, figs, raisins)

BREAD, FLOUR & GRAINS

All-purpose flour
Buckwheat flour
Whole-wheat flour
Whole-grain pastry flour
Oats (old-fashioned rolled, quick-cooking)
Yellow cornmeal
Plain dry bread crumbs, preferably whole-wheat
Pasta (whole-wheat and regular, in a variety of shapes)
Soba noodles
Bulgur wheat
Pearl barley
Rice (brown, wild, Arborio, white long grain)
Whole-wheat couscous

IN THE FREEZER

Packages of unsweetened sliced peaches
Packages of unsweetened berries (strawberries, raspberries, blueberries)
Artichoke hearts
Broccoli
Corn
Lima beans
Peas
Puréed winter squash
Shelled edamame
Shrimp
Spinach

A Word about Serving Sizes

Everyone has a different appetite and calorie needs, so in reality there is always a range of how many a given recipe serves. My husband eats about twice what I do, so a dish that would make four helpings for me would only make two for him. But in order to do the nutrition analysis I had to pick a number. So I chose to base the serving sizes on portions that would satisfy the average woman. If you are serving a group of lumberjacks or marathon runners (or if you are one yourself!), adjust the portions accordingly. The same goes for a family of hungry teenagers.

Crave It, Make It, Enjoy It!

Now that you have delved into this book, you are already on your way to eating and cooking better. And the best is yet to come. There are some seriously delicious foods in this book to explore. All are easy to prepare and designed to make the most of your time in the kitchen. As you explore them, keep in mind that enjoying a great meal doesn't start with the first forkful. It starts with the pleasure of choosing and purchasing sumptuous fresh ingredients and extends to the joy of preparing it, surrounding yourself with aromas and textures, and anticipating the first bite. Finally, there's the glory of eating it. And with this food there is another big payoff: how much better you will feel and look from enjoying food in this new way. It's really more than just cooking, it's a cooking way of life, and it is one that is ultimately fulfilling. So don't start tomorrow. Start right now!

breakfast

Whole-Wheat Pancakes with Strawberry Sauce

These pancakes are a weekend favorite at my house. My five-year-old daughter, Bella, begs to make these with me, and I am happy to oblige. The funny thing is, she always wants to "play Food Network," where she pretends to host her own show. My favorite part is when she tells the "camera" that it is important to use whole grain. Like mother, like daughter!

In these pancakes I use half whole-wheat flour, for all the antioxidants and fiber it contains, and half all-purpose to ensure they are extra light and fluffy. The brilliant red strawberry sauce cradles them in a perfect juicy balance of tangy and sweet. These are also fun to cut into heart shapes with a cookie cutter for Valentine's Day.

¾ cup all-purpose flour

¾ cup whole-grain pastry flour or whole-wheat flour

1½ teaspoons baking powder

½ teaspoon baking soda

¼ teaspoon salt

2 large eggs

1 cup lowfat buttermilk

¾ cup nonfat milk

1 tablespoon honey

¼ teaspoon vanilla extract

Cooking spray

Strawberry Sauce (recipe follows)

Confectioners' sugar (optional)

SERVES 4
MAKES TWELVE 4-INCH PANCAKES; SERVING SIZE: 3 PANCAKES AND ⅓ CUP SAUCE

PER SERVING
CALORIES: 310;
TOTAL FAT: 3.5G
MONO: 0G,
POLY: 0G;
SAT: 1G,
PROTEIN: 13G;
CARB: 59G;
FIBER: 5G;
CHOL: 110MG;
SODIUM: 420MG

EXCELLENT SOURCE OF CALCIUM, FIBER, FOLATE, IODINE, MANGANESE, PHOSPHORUS, PROTEIN, RIBOFLAVIN, SELENIUM, THIAMIN, VITAMIN C

GOOD SOURCE OF COPPER, IRON, MAGNESIUM, NIACIN, PANTOTHENIC ACID, POTASSIUM, VITAMIN B6, ZINC

In a large bowl, whisk together the flours, baking powder, baking soda, and salt. In a medium bowl, beat together the eggs, buttermilk, nonfat milk, honey, and vanilla.

Coat a large nonstick griddle or skillet with cooking spray and preheat over medium-low heat. Stir the wet ingredients into the dry ingredients, mixing only enough to combine them. The batter will be somewhat lumpy. Use a ¼-cup measure to ladle the batter onto the griddle or skillet. Flip the pancakes when they are golden brown on the bottom and bubbles are forming on top, about 1½ minutes. Cook the other side until golden brown, about another 1½ minutes. Keep the pancakes warm in a 200°F oven as you finish cooking the remaining ones.

Ladle about ⅓ cup of the strawberry sauce onto each plate, place the pancakes on top, sprinkle with confectioners' sugar, if using, and serve.

Strawberry Sauce

This luscious sauce is also a delicious way to flavor your morning oatmeal and is fabulous drizzled over light ice cream or angel food cake.

2 pints (16 ounces) fresh strawberries, hulled, or 4 cups frozen unsweetened
   strawberries, thawed
1 teaspoon fresh lemon juice
2 tablespoons pure maple syrup

Place the strawberries in a food processor and process them into a chunky purée. Transfer the purée to a small saucepan over low heat and heat just until warm. Stir in the lemon juice and maple syrup.

SERVES 4
MAKES 1⅓ CUPS;
SERVING SIZE:
⅓ CUP

PER SERVING
CALORIES: 63;
TOTAL FAT: 0G;
PROTEIN: 0.7G;
CARB: 15.5G;
FIBER: 2.2G;

CHOL: 0MG;
SODIUM: 2MG

**EXCELLENT
SOURCE OF**
MANGANESE,
VITAMIN C

**GOOD
SOURCE OF**
FIBER

* **DID YOU KNOW?**
Although strawberries taste sweet, they have one of the lowest sugar contents of any fruit and are packed with vitamin C and fiber. Just 1 cup of strawberries has more vitamin C than a medium-size orange!

Blueberry Buckwheat Pancakes

There is something ultrasatisfying about the bold, nutty taste and hearty texture of buckwheat. After eating these pancakes I feel like I am ready for just about anything! They are moist and rich and the blueberries inside become warm, juice-bursting globes embedded in the fragrant cake.

¾ cup buckwheat flour

¾ cup whole-grain pastry flour or whole-wheat flour

1½ teaspoons baking powder

½ teaspoon baking soda

¼ teaspoon salt

1 cup lowfat buttermilk

¾ cup nonfat milk

1 tablespoon honey

2 large eggs

2 tablespoons canola oil

2 cups fresh or (thawed) frozen unsweetened blueberries

Cooking spray

½ cup pure maple syrup

SERVES 4
MAKES TWELVE 4-INCH PANCAKES; SERVING SIZE: 3 PANCAKES PLUS ¼ CUP EXTRA BLUEBERRIES AND 2 TABLESPOONS MAPLE SYRUP

EXCELLENT SOURCE OF
CALCIUM, FIBER, IODINE, MANGANESE, PROTEIN, RIBOFLAVIN, THIAMIN, VITAMIN K

PER SERVING
CALORIES: 435;
TOTAL FAT: 11G
  MONO: 5G;
  POLY: 2.5G;
  SAT: 1.5G,
PROTEIN: 13G;
CARB: 73G;
FIBER: 7G;
CHOL: 110MG;
SODIUM: 640MG

GOOD SOURCE OF
IRON, PHOSPHORUS, POTASSIUM, SELENIUM, VITAMIN C, ZINC

In a large bowl, whisk together the flours, baking powder, baking soda, and salt. In a medium bowl, beat together the buttermilk, nonfat milk, honey, eggs, and oil. Stir the wet ingredients into the dry ingredients, mixing only enough to combine them. The batter will be somewhat lumpy. Stir in 1 cup of the berries.

Coat a large nonstick griddle or skillet with cooking spray and preheat over medium heat. Use a ¼-cup measure to ladle the batter onto the griddle or skillet. Flip the pancakes when they are golden brown on the bottom and bubbles are forming on top, about 1½ minutes. Cook the other side until golden brown, about another 1½ minutes. Keep the pancakes warm in a 200°F oven as you finish cooking the remaining ones.

Serve topped with the remaining blueberries and the maple syrup.

Pumpkin Pie Muffins

These scrumptious muffins are brimming with fragrant pumpkin pie spices that will fill your kitchen with their aroma as they bake and heighten your anticipation of that first warm bite.

Cooking spray
1 cup all-purpose flour
1 cup whole-grain pastry flour or whole-wheat flour
1 teaspoon baking soda
½ teaspoon salt
1 teaspoon ground cinnamon
½ teaspoon ground ginger
¼ teaspoon ground cloves
⅛ teaspoon ground nutmeg
¾ cup firmly packed dark brown sugar
3 tablespoons unsulfured molasses
¼ cup canola oil
2 large eggs
1 cup canned solid-pack pumpkin
1 teaspoon vanilla extract
¾ cup lowfat buttermilk
¼ cup unsalted raw pumpkin seeds

SERVES 12
SERVING SIZE:
1 MUFFIN

EXCELLENT
SOURCE OF
THIAMIN,
VITAMIN A

PER SERVING
CALORIES: 205;
TOTAL FAT: 7G
    MONO: 3.5G,
    POLY: 2 G;
    SAT: 1G,
PROTEIN: 5G;
CARB: 32G;
FIBER: 2G;
CHOL: 36MG;
SODIUM: 233MG

GOOD
SOURCE OF
MANGANESE,
PROTEIN,
VITAMIN K

Preheat the oven to 400°F. Coat a 12-cup muffin pan with cooking spray.

In a medium bowl, whisk together both flours, the baking soda, salt, and spices. In a large bowl, whisk together the sugar, molasses, oil, and one of the eggs until combined. Add the other egg and whisk well. Whisk in the pumpkin and vanilla. Stir in the flour mixture in two batches, alternating with the buttermilk, just until combined. Pour the batter into the prepared muffin pan, filling each about two-thirds full, and sprinkle the tops with the pumpkin seeds. Tap the pan on the counter a few times to remove any air bubbles. Bake until a toothpick inserted in the center of one of the muffins comes out clean, about 20 minutes.

Let cool on a wire rack for 15 minutes. Run a knife around the muffins to loosen them and unmold. Enjoy warm or let cool completely before storing in an airtight container in the refrigerator for up to 3 days or in the freezer for up to 3 months.

*

DID YOU KNOW?
Canned pumpkin is so good there is no need to fuss with fresh if you are not so inclined. It is also packed with nutrients; 1 cup contains more potassium than a medium banana and more vitamin A than a cup of carrots. Buy plain canned pumpkin, sold as solid-pack, not pumpkin pie filling, which has added flavorings.

Apple-Pecan Muffins

These muffins are unbelievably moist and tender, with just the right touch of sweetness. Each bite yields a chunk of sweet baked apple, and they have a delightfully crunchy pecan crumb topping. Yes, you have finally found it: a truly delicious, crave-able muffin that you can feel good about eating for breakfast.

Cooking spray

¾ cup plus 2 tablespoons firmly packed dark brown sugar

¼ cup chopped pecans

½ teaspoon ground cinnamon

1 cup all-purpose flour

1 cup whole-grain pastry flour or whole-wheat flour

1 teaspoon baking soda

½ teaspoon salt

¼ cup canola oil

2 large eggs

1 cup natural unsweetened applesauce

1 teaspoon vanilla extract

¾ cup lowfat buttermilk

1 Golden Delicious apple, cored, peeled, and cut into ¼-inch pieces

SERVES 12
SERVING SIZE:
1 MUFFIN

CARB: 35G;
FIBER: 2G;
CHOL: 36MG;
SODIUM: 236MG

PER SERVING
CALORIES: 213;
TOTAL FAT: 8G
MONO: 3G,
POLY: 1.5G;
SAT: 1G,
PROTEIN: 4G;

**EXCELLENT
SOURCE OF**
THIAMIN

Preheat the oven to 400°F. Coat a 12-cup muffin pan with cooking spray.

In a small bowl, mix together 2 tablespoons of the brown sugar, the pecans, and cinnamon. Set aside.

In a medium bowl, whisk together both flours, the baking soda, and salt.

In a large bowl, whisk the remaining ¾ cup brown sugar and the oil until combined. Add the eggs, one at a time, whisking well after each addition. Whisk in the applesauce and vanilla. Stir in the flour mixture in two batches, alternating with the buttermilk, just until combined. Gently stir in the apple chunks.

Pour the batter into the prepared muffin pan, filling each about two-thirds full, and sprinkle evenly with the pecan mixture. Tap the pan on the counter a few times to remove any air bubbles. Bake until a toothpick inserted in the center of one of the muffins comes out clean, about 20 minutes.

Let cool on a wire rack for 15 minutes. Run a knife around the muffins to loosen them and unmold. Enjoy warm or let cool completely before storing in an airtight container in the refrigerator for up to 3 days or in the freezer for up to 3 months.

Building a Better Muffin

Most of the muffins I have tried fall into one of two categories: 1. Those that are essentially cake but are called a muffin so people don't have to admit to eating cake for breakfast, or 2. Those that are fat-free, dairy-free, sugar-free, wheat-free, dare I say taste-free rubbery things that happen to have been baked in a muffin tin. If you have had a similar experience, you are really going to appreciate my muffin recipes. They are the muffins you have been dreaming of: moist, tender, delicious morsels that you can feel good about eating for breakfast. I employ some simple tricks that make them that way:

1. CUT THE FAT BUT DON'T ELIMINATE IT.
You need some fat in the muffin to keep it moist and tender. You just don't need as much as a traditional recipe calls for. I use just ¼ cup oil in the whole batter, which yields 1 teaspoon of fat per muffin.

2. USE HEART-HEALTHY CANOLA OIL.
Instead of saturated-fat laden butter, I use monounsaturated-rich, heart-healthy canola oil. It is perfect for baking because it has a light, neutral taste.

3. BOOST MOISTURE AND TENDERNESS WITH FRUIT OR VEGETABLE PURÉES.
Fruit and vegetable purées like applesauce and pumpkin purée lend moisture, tenderness, and a touch of sweetness, so you can use less fat and a little less sugar without compromising taste.

4. USE WHOLE-GRAIN PASTRY FLOUR.
Whole-grain pastry flour is one of my favorite secret ingredients. It is made from a variety of wheat that is very tender, so while it is a whole grain, with all that antioxidant power, it has a much lighter texture and taste. I like to use half whole-grain pastry flour and half all-purpose for a muffin that has a real cakey texture. If you can't find whole-grain pastry flour, it is fine to substitute regular whole-wheat flour.

New York Breakfast

Growing up, smoked fish was such a big part of our weekend breakfast ritual that my dad was on a first-name basis with the guy behind the fish counter. We'd pile the fish on fresh bagels spread with cream cheese, then top it with tomatoes and onions. There is something about that combination—soft cream cheese, silky, smoky fish, the crunchy bite of onion, and a juicy slice of tomato—that is more than the sum of its parts.

Nowadays I usually skip the bagel (which is equivalent to 4 to 5 pieces of bread) in favor of thinly sliced dark pumpernickel bread for a breakfast that's simple, sophisticated, modern, and classic all at once.

8 pieces thin pumpernickel bread (3½ inches square)
¼ cup whipped cream cheese
8 ounces thinly sliced smoked salmon
½ red onion, thinly sliced
¼ English cucumber, thinly sliced
2 medium ripe tomatoes, cored, seeded, and diced
2 teaspoons chopped fresh chives
Salt and freshly ground black pepper to taste

SERVES 4
SERVING SIZE:
2 PIECES

PER SERVING
CALORIES: 222;
TOTAL FAT: 7G
  MONO: 1.5G,
  POLY: 1G;
  SAT: 3G,
PROTEIN: 15G;
CARB: 24G;
FIBER: 4G;
CHOL: 26MG;
SODIUM: 760MG

EXCELLENT SOURCE OF
MANGANESE,
NIACIN,
PHOSPHORUS,
SELENIUM,
VITAMIN B$_{12}$,
VITAMIN C

GOOD SOURCE OF
COPPER, FIBER,
FOLATE, IRON,
MAGNESIUM,
POTASSIUM,
RIBOFLAVIN,
THIAMIN,
VITAMIN A,
VITAMIN B$_6$,
VITAMIN K

Toast the bread, then spread 1½ teaspoons of cream cheese on top of each piece. Put a slice of smoked salmon, a couple of slices of onion, a slice or two of cucumber, and about 1 tablespoon of chopped tomato on top. Sprinkle with the chives and season with salt and pepper.

* **EATING WELL TIP**
Whipped regular cream cheese has the same calories per tablespoon as reduced-fat cream cheese because it has air whipped into it, making it less dense. Great tasting and easy to spread, whipped is my choice for spreading. For baking, as in the cheesecake on page 281, I use unwhipped reduced-fat cream cheese because there you need that density.

Vegetable Cheese Strata

You will definitely get "oohs" and "ahhhs" when you pull this dish out of the oven. It rises up beautifully golden brown above the baking dish—almost like a soufflé—and its rich aroma draws you right in. But its taste is the real reward: a delicate crust outside, with a tender eggy inside brimming with cheese and savory vegetables. Since you prepare it the night before, it is the perfect dish for overnight guests or a party. You can relax and enjoy it as much as your guests will the next day.

4 teaspoons olive oil
1 large onion, diced (about 2 cups)
3 cloves garlic, minced (about 1 tablespoon)
8 ounces white mushrooms, sliced (about 3 cups)
Cooking spray
1 whole-wheat baguette, cubed (about 5 cups)
8 large eggs
8 large egg whites
2 cups nonfat milk
1 tablespoon Dijon mustard
10 ounces broccoli, steamed until tender but still firm, cooled, and chopped, or one 10-ounce package frozen broccoli, thawed and chopped
⅓ cup freshly grated Parmesan cheese
4 ounces part-skim mozzarella cheese, shredded (1 cup)
½ cup thinly sliced sun-dried tomatoes (not oil-packed), soaked in hot water until soft, then drained
1 tablespoon minced fresh thyme
½ teaspoon salt
½ teaspoon freshly ground black pepper

SERVES 8
SERVING SIZE:
1½ CUPS

PER SERVING
CALORIES: 255;
TOTAL FAT: 12G
    MONO: 5G,
    POLY: 2G;
    SAT: 3.5G,
PROTEIN: 21G;
CARB: 17G;
FIBER: 4.5G;
CHOL: 215MG;
SODIUM: 605MG

EXCELLENT SOURCE OF
CALCIUM, FIBER, IODINE, PHOSPHORUS, PROTEIN, RIBOFLAVIN, SELENIUM, VITAMIN A, VITAMIN C

GOOD SOURCE OF
COPPER, FOLATE, IRON, MANGANESE, MOLYBDENUM, NIACIN, PANTOTHENIC ACID, POTASSIUM, THIAMIN, VITAMIN B_6, VITAMIN B_{12}, VITAMIN D

Heat 2 teaspoons of the oil in a medium nonstick skillet over medium-high heat. Add the onion and cook, stirring, until softened and beginning to brown, 3 to 5 minutes. Add the garlic and continue to cook for 1 minute. Transfer the onion mixture to a medium bowl and let cool.

Heat the remaining 2 teaspoons oil in the same skillet over medium-high heat and cook the mushrooms, stirring a few times, until their water evaporates and they begin to brown, 5 to 7 minutes. Remove from the heat and let cool completely.

The Story on Eggs

Back when I began studying nutrition (now I am dating myself!), eggs were considered a big no-no because they are high in cholesterol—one egg has 213mg—most of the currently held upper limit of 300mg a day. But it turns out that eggs are not the villain they were once thought to be. We now know that it is not so much the cholesterol you eat that raises your blood choles-terol; saturated fat is a much more potent culprit. So while you still want to watch cholesterol, it is far more important to limit saturated fat. Eggs are low in total fat and saturated fat (5 grams and 1.5 grams respectively) and one egg has only 75 calories and contains 13 different essential nutrients. Eggs are also one of the best sources of protein going.

Interestingly, nearly all of an egg's fat and cholesterol are in the yolk, but so are the bulk of its nutrients. The whites are pretty much pure protein. The bottom line is that it is okay to enjoy eggs, just keep it to one whole egg a day for a healthy balance. That's why my rule of thumb for egg dishes is to allow one whole egg and one or two whites per person. This way you get the beautiful yellow color, rich texture, flavor, and nutrients from the yolk without overdoing the cholesterol.

Coat a large baking dish (about 9 x 13 inches) with cooking spray. Arrange the bread cubes over the bottom. In a large bowl, beat the whole eggs, egg whites, milk, and mustard together until incorporated. Add the mushrooms, onion-garlic mixture, broccoli, both cheeses, the sun-dried tomatoes, thyme, salt, and pepper and stir to incorporate. Pour the mixture over the bread, making sure the liquid saturates the bread. Cover with plastic wrap and refrigerate overnight or at least 8 hours.

Preheat the oven to 350°F. Remove the plastic wrap from the strata and bake until the top forms a light brown crust, 60 to 70 minutes.

Scrumptious Scramble

There is always a line out the door for breakfast at one of my favorite NYC eateries, aptly named Good Enough to Eat. This riff on scrambled eggs is inspired by the special scramble on their menu. It amazes me how the easy addition of tomatoes, onion, and dill can turn ho-hum eggs into a sublime dish. The deep red chunks of tomato mingling with savory onion and the sweet, earthy aroma of the dill summon you to dig right in! I like to serve this with a slice of hearty whole-grain toast spread with ripe avocado instead of butter.

1 teaspoon olive oil
½ cup diced red onion
1 medium ripe tomato, cored, seeded, and diced (about 1 cup)
4 large eggs
4 large egg whites
2 tablespoons water (optional)
1 tablespoon finely chopped fresh dill or 1 teaspoon dried
Salt and freshly ground black pepper to taste

SERVES 4
SERVING SIZE:
¾ CUP

PER SERVING
CALORIES: 118;
TOTAL FAT: 6G
    MONO: FAT 3G,
    POLY: 1G;
    SAT: 1.5G,
PROTEIN: 11G;
CARB: 4G;
FIBER: 1G;
CHOL: 212MG;
SODIUM: 128MG

EXCELLENT SOURCE OF
IODINE, PROTEIN,
RIBOFLAVIN,
SELENIUM

GOOD SOURCE OF
MOLYBDENUM,
PHOSPHORUS,
VITAMIN A,
VITAMIN, B$_{12}$,
VITAMIN C

In a medium nonstick skillet, heat the oil over medium heat. Add the onion and cook for 2 minutes, stirring once or twice. Add the tomato and cook for 1 minute more. Transfer the onion-tomato mixture to a bowl and set aside.

In a medium bowl, lightly beat together the whole eggs, egg whites, and water, if using. Pour the egg mixture into the skillet and cook over medium-low heat, stirring frequently, until the eggs are almost set. Drain any excess water from the tomato mixture and stir the mixture gently into the eggs. Toss in the dill, season with salt and pepper, and serve.

Southwestern Hash and Eggs

This dish is a hearty skillet breakfast I imagine a rugged cowboy might whip up while out on the range. It's an aromatic hash of black beans and potatoes deeply flavored with chili, cumin, and garlic, then brightened with tomatoes and fresh cilantro and crowned with a sunny-side-up egg. It is amazing that such a stick-to-your-ribs breakfast just happens to be meatless.

1 pound small red potatoes, cut into ½-inch cubes

1 tablespoon olive oil

1 small onion, diced (about 1 cup)

1 medium red bell pepper, seeded and diced (about 1 cup)

3 cloves garlic, minced (about 1 tablespoon)

¼ teaspoon ground cumin

½ teaspoon dried oregano

1 teaspoon ancho chile powder or regular chili powder

3 medium ripe tomatoes, diced (about 3 cups)

One 15.5-ounce can black beans, preferably low-sodium, drained and rinsed

Salt and freshly ground black pepper to taste

⅓ cup chopped fresh cilantro

Cooking spray

4 large eggs

Hot pepper sauce for serving

SERVES 4
SERVING SIZE: 1¼ CUPS HASH AND 1 EGG

PER SERVING
CALORIES: 340;
TOTAL FAT: 10G
   MONO: 5G;
   POLY: 1G;
   SAT: 2G,
PROTEIN: 16G;
CARB: 46G;
FIBER: 10G;
CHOL: 212MG;
   SODIUM: 109MG

EXCELLENT SOURCE OF
FIBER,
FOLATE, IRON,
MAGNESIUM,
PHOSPHORUS,
POTASSIUM,
RIBOFLAVIN,
SELENIUM,
THIAMIN,
VITAMIN A,
VITAMIN B6,
   VITAMIN C

GOOD SOURCE OF
CALCIUM,
IODINE, NIACIN,
VITAMIN B12,
VITAMIN K

Place the potatoes in a large nonstick skillet. Cover with water, bring to a boil, and cook until the potatoes are fork-tender, about 8 minutes. Drain and transfer the potatoes to a bowl.

Dry the skillet with a paper towel. Add the oil and heat over medium-high heat. Add the onion and bell pepper and cook, stirring, until the vegetables have softened, about 6 minutes. Stir in the potatoes, garlic, cumin, oregano, and ancho powder. Add the tomatoes and beans and simmer until heated through, about 5 minutes. Season with salt and black pepper. Stir in the cilantro.

Transfer the hash to serving plates. With the heat off, wipe out the pan again. Coat it with cooking spray, turn the heat to medium-low, and cook the eggs sunny side up or over, however you prefer. Put an egg on top of each mound of hash. Serve with hot sauce.

10 Grab-and-Go Breakfasts

It's great to be able to sit down to breakfast, even if you have just 15 minutes. But sometimes even that little bit of time just isn't in the cards. If you have to eat on the go, the muffins on pages 21–22 and energy bars on page 39 are great make-ahead options. I like to wrap them individually and freeze them. Just take them out to thaw the night before and, in the morning, grab and go with a piece of fruit. Also, the smoothies on pages 41–43 can be made the night before and stored in the refrigerator. The next day, just give them a good shake and pour into a to-go cup.

Here are ten more portable, easy-to-pull-together breakfast ideas:

1. Peanut butter on a whole-wheat English muffin with sliced banana and a drizzle of honey
2. A snack bag filled with dried cereal, walnuts, and dried cherries
3. A hard-boiled egg (made ahead), tangerine, and a handful of whole-grain crackers
4. A stick of part-skim mozzarella cheese, a chunk of whole-grain baguette, and some grapes
5. A whole-wheat tortilla sprinkled with shredded reduced-fat cheddar, topped with slices of green apple, and rolled up
6. A whole-wheat pita stuffed with lowfat cottage cheese and sliced peaches or blueberries with a drizzle of honey
7. Some smoked salmon, a slice of tomato, and a little whipped cream cheese on pumpernickel bread
8. A single-serving container of lowfat yogurt and a banana
9. A whole-grain frozen waffle, toasted and spread with peanut butter and some unsweetened applesauce
10. Two pieces of whole-grain crisp bread spread with soft goat cheese and topped with sliced strawberries

Broccoli and Cheddar Frittata

A frittata is a classic Italian egg dish that is basically a crustless quiche. It makes a lovely light lunch or dinner with soup or a salad, and it is perfect cut into smaller wedges for a party buffet. It is delicious served warm or at room temperature and it takes less than 15 minutes to make. Pretty good resumé, don't you think?

Since everyone loves a classic broccoli and cheddar quiche, I figured why not bring that all-American flavor to my frittata? Cooked on the stove and finished in the oven, it comes out golden brown, bubbling with cheese, and chock-full of bright, tender broccoli.

4 large eggs

4 large egg whites

2 tablespoons water

2 teaspoons olive oil

1 small red onion, cut in half, then thinly sliced into half-moons

2 cups chopped cooked or thawed frozen broccoli

¼ teaspoon salt

Freshly ground black pepper to taste

2 ounces extra-sharp cheddar cheese, shredded (½ cup)

SERVES 4
SERVING SIZE:
2 WEDGES

PER SERVING
CALORIES: 215;
TOTAL FAT: 12G
MONO: 3.7G,
POLY: 1G;
SAT: 4G,
PROTEIN: 17G;
CARB: 11G;
FIBER: 4G;
CHOL: 227MG;
SODIUM: 385MG

EXCELLENT SOURCE OF
CALCIUM, FOLATE, IODINE, PROTEIN, RIBO-FLAVIN, SELE-NIUM, VITAMIN A, VITAMIN C

GOOD SOURCE OF
FIBER, IRON, MOLYBDENUM, PHOSPHORUS, POTASSIUM, THIAMIN, VITAMIN B6, VITAMIN B12

Preheat the broiler.

Combine the whole eggs, egg whites, and water in a medium bowl and whisk well.

In a medium ovenproof nonstick skillet, heat the oil over medium heat. Add the onion and cook, stirring, until it begins to soften, about 3 minutes. Add the broccoli and cook for another 2 minutes. Season with salt and pepper. Pour the egg mixture over the vegetables in the skillet, covering them evenly. Reduce the heat to medium-low, cover, and let cook until the egg mixture has set around the edges of the pan but is still somewhat liquid in the middle, about 8 minutes. Sprinkle with the cheese.

Place the skillet under the broiler about 2 inches from the heat until the surface is set and golden brown, 1 to 2 minutes. Be careful not to overcook or the egg mixture will become tough.

Cut the frittata into 8 wedges and serve.

✳ **EATING WELL TIP**
I use full-fat cheddar strategically, so a little goes a long way. That means using extra-sharp to get the most flavor and sprinkling it right on top where you can see every bit of its melting goodness. We eat with our eyes, so putting the cheese front and center helps us get the most bang out of it.

Poached Eggs with Herb-Roasted Turkey Breast and Sweet Potato Hash

You know someone is a big fan of leftovers when they cook extra just to be sure to wind up with them. Guilty as charged! Whenever I make my Herb-Roasted Turkey Breast (page 219), I pop a couple of sweet potatoes in the oven and I make sure I have enough turkey left over to make this simple, yet outstanding, hash the next morning. It makes a perfect sweet-savory, herb-perfumed bed for poached eggs. I don't know what is better, the moment I break the egg and watch the yolk flow decadently over the hash or my first satisfying bite.

2 medium sweet potatoes
2 teaspoons olive oil
1 small onion, diced (about 1 cup)
1 teaspoon chopped fresh thyme
1½ cups diced Herb-Roasted Turkey Breast (page 219)
¼ teaspoon salt
Freshly ground black pepper to taste
¼ cup low-sodium chicken broth
1 teaspoon white vinegar
4 large eggs
Hot pepper sauce for serving

SERVES 4
SERVING SIZE: ABOUT 1 CUP HASH AND 1 EGG

PER SERVING
CALORIES: 250;
TOTAL FAT: 9G
  MONO: 4G,
  POLY: 1G;
  SAT: 2G;
PROTEIN: 25G;
CARB: 17G;
FIBER: 2G;
CHOL: 253MG;
SODIUM: 350MG

EXCELLENT SOURCE OF
IODINE, NIACIN, PHOSPHORUS, PROTEIN, RIBOFLAVIN, SELENIUM, VITAMIN A, VITAMIN B$_6$, VITAMIN C

GOOD SOURCE OF
COPPER, FIBER, FOLATE, MAGNESIUM, MANGANESE, MOLYBDENUM, PANTOTHENIC ACID, POTASSIUM, VITAMIN B$_{12}$, ZINC

Preheat the oven to 400°F. Bake the sweet potatoes for 40 minutes; cool, peel, and dice.

In a large nonstick skillet, heat the oil over medium heat. Add the onion and thyme and cook, stirring, until softened and beginning to brown, 3 to 5 minutes. Add the sweet potatoes, turkey, salt, and some pepper and cook, stirring occasionally, until the potatoes begin to brown, about 3 minutes longer. Add the broth, scraping up any brown bits that may have formed on the bottom of the pan. Keep warm while you poach the eggs.

Fill a sauté pan with 1½ inches of water, add the vinegar, and bring to a simmer. Break 1 egg into a small bowl, then carefully pour it into the water. Repeat with the remaining eggs, spacing them so they do not touch. Poach at a gentle simmer until the whites are firm but the yolks are still runny, 3 to 4 minutes. With a slotted spoon, transfer the eggs to paper towels and season with salt and pepper.

Divide the hash between 4 plates and top each serving with a poached egg. Serve with hot sauce.

Peach French Toast Bake

When you want a hot, homey breakfast that's special enough for company but without the morning fuss, this French toast bake is the answer. You pull it together the night before and while you sleep the eggy goodness seeps into the bread and all the flavors meld together. In the morning you just need to pop it in the oven. It comes out fragrant, with juicy, brown sugar–laced peaches atop tender vanilla and cinnamon–scented bread that has just the right amount of chewiness from the baguette crust. A drizzle of maple syrup and a dollop of cool, creamy yogurt complete the picture and everyone's left wondering just how you manage to do it all with such grace.

Cooking spray
1 large whole-wheat baguette (about 8 ounces)
4 large eggs
4 large egg whites
1 cup nonfat milk
1 teaspoon vanilla extract
5 cups frozen unsweetened sliced peaches, thawed
2 tablespoons firmly packed brown sugar
¼ teaspoon ground cinnamon
1½ cups plain nonfat yogurt (optional)
¾ cup pure maple syrup (optional)

SERVES 6
SERVING SIZE:
ONE 4½ X
4-INCH SLICE

PER SERVING
CALORIES: 254;
TOTAL FAT: 6G
    MONO: 2G,
    POLY: 1.4G;
    SAT: 1.6G,
PROTEIN: 12.5G;
CARB: 40G;
FIBER: 5G;
CHOL: 144MG;
SODIUM: 288MG

**EXCELLENT
SOURCE OF**
FIBER, IODINE,
MANGANESE,
PROTEIN, RIBOFLA-
VIN, SELENIUM

**GOOD
SOURCE OF**
CALCIUM, COPPER,
IRON, MAGNESIUM,
NIACIN, PANTO-
THENIC ACID,
PHOSPHORUS,
POTASSIUM, THIA-
MIN, VITAMIN A,
VITAMIN C, ZINC

Coat a 9 x 13-inch baking pan with cooking spray. Cut the baguette into ½-inch-thick slices and arrange them in a single layer in the pan.

In a medium bowl, whisk together the whole eggs, egg whites, milk, and vanilla. Pour the egg mixture over the bread in the pan. Scatter the peach slices evenly over the bread. Sprinkle with the brown sugar and cinnamon. Cover with plastic wrap and refrigerate overnight.

Preheat the oven to 350°F. Uncover and bake until it is slightly puffed and the bread is golden brown, about 40 minutes. Top with yogurt and drizzle with maple syrup, if desired.

✳ **EATING WELL TIP**
Frozen fruit is nutritionally comparable to fresh, and it is perfectly suited for baking and blending. In fact, I prefer to use frozen fruit in a smoothie because it makes it ultracool and frothy. Just be sure to buy it unsweetened. I use frozen peaches in this recipe to make it an easy year-round dish, but feel free to use fresh ripe peaches if they are in season.

Cherry Vanilla Oatmeal

The addition of sweet-tart dried cherries transforms ordinary oatmeal into something to wake up for.

3½ cups water
¼ teaspoon salt (optional)
2 cups old-fashioned or quick-cooking rolled oats
½ cup dried cherries
1 teaspoon vanilla extract
¼ cup cherry jam, or to taste
1 cup nonfat milk, or to taste

SERVES 4	CHOL: 4MG;
SERVING SIZE:	SODIUM: 35MG
1¼ CUPS	
	EXCELLENT
PER SERVING	**SOURCE OF**
CALORIES: 280;	MAGNESIUM,
TOTAL FAT: 4G	PHOSPHORUS
MONO: 1G,	
POLY: 1G;	**GOOD**
SAT: 1G;	**SOURCE OF**
PROTEIN: 8G;	CALCIUM, FIBER,
CARB: 56G;	IRON, PROTEIN,
FIBER: 4G;	THIAMIN,
	VITAMIN A

Combine the water, salt (if using), oats, and cherries in a medium saucepan. Bring to a boil, reduce the heat to low and simmer, stirring a few times, until the oats are tender, about 5 minutes for old-fashioned oats or 1 minute for quick-cooking oats. Remove from the heat. Stir in the vanilla and cherry jam. Divide the oatmeal between 4 serving bowls, pour ¼ cup of milk over each bowl, and serve.

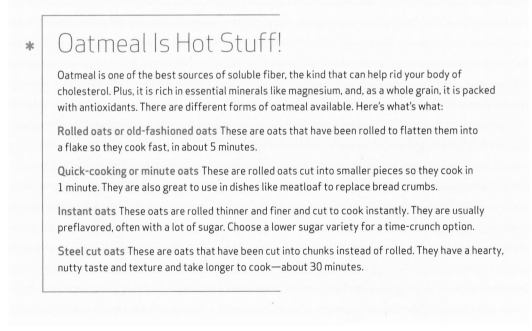

* Oatmeal Is Hot Stuff!

Oatmeal is one of the best sources of soluble fiber, the kind that can help rid your body of cholesterol. Plus, it is rich in essential minerals like magnesium, and, as a whole grain, it is packed with antioxidants. There are different forms of oatmeal available. Here's what's what:

Rolled oats or old-fashioned oats These are oats that have been rolled to flatten them into a flake so they cook fast, in about 5 minutes.

Quick-cooking or minute oats These are rolled oats cut into smaller pieces so they cook in 1 minute. They are also great to use in dishes like meatloaf to replace bread crumbs.

Instant oats These oats are rolled thinner and finer and cut to cook instantly. They are usually preflavored, often with a lot of sugar. Choose a lower sugar variety for a time-crunch option.

Steel cut oats These are oats that have been cut into chunks instead of rolled. They have a hearty, nutty taste and texture and take longer to cook—about 30 minutes.

Nutty Granola

You can't buy granola this good, and it couldn't be simpler to make. All the flavors come through crisp and clear: crunchy toasted nuts, chewy oats, and caramelized raisins perfectly sweetened with the unmistakable flavor of real maple syrup and humming with cinnamon.

Cooking spray
3 cups old-fashioned rolled oats
½ cup chopped walnuts
½ cup chopped almonds
½ cup chopped pecans
½ cup pure maple syrup
¼ teaspoon salt
¼ teaspoon ground cinnamon
½ cup raisins (optional)

SERVES 9	EXCELLENT
MAKES 4½ CUPS	SOURCE OF
SERVING SIZE:	MAGNESIUM,
½ CUP	MANGANESE
PER SERVING	GOOD
CALORIES: 280;	SOURCE OF
TOTAL FAT: 15G	FIBER,
MONO: 3.7G;	PHOSPHORUS,
POLY: 4.7G;	PROTEIN,
SAT: 1.5G;	THIAMIN, ZINC
PROTEIN: 7G;	
CARB: 34G;	
FIBER: 4.5G;	
CHOL: 0MG;	
SODIUM: 67MG	

Preheat the oven to 300°F. Coat a large baking sheet with cooking spray.

In a medium bowl, combine all the ingredients, mixing well to coat everything with the maple syrup. Spread on the baking sheet and bake until golden brown, stirring occasionally, about 30 minutes.

Transfer the sheet to a wire rack and let cool completely. Store in the refrigerator in an airtight container for about 2 weeks.

* Getting Nutty

Nuts are loaded with protein, minerals, and cholesterol-lowering compounds. Yes, they are high in fat and calories, but it's heart-healthy fat, and research shows nuts may actually aid in weight control. But don't sit there munching a whole can of cashews—a serving of nuts is 1 ounce, a small handful.

I recommend eating a variety of nuts each week because each one has its own star quality. Walnuts contain a significant amount of health-protective omega-3 fat; 1 ounce covers your need for the day. Almonds are a top source of vitamin E, a fat-soluble vitamin and antioxidant, and just one Brazil nut gives you a day's worth of the essential mineral selenium.

Energy Bars

I find most packaged energy bars either unbearably sweet or like leaden masses of mortar. Besides, so many are filled with bizarre ingredients. Mine are true fruit, nut, and grain bars—chewy, crunchy, and satisfying, with just the right touch of sweetness, provided by real maple syrup. A viewer once emailed me that she made the "mistake" of sharing some with her coworkers, who loved them so much they roped her into making them for everyone regularly. Consider yourself fairly warned!

Cooking spray
1 cup quick-cooking rolled oats
½ cup shelled unsalted raw sunflower seeds
½ cup toasted wheat germ
¼ cup whole-grain pastry flour or whole-wheat flour
½ cup dried apricots
½ cup raw almonds
½ cup raisins
½ cup pitted dried dates
½ cup nonfat dry milk
½ teaspoon ground cinnamon
⅓ cup pure maple syrup
2 large eggs

SERVES 24
MAKES 24 BARS,
EACH ABOUT
3 X 1½ INCHES
SERVING SIZE:
1 BAR

PER SERVING
CALORIES: 133;
TOTAL FAT: 5G;
  MONO: 1.8G,
  POLY: 2G;
  SAT: 0.6G,
PROTEIN: 5G;
CARB: 20G;

FIBER: 2.5G;
CHOL: 21MG;
SODIUM: 19MG

**EXCELLENT
SOURCE OF**
MANGANESE

**GOOD
SOURCE OF**
FIBER,
PHOSPHORUS,
PROTEIN,
THIAMIN

Preheat the oven to 350°F. Coat a 9 x 13-inch baking pan with cooking spray.

Place all the ingredients, except the maple syrup and eggs, in a food processor and pulse until everything is finely chopped. Add the syrup and eggs and pulse until the mixture is well combined. It will resemble a coarse paste.

Transfer to the baking pan and spread evenly to cover the bottom. Bake until lightly browned, about 20 minutes. Allow to cool for 15 minutes, then cut into 24 bars. Store in an airtight container at room temperature for about 3 days or wrap individually and freeze for up to 3 months.

Blueberry Blast Smoothie and Energy Bars (page 39)

Blueberry Blast Smoothie

This cold, frothy shake is a vibrant shade of purple and as delicious as it is beautiful.

½ cup nonfat milk
½ cup plain nonfat yogurt
1 cup frozen unsweetened blueberries
1 teaspoon honey

Put all the ingredients into a blender and process until smooth.

SERVES 1
SERVING SIZE :
2 CUPS

PER SERVING
CALORIES: 195;
TOTAL FAT: 1G
  MONO: 0G,
  POLY: 0G;
  SAT: 0,
PROTEIN: 10G;
CARB: 40G;
FIBER: 4G;
CHOL: 5MG
SODIUM: 134MG

EXCELLENT SOURCE OF
CALCIUM,
PROTEIN,
VITAMIN A,
VITAMIN C,
VITAMIN K

GOOD SOURCE OF
FIBER,
MANGANESE,
PHOSPHORUS,
RIBOFLAVIN,
VITAMIN D

*

Three Reasons to Eat Breakfast

The research is compelling that breakfast is much more than delicious. It just may just be the most important meal of the day.

1. BREAKFAST CAN HELP KEEP YOU HEALTHIER

People who eat breakfast have better overall nutrient intakes, lower cholesterol levels, and better blood sugar regulation (risk factors for heart disease and diabetes) than breakfast skippers.

2. BREAKFAST CAN HELP MANAGE YOUR WEIGHT

Research shows that breakfast eaters tend to eat fewer calories over the course of the day than breakfast skippers. They are less likely to be obese, and eating breakfast has been identified by the National Weight Control Registry as one of the key habits of successful weight losers.

3. BREAKFAST CAN HELP BOOST YOUR BRAIN POWER

After fasting all night, your blood sugar level is low and your brain basically has to run on empty until you eat something. That's why people who have eaten breakfast do better on memory tests and with skills involving memory than those who don't.

Peanut Butter Split Smoothie

This smoothie is a great way to use overripe bananas. Just peel them, cut them into chunks, and freeze them in a plastic bag. Then they'll be at the ready when you need them.

1 ripe banana, peeled, quartered, and frozen
½ cup nonfat milk
¼ cup plain nonfat yogurt
1½ tablespoons creamy natural peanut butter

Put all the ingredients in a blender and process until smooth.

SERVES 1
SERVING SIZE:
1½ CUPS

PER SERVING
CALORIES: 325;
TOTAL FAT: 12.5G
   MONO: 0G,
   POLY: 0G;
   SAT: 1.5G,
PROTEIN: 13.5G;
CARB: 43.5G;
FIBER: 4.5G;
CHOL: 3MG
SODIUM: 190MG

EXCELLENT
SOURCE OF
CALCIUM, FIBER,
PROTEIN,
VITAMIN B$_6$,
VITAMIN C

GOOD
SOURCE OF
MANGANESE,
POTASSIUM,
VITAMIN A,
VITAMIN D

---

*

How to Choose the Best Cereal

If you pick the right cereal and have it with fruit and lowfat milk or yogurt, you get a huge nutritional bang for your buck. The trick is picking a good one. Here's a checklist to help guide you through.

LOOK FOR:
• 6 grams of sugar or less per serving or 16 grams if the cereal contains fruit
• at least 3 grams of fiber per serving
• whole grain as the first ingredient on the list

AVOID:
• partially hydrogenated oil, high fructose corn syrup, and artificial colors

BE AWARE:
• the words "less sugar" on the box may not mean the cereal is less sweet. It may contain an artificial sweetener
• serving sizes vary widely because some cereals are more concentrated than others

Mango Lassi

This is my take on the classic Indian drink, which is traditionally made with lots of white sugar. I use a bit of honey to bring out the natural sweetness of the mango and the result is nirvana—a silky-smooth delight that is sunny shade of yellow.

2 ripe mangos
1½ cups plain nonfat yogurt
2 tablespoons honey
2 cups ice (1 tray of cubes)

SERVES 4	**EXCELLENT**
SERVING SIZE:	**SOURCE OF**
1 CUP	VITAMIN A,
	VITAMIN C
PER SERVING	
CALORIES: 140;	**GOOD**
TOTAL FAT: 0G;	**SOURCE OF**
PROTEIN: 4.5G;	CALCIUM
CARB: 33G;	
FIBER: 2G;	
CHOL: 2MG;	
SODIUM: 53MG	

To peel and cut the mango, cut ¼ inch off the top and bottom of the fruit and sit it on its larger end on a cutting board. At the top end, find the pit with your knife and cut down alongside it (a mango's pit is flat). Do the same with the other side. Cut each half lengthwise into 4 slices. Cut the peel from each slice and slice the mango crosswise into chunks.

   Place the mango chunks in a blender and process until smooth. Add the yogurt, honey, and ice and process until the ice is crushed and the drink is frothy. Serve in tall glasses with additional ice, if desired.

＊ **DID YOU KNOW?**
Mango is one of the best sources of beta-carotene, a powerful antioxidant that imparts a yellow-orange hue to foods. The nutrient, which is a form of vitamin A, gives pumpkin and carrots their glorious color, too.

nibbles & noshes

Honey-Mustard Turkey Roll-Ups

I love when you can take everyday ingredients that might usually elicit a yawn and combine them in a fresh, exciting way that positively lights you up. That's the case here, where I turn deli turkey breast and some salad vegetables into a zingy honey-mustard-doused roll-up. Whatever you do, don't forget the fresh basil—it makes the dish.

2 teaspoons Dijon mustard

2 teaspoons honey

8 slices turkey breast (about 8 ounces)

2 large red-leaf lettuce leaves, spines removed and each leaf torn into 4 pieces

¼ large English cucumber, seeded and cut into 3-inch-long sticks

¼ large red bell pepper, cut into thin strips

8 large fresh basil leaves

SERVES 4	CHOL: 4MG;
MAKES 8	SODIUM: 111MG
ROLL-UPS;	
SERVING SIZE:	**EXCELLENT**
2 ROLL-UPS	**SOURCE OF**
	VITAMIN A
PER SERVING:	
CALORIES: 21;	**GOOD**
TOTAL FAT: 0G;	**SOURCE OF**
PROTEIN: 2G;	VITAMIN C,
CARB: 3G;	VITAMIN K
FIBER: 0G;	

In a small bowl, mix together the mustard and honey until well combined.

Lay a slice of turkey on a plate or cutting board. Spread ½ teaspoon of the honey-mustard along the turkey about 2 inches from the end of the slice. Place a piece of lettuce on top of that, then a couple of sticks of cucumber and slices of red pepper. Top with a basil leaf and roll it all up in the turkey. Repeat with the remaining ingredients. These may be prepared several hours in advance and stored, covered, in the refrigerator.

Smoked Turkey-Wrapped Asparagus

In this dish, the smoked turkey crisps a little in the oven and seals itself around the tender asparagus, making for a gorgeous presentation. If you feel like taking the extra step, the chive "bow" tied around each spear really ups the ante, but you can also skip it for a premeal nibble that gives maximum effect for minimal effort. Make sure you get turkey that is not too crumbly so it is easy to wrap.

12 asparagus spears
1½ teaspoons extra-virgin olive oil
4 thin slices smoked turkey (about ¼ pound)
12 fresh chives (optional)

SERVES 2
MAKES 12
ROLL-UPS;
SERVING
SIZE: 6 PIECES

PER SERVING
CALORIES: 114;
TOTAL FAT: 5G
  MONO: 2.7G,
  POLY: 0G;
  SAT FAT: 1G,
PROTEIN: 13G;
CARB: 7G;
FIBER: 2G;

CHOL: 26MG;
SODIUM: 495MG

**EXCELLENT
SOURCE OF**
PROTEIN,
VITAMIN K

**GOOD
SOURCE OF**
COPPER, IRON,
THIAMIN,
VITAMIN A

Preheat the oven to 400°F.

Break the woody end off each asparagus spear and peel the outermost layer off the lower three-quarters of the spear with a vegetable peeler. Place the asparagus on a large plate, drizzle with the oil, and toss gently to coat.

Cut each slice of turkey lengthwise into three strips. Wrap one strip around each asparagus spear, leaving the tips of the asparagus unwrapped. If using, tie a blade of chive around each wrapped spear. Place the wrapped asparagus on a baking sheet and bake, turning once, until the asparagus are firm but tender and the turkey begins to brown, about 12 minutes. Alternatively, you can put them on a large microwave-proof plate and microwave, uncovered, for 3 minutes if the asparagus are thin and 4 minutes if they are thicker.

✳ DID YOU KNOW?
Asparagus is one of the best sources of folate, which is important for heart health and for pregnant women to prevent birth defects. A half-cup of cooked asparagus contains about one-third of the daily requirement for folic acid.

Grilled Zucchini Roll-Ups with Herbs and Cheese

These bite-sized morsels are just the thing to add a touch of simple elegance to a meal. They are absolutely beautiful, with tender spinach and basil leaves peeking out of delicate grilled zucchini rolls filled with creamy herbed goat cheese. These are ideal for a special picnic or an hors d'oeuvre at a cocktail party. When served atop a basic green salad, they turn it into something to celebrate.

3 small zucchini (about ½ pound each), cut lengthwise into ¼-inch-thick slices
1 tablespoon olive oil
⅛ teaspoon salt, plus more to taste
Pinch of freshly ground black pepper, plus more to taste
1½ ounces fresh goat cheese, preferably reduced-fat
1 tablespoon minced fresh parsley
½ teaspoon fresh lemon juice
2 ounces baby spinach leaves (2 cups lightly packed)
⅓ cup fresh basil leaves

SERVES 4
MAKES
16 ROLL-UPS;
SERVING SIZE:
4 ROLLS

PER SERVING
CALORIES: 80;
TOTAL FAT: 5G
    MONO: 3G;
    POLY: 0.5G;
    SAT: 1.5G;
PROTEIN: 3G;
CARB: 7.5G;
FIBER: 2.5G;
CHOL: 2MG;
SODIUM: 160MG

EXCELLENT
SOURCE OF
MOLYBDENUM,
VITAMIN A,
VITAMIN B6,
VITAMIN C,
VITAMIN K

GOOD
SOURCE OF
FIBER,
MANGANESE,
POTASSIUM,
RIBOFLAVIN

Preheat a grill or grill pan over medium heat.

Discard the outermost slices of zucchini and brush the rest with the oil on both sides. Sprinkle with the salt and pepper. Grill until tender, about 4 minutes per side. You can make the grilled zucchini a day ahead and store in an airtight container in the refrigerator.

In a small bowl, combine the goat cheese, parsley, and lemon juice, mashing them together with a fork.

Put ½ teaspoon of the cheese mixture about ½ inch from the end of a zucchini slice. Top with a few spinach leaves and one small or half of a large basil leaf. Roll up and place seam side down on a platter. Repeat with the rest of the zucchini slices. You can make these up to a day before you are ready to serve and store them in an airtight container in the refrigerator.

Figs with Ricotta, Pistachios, and Honey

This dish just oozes with sex appeal. Sweet figs are split to reveal their tender centers, then filled with creamy, cool ricotta cheese, drizzled with golden honey, and jeweled with a crunch of emerald pistachios. It is one of the few dishes that can bookend a meal on either side, as a luscious appetizer or dessert.

¼ cup unsalted shelled pistachios
8 dried figs
¼ cup part-skim ricotta cheese
1 tablespoon honey
Salt to taste

SERVES 4
MAKES 16 STUFFED FIG HALVES;
SERVING SIZE: 4 STUFFED FIG HALVES

PER SERVING
CALORIES: 150;
TOTAL FAT: 2.5G
MONO: 0.5G,
POLY: 0.5G;
SAT: 1G,

PROTEIN: 3G;
CARB: 30G;
FIBER: 4G;
CHOL: 9MG;
SODIUM: 64MG

GOOD SOURCE OF FIBER, MANGANESE

Toast the pistachios in a small dry skillet over medium-high heat until fragrant, 3 to 5 minutes, stirring frequently. Set aside to cool, then chop coarsely.

Cut each fig in half crosswise and place the fig pieces on a serving dish, cut side up. Make a small indentation into the cut side of each fig half with a small spoon or your finger. Put ½ teaspoon of the ricotta on each piece of fig and sprinkle with pistachios. Drizzle with honey, sprinkle with salt, and serve. These may be made several hours ahead and stored in the refrigerator.

*

DID YOU KNOW?
Figs are eaten as a fruit but they are actually inverted flowers that fold in on themselves instead of opening to bloom. They contain more fiber, minerals, and polyphenols (the same heart-protective compound found in red wine and tea) than most fruits.

Italian Sausage Skewers

Grilled sausage is standard appetizer fare, sliced and served on toothpicks. In this recipe I step the ordinary up to extraordinary by skewering grilled Italian-style poultry sausage with three fresh Italian tastes: tomato, olives, and basil. It is a modern take on an old-world combination that really works.

8 ounces Italian-style poultry sausage
8 large fresh basil leaves
12 pitted calamata olives, cut in half
24 grape tomatoes
Twenty-four 6-inch wooden skewers

SERVES 6	PROTEIN: 8G;
MAKES 24	CARB: 3G;
SKEWERS;	FIBER: 1G;
SERVING SIZE:	CHOL: 33MG;
4 SKEWERS	SODIUM: 350MG

PER SERVING	GOOD
CALORIES: 100;	SOURCE OF
TOTAL FAT: 5.5G	PROTEIN,
MONO: 1.5G,	VITAMIN A,
POLY: 0G;	VITAMIN C
SAT: 1G,	

Cook the sausage according to package directions and cut it into 1-inch-thick rounds. Cut the basil leaves lengthwise into thirds.

Work an olive half about one-third of the way down onto a skewer. Then add one strip of basil, folding so it fits nicely on the skewer. Follow with one tomato and a round of sausage. Position everything on the end of the skewer so the skewer can stand up on its sausage end. Repeat with the remaining skewers and ingredients. These skewers may be prepared several hours in advance and stored in the refrigerator. Allow them to come to room temperature before serving.

Marinated Feta and Olive Skewers

These scrumptious mouthfuls blast your taste buds with an array of bold, exciting flavors. Each skewer has it all: salty cheese and olives balanced with the refreshing tang of orange and fennel seed, a spicy kick from cracked pepper, and a cooling effect from cucumber and mint. Visually they are like little works of art—totem poles of color and texture with a bright green flag of mint set proudly on top.

2 teaspoons fennel seeds

2 teaspoons finely grated orange zest

3 tablespoons orange juice

1 teaspoon cracked black peppercorns

4 ounces feta cheese, cut into twenty-four ½-inch cubes

24 fresh mint leaves

12 pitted green olives, cut in half

¼ large English cucumber (seeded, if desired), cut into ½-inch chunks

Twenty-four 6-inch skewers

SERVES 6	PROTEIN: 3G;
MAKES 24	CARB: 3.5G;
SKEWERS;	FIBER: 0.5G;
SERVING SIZE:	CHOL: 17MG;
4 SKEWERS	SODIUM: 35MG
PER SERVING	GOOD
CALORIES: 80;	SOURCE OF
TOTAL FAT: 6G	CALCIUM,
MONO: 2.5G,	RIBOFLAVIN
POLY: 0.5G;	
SAT: 3G,	

In a medium bowl, combine the fennel seeds, orange zest and juice, and pepper. Gently stir in the feta and marinate for 1 hour at room temperature or up to 3 hours in the refrigerator.

To make the skewers, place a mint leaf about ¾ inch up the skewer, then add a chunk of cucumber, and an olive half. Gently place a cube of the marinated feta on the end. These can be made several hours in advance and stored in the refrigerator until ready to serve. Allow to come to room temperature before serving.

✱ DID YOU KNOW?
Soft cheeses like feta and fresh goat cheese naturally have about a third less fat than hard cheeses like cheddar.

Chicken Saté with Spicy Peanut Dipping Sauce

Just about every culture has some version of skewered grilled meat eaten as an appetizer or a snack. The Indonesian variation, called saté, takes it to its greatest heights, with chicken made succulent, flavorful, and fragrant with a bold marinade, then grilled to perfection and served with a rich peanut sauce that echoes the tastes in the marinade and adds a nice hit of spiciness.

½ cup low-sodium chicken broth

½ cup unsweetened light coconut milk

2 tablespoons low-sodium soy sauce

1 shallot, thinly sliced

1 clove garlic, minced

1½ teaspoons Asian fish sauce (or 2 more teaspoons low-sodium soy sauce)

1 tablespoon firmly packed dark brown sugar

½ teaspoon finely grated lime zest

1 tablespoon peeled and minced fresh ginger

1 pound skinless, boneless chicken breast halves, pounded slightly between 2 sheets of waxed paper and cut across into 1-inch-thick strips

Cooking spray

Eight 8-inch bamboo skewers, soaked in water for 20 minutes

½ cup Spicy Peanut Dipping Sauce (recipe follows)

2 tablespoons minced fresh basil or cilantro

¼ cup chopped unsalted peanuts

SERVES 4
MAKES 8 SKEWERS; SERVING SIZE: 2 SKEWERS AND 2 TABLESPOONS DIPPING SAUCE

PER SERVING
CALORIES: 290;
TOTAL FAT: 13G
MONO: 2.5G,
POLY: 2G;
SAT: 2G,
PROTEIN: 33G;
CARB: 10G;
FIBER: 2G;
CHOL: 66MG;
SODIUM: 385MG

EXCELLENT SOURCE OF NIACIN, PHOSPHORUS, PROTEIN, SELENIUM, VITAMIN B6, VITAMIN K

GOOD SOURCE OF MAGNESIUM, MANGANESE, PANTOTHENIC ACID, POTASSIUM, VITAMIN A

In a medium bowl, whisk together the broth, coconut milk, soy sauce, shallot, garlic, fish sauce, brown sugar, lime zest, and ginger. Add the chicken strips, toss to coat them evenly, cover with plastic wrap, and marinate in the refrigerator for 1 hour.

Remove the chicken from the marinade and discard the marinade.

Coat a nonstick grill pan with cooking spray and set it over medium-high heat. While the pan is heating, thread the chicken onto the skewers. Place the skewers in the hot pan and sear until cooked through and the chicken has light grill marks, 2 to 3 minutes per side.

Serve the chicken skewers with the dipping sauce, garnished with the basil and chopped peanuts.

Spicy Peanut Dipping Sauce

This is also sublime as a dip for raw vegetables or tossed with cooked whole-wheat spaghetti.

½ cup creamy natural peanut butter
¼ cup low-sodium chicken broth
3 tablespoons low-sodium soy sauce
1½ tablespoons packed dark brown sugar
1½ tablespoons peeled and minced fresh ginger
2 tablespoons fresh lime juice
1 clove garlic, minced (about 1 teaspoon)
½ teaspoon red pepper flakes
1 teaspoon red curry paste (you can substitute curry powder)
1 medium shallot, roughly chopped

SERVES 10
MAKES ABOUT
1¼ CUPS;
SERVING SIZE:
2 TABLESPOONS

PROTEIN: 3.5G;
CARB: 6G;
FIBER: 1G;
CHOL: 0MG;
SODIUM:
202MG

PER SERVING
CALORIES: 97;
TOTAL FAT: 6.5G
    MONO: 0G,
    POLY: 0G;
    SAT: 1G

Place all the ingredients in a blender and blend until smooth. It will keep in the refrigerator for 3 days.

Smart Snacking

Many of my nibbles make ideal between-meal snacks. Snacking can help keep your energy up throughout the day and prevent impulsive eating and overeating at meals. The key is to snack right.

PLAN, DON'T PICK
Enjoy one or two well-planned snacks each day—one in the midmorning and one midafternoon. A healthy bite at 4 p.m. is helpful for combating afternoon energy dips and sugar cravings.

PORTION RIGHT
Try to keep snacks between 100 and 300 calories, depending on your personal needs. That equals 1 cup of fruit and some yogurt, or about a handful of nuts. Preportion nibbles in little snack bags so they are easy to grab and go, and you don't have to worry about overeating.

PROTEIN POWER
Try to include some protein at each snack—lean meat, lowfat dairy, nuts, or beans. Protein will help keep your blood sugar stable and keep you feeling satisfied and energized longer.

Soft Asian Summer Rolls
with Sweet and Savory Dipping Sauce

Summer rolls are one of my all-time favorite starters. Served cold, they are the essence of freshness—cool, crisp vegetables, fresh herbs, and shrimp tucked in a delicate rice noodle wrapper, served alongside a tangy-spicy dipping sauce. They look so stunning, I had always assumed they'd be hard to make. When I finally did it, I was shocked at how easy they are. The trick is to get all the ingredients prepped and laid out before you start to make the rolls.

For the dipping sauce

1 tablespoon sugar

2 teaspoons warm water

¼ cup rice vinegar

1 teaspoon chili sauce, such as Sriracha

1 tablespoon fresh lime juice

1 teaspoon Asian fish sauce or low-sodium soy sauce

1 tablespoon finely shredded carrot

1 scallion (white and green parts), thinly sliced

For the rolls

6 medium shrimp, peeled and deveined

2 ounces Vietnamese or Thai rice noodles

6 rice-paper rounds (about 8½ inches in diameter)

12 fresh Thai or regular basil leaves

½ cup shredded carrot

12 large fresh mint leaves

3 red-leaf lettuce leaves, spines removed, making 6 halves

SERVES 6	PROTEIN: 3G;
MAKES 6	CARB: 18G;
SUMMER ROLLS;	FIBER: 1G;
SERVING SIZE:	CHOL: 9MG;
1 WHOLE ROLL	SODIUM:
PLUS 1	100MG
TABLESPOON	
DIPPING SAUCE	EXCELLENT
	SOURCE OF
PER SERVING	VITAMIN A,
CALORIES: 90;	VITAMIN K
TOTAL FAT: 0G;	

To make the dipping sauce, in a small bowl, dissolve the sugar in the warm water, then add the remaining sauce ingredients and stir until well combined. Refrigerate until ready to use. You can prepare the dipping sauce a day in advance.

To make the rolls, cook the shrimp in boiling water for 2 minutes, and cut in half lengthwise; set aside. Bring a medium saucepan of water to a boil and cook the rice noodles according to the package directions. Drain, rinse, and let cool.

Line up the remaining ingredients in small bowls before beginning to make rolls. Fill a large bowl or saucepan with very warm water that is not too hot to touch. Place a rice paper round in the hot water and soak for 30 to 60 seconds, until it is pliable and the pattern on the round is barely visible. Remove from the water and place on a clean work surface. Place 2 basil leaves on the inner edge of the moistened round, about 1 inch from the edge and leaving about 1 inch on each side. Top with about ¼ cup of the cooked rice noodles. Place 2 shrimp halves on top. Top with a heaping tablespoon of the carrots, then 2 leaves of mint.

Fold one piece of lettuce leaf and place on top of the pile. Bring the edge of the round over the filling, fold in the sides, and roll. Place the finished roll under a damp cloth or paper towel. Repeat with the remaining rice paper rounds and filling ingredients. The rolls may be prepared several hours before serving and stored covered by a damp paper towel in an airtight container in the refrigerator.

When ready to serve, slice the rolls in half on the diagonal and serve, cut ends up, with the dipping sauce.

Crab Salad in Crisp Wonton Cups

Wonton wrappers baked in a mini-muffin tin make perfect crunchy cups to hold this succulent crab salad spiked with sweet mango, cilantro, scallion, and lime. This appetizer has a huge wow factor and is surprisingly easy to make.

For the wonton cups
Cooking spray
18 wonton wrappers, thawed if frozen
2 teaspoons canola oil
¼ teaspoon salt

For the dressing
2 tablespoons fresh lime juice
1 teaspoon finely grated lime zest
¼ teaspoons salt
⅛ teaspoon freshly ground black pepper
½ teaspoon red pepper flakes
2 tablespoons olive oil

For the salad
½ pound lump crabmeat, picked over for shells and cartilage
1 stalk celery, finely diced (¼ cup)
½ cup peeled and finely diced ripe mango
¼ cup thinly sliced scallions (white and green parts)
2 tablespoons coarsely chopped fresh cilantro

SERVES 6
MAKES 18 WONTON CUPS;
SERVING SIZE: 3 WONTON CUPS

PER SERVING
CALORIES: 170;
TOTAL FAT: 7G
MONO: 5G,
POLY: 1G;
SAT: 1G,
PROTEIN: 9G;
CARB: 17G;
FIBER: 1G;

CHOL: 32MG;
SODIUM: 448MG

EXCELLENT
SOURCE OF
SELENIUM,
VITAMIN B12

GOOD
SOURCE OF
FOLATE, NIACIN,
PHOSPHORUS,
PROTEIN, THIAMIN,
VITAMIN C,
VITAMIN K, ZINC

Preheat the oven to 375°F. Coat two mini-muffin tins with cooking spray.

To make the wonton cups, brush both sides of the wonton wrappers with the canola oil and place each wrapper into a section of a mini-muffin tin. Gently press each wrapper into the tin and arrange so that it forms a cup shape. The wrapper will stick up out of the cup. Sprinkle with the salt and bake until browned and crisp, 8 to 10 minutes. Allow the cups to cool, then remove from the tin. These can be prepared the day before and stored at room temperature in an airtight container.

To make the dressing, whisk together the lime juice and zest, the salt, black pepper, and red pepper. Add the olive oil and whisk until well combined.

To make the salad, in a medium bowl, gently toss together the crabmeat, celery, mango, scallions, and cilantro, trying not to break up the crab too much. Add the dressing and gently toss to combine. This can be prepared the day before and stored in the refrigerator in an airtight container.

Fill each cup with the crab salad and serve immediately.

Maple-Glazed Walnuts

It amazes me that just three simple ingredients can make such a deeply flavored, versatile treat. The maple syrup gives the rich toasted walnuts a sweet caramelized coating, and a hint of salt adds a touch of savory complexity. Enjoy these nuts as a snack on their own, tossed in salads, or served on top of mashed sweet potatoes.

2 cups walnut halves
⅓ cup pure maple syrup
⅛ teaspoon salt

SERVES 6
MAKES 2 CUPS;
SERVING SIZE:
⅓ CUP

PER SERVING
CALORIES: 265;
TOTAL FAT: 22G
MONO: 3G,
POLY: 16G;
SAT: 2G,
PROTEIN: 5G;
CARB: 16.5G;
FIBER: 2G;

CHOL: 0MG;
SODIUM: 51MG

**EXCELLENT
SOURCE OF**
COPPER,
MANGANESE

**GOOD
SOURCE OF**
MAGNESIUM,
MOLYBDENUM,
PHOSPHORUS,
PROTEIN, ZINC

Preheat a dry medium skillet over medium-high heat until hot. Add the walnuts, maple syrup, and salt. Cook, stirring frequently, until the syrup is caramelized and the nuts are toasted, about 3 minutes. Let cool. The nuts will keep in an airtight container in the refrigerator for up to 2 weeks.

Spiced Mixed Nuts

Whenever I make a batch of these nuts, they get gobbled up instantly. I love watching people's expressions of surprise and delight when they eat them for the first time because the mix is so scrumptious, but no one can ever pinpoint what they are spiced with. The flavorings are a unique combination of aromatic curry powder and rosemary, with a hint of maple sweetness and a kick of cayenne heat. It is one of those flavor combinations you just can't stop thinking about long after you have eaten the last bite.

½ cup raw pecans
½ cup raw almonds
⅓ cup shelled raw pistachios
⅓ cup raw cashews
⅓ cup shelled raw pumpkin seeds
1 tablespoon pure maple syrup
½ teaspoon curry powder
⅛ teaspoon cayenne pepper, or more to taste
½ teaspoon dried rosemary
¼ teaspoon salt
Cooking spray

SERVES 6
MAKES 2 CUPS;
SERVING SIZE:
⅓ CUP

PER SERVING
CALORIES: 275;
TOTAL FAT: 23G
  MONO: 8.5G;
  POLY: 4.5G;
  SAT: 2G,
PROTEIN: 8G;
CARB: 12G;
FIBER: 3.5G;
CHOL: 0MG;
SODIUM: 100MG

**EXCELLENT
SOURCE OF**
COPPER,
MAGNESIUM,
MANGANESE,
PHOSPHORUS

**GOOD
SOURCE OF**
FIBER, IRON,
RIBOFLAVIN,
THIAMIN,
VITAMIN B6,
VITAMIN K, ZINC

Preheat the oven to 325°F. Combine the nuts and seeds in a medium bowl. Add the maple syrup, spices, rosemary, and salt and toss to combine.

Coat a baking sheet with cooking spray, then transfer the coated nuts to the sheet and spread evenly in a single layer. Bake, stirring once, until the nuts are fragrant and lightly toasted, 15 to 20 minutes. Remove from the oven and let cool. The nuts will keep in an airtight container in the refrigerator for up to 2 weeks.

Devilish Eggs

These deviled eggs have an indulgent filling boldly flavored with all the classic tongue-tingling tastes: mustard, hot sauce, and a spike of horseradish. They are garnished old-school style with a sprinkle of paprika, giving you everything you expect from traditional deviled eggs. The only unexpected thing is that these are good for you, thanks to my secret ingredient, silken tofu, which is so creamy and rich it lets you use less egg yolk and mayonnaise. Don't tell your guests and they'll never know. Just ask my husband, a self-proclaimed deviled egg connoisseur, who couldn't stop eating them.

1 dozen large eggs
2/3 cup silken tofu, drained
1 tablespoon mayonnaise
1 tablespoon Dijon mustard
1/2 teaspoon hot pepper sauce, plus more to taste
2 teaspoons prepared horseradish
2 tablespoons chopped fresh chives, plus more for garnish
Salt and freshly ground black pepper to taste
1/4 teaspoon paprika

SERVES 12
MAKES 24
DEVILED EGGS;
SERVING SIZE:
2 DEVILED EGGS

PER SERVING
CALORIES: 64;
TOTAL FAT: 4G
    MONO: 1G,
    POLY: 0.6G;
    SAT: 6G,
PROTEIN: 7G;
CARB: 1G;
FIBER: 0G;

CHOL: 106MG;
SODIUM:
114MG

**GOOD
SOURCE OF**
IODINE, PROTEIN,
RIBOFLAVIN,
SELENIUM

Place the eggs in a large saucepan and cover with water. Place over high heat and bring to a boil. Reduce the heat to low and simmer for 9 minutes. Remove the eggs from the water and run under cold water for about 1 minute, until cool enough to touch. Peel the eggs under cold running water. Pat them dry.

Slice the eggs in half lengthwise. Scoop out the yolks and discard 6 of them. Set aside the whites. Place the remaining yolks in a medium bowl and mash with the tofu, mayonnaise, mustard, hot sauce, horseradish, and chives. Season with salt and pepper. (You can prepare the filling and store it separately from the egg whites in the refrigerator in airtight containers for up to 2 days.)

Spoon the yolk mixture into the corner of a plastic bag and snip off the end. Pipe the yolk mixture into the egg whites. Arrange on a platter and sprinkle with paprika and chives. You can hold the stuffed eggs in the refrigerator for up to a few hours before serving.

Portobello Panini with Gorgonzola and Sun-Dried Tomatoes

Succulent, meaty portobello mushrooms are the "bread" in this sumptuous grilled sandwich. The center oozes with pungent Gorgonzola cheese and the slightly chewy sun-dried tomatoes add a concentrated tomato flavor and slight sweetness.

4 sun-dried tomatoes (not oil packed)
Boiling water
4 portobello mushrooms (2 ounces each)
¼ cup crumbled Gorgonzola cheese
1 tablespoon plus 1 teaspoon olive oil
Salt and freshly ground black pepper to taste

SERVES 4
MAKES 4 PANINI;
SERVING SIZE:
1 PANINI

PER SERVING
CALORIES: 90;
TOTAL FAT: 7G
  MONO: 3.3G,
  POLY: 0.7G;
  SAT: 2G,
PROTEIN: 3G;
CARB: 5G;
FIBER: 2G;
CHOL: 5MG;
SODIUM: 100MG

GOOD SOURCE OF
COPPER, NIACIN,
POTASSIUM,
RIBOFLAVIN,
SELENIUM

Reconstitute the sun-dried tomatoes by soaking them in boiling water for 10 minutes. Remove the tomatoes from the water, pat dry, and chop them.

Slice the stems off the mushrooms so they can lay completely flat. Slice each cap in half so you have 8 round mushroom slices. Top half of the mushrooms with 1 tablespoon of the chopped tomatoes and 1 tablespoon of the cheese. Top with the remaining mushroom slices. Brush the top side of each "sandwich" with some of the oil.

Preheat a large nonstick skillet or grill pan over medium-high heat until good and hot. Place the mushroom sandwiches in the hot pan carefully, oiled side down, and cook for 2 minutes. Brush the top half with the remaining oil, flip with a spatula, and cook until the mushroom softens and begins to brown and the cheese is melted, about another 2 minutes. Season with salt and pepper and serve.

*
DID YOU KNOW?
It turns out there are five basic tastes our tongues can detect: sweet, sour, salty, bitter, and, only recently recognized by western science, umami, a Japanese word that loosely translates to "deliciousness." The umami taste is often described as rich, savory, and mouthwatering. Tomatoes, mushrooms, and cheese are all full of umami, which helps explain why these portobello panini are so irresistible.

Herbed Goat Cheese Dip

Blending soft tangy goat cheese with a little yogurt and a drizzle of olive oil makes a silken white base for flecks of fresh green herbs. Sumptuous and refreshing all at once, this dip is one you will make over and over. It is also delicious served as a sauce with grilled meat.

6 ounces fresh goat cheese, preferably reduced-fat

1 tablespoon plain nonfat yogurt

2 teaspoons olive oil

⅓ cup chopped fresh flat-leaf parsley

2 teaspoons chopped fresh thyme

2 teaspoons chopped fresh mint

Salt and freshly ground black pepper to taste

Celery stalks or other raw vegetables for dipping

SERVES 4
MAKES ¾ CUP;
SERVING SIZE:
3 TABLESPOONS

PER SERVING
CALORIES: 85;
TOTAL FAT: 7G
MONO: 2G;
POLY: 0G;
SAT: 3.3G,
PROTEIN: 3G;
CARB: 2G;

FIBER: 0G;
CHOL: 7.5MG;
SODIUM: 200MG

EXCELLENT SOURCE OF
VITAMIN K

GOOD SOURCE OF
VITAMIN A,
VITAMIN C

Put the cheese, yogurt, and oil in a food processor and process until smooth. Stir in the herbs, season with salt and pepper, cover with plastic wrap, and chill in the refrigerator for at least 1 and up to 3 hours.

Serve chilled with vegetables for dipping.

The Scoop on Dips

What could be simpler to make or more enjoyable to eat than a good dip? It's no wonder dips are on the A list for every party. They are a social food, calling you to gather 'round and share from the same dish (no double dipping, please!). And they're fun to eat. Maybe that's why you can get a child to eat pretty much anything if you make it dipable. Dip variations are endless, for both the dip and what accompanies it. But some are decidedly better for you than others. Here's the scoop on making the most of your dips.

USE CREAMY SWAP-OUTS
You can have your favorite thick, creamy dip with a lot less fat and fewer calories by swapping out some or all of the full-fat sour cream and mayonnaise with plain yogurt, reduced-fat sour cream, or silken tofu.

LOOK TO THE MEDITERRANEAN OR MEXICO
Some classic dips are perfectly healthful as is. Many Mediterranean dips start with bean or vegetable purées or thickened yogurt as a base. And everyone's favorite Mexican dips—salsas, bean dips, and guacamole—are loaded with nutrition.

RETHINK THE CHIPS
Instead of the standard fried tortilla chips or potato chips, try some of the new baked chips on the market. They give you the same crispy crunch without many downsides. You can also make your own by brushing a little oil on slices of baguette, pita, or tortilla, sprinkling with a little salt, and toasting them on a baking sheet in a 375°F oven until crispy.

Edamame "Hummus" with Spiced Pita Chips

This fresh green, creamy dip has all the classic hummus flavors of garlic, cumin, and lemon. But it is light on the cumin and garlic in favor of a big citrus punch. Its mellow, bright flavor and smooth texture make it the perfect companion to the bold spicy shards of pita.

2 cups frozen shelled edamame, cooked according to package directions
1 cup silken tofu, drained
½ teaspoon salt, plus more to taste
Pinch of white pepper, plus more to taste
1½ teaspoons ground cumin, plus more for garnish
3 cloves garlic, minced (about 1 tablespoon)
¼ cup olive oil
⅓ cup fresh lemon juice, plus more to taste
Spiced Pita Chips (recipe follows)

SERVES 12
MAKES 3 CUPS;
SERVING SIZE:
¼ CUP HUMMUS
PLUS 4 PITA CHIPS

PER SERVING
CALORIES: 195;
TOTAL FAT: 12G
  MONO: 7G,
  POLY: 1.5G;
  SAT: 1.5G,
PROTEIN: 6G;
CARB: 18G;

FIBER: 3.5G;
CHOL: 0MG;
SODIUM: 326MG

EXCELLENT SOURCE OF
MANGANESE

GOOD SOURCE OF
FIBER, PROTEIN, SELENIUM

Set 1 tablespoon of the edamame aside for a garnish. Place the rest, along with the tofu, salt, pepper, cumin, garlic, oil, and lemon juice, in a food processor and process until very smooth, about 2 minutes. Taste and adjust the seasoning with more salt, pepper, and lemon juice, if desired. At this point, you can refrigerate the hummus in an airtight container for up to 3 days.

Transfer the hummus to a serving bowl and garnish with the reserved edamame and a sprinkle of cumin. Serve with the spiced pita chips.

✱ **EATING WELL TIP**

Edamame are young green soy beans. Once considered an exotic Japanese ingredient, you can now find them shelled and unshelled in the freezer case in most grocery stores. In Japan, edamame are usually eaten as a snack, boiled or steamed in their shells and lightly salted. Served that way, they are a fun finger-food. You just scrape the beans into your mouth with your teeth and discard the shell.

Shelled edamame are bright green nuggets that can be used just as you would any bean, hot or cold. They just need to be steamed for about 4 minutes from frozen and they are ready to go.

Spiced Pita Chips

These are the kind of chips that you just can't stop eating. They are great on their own, but even better for dipping.

¼ cup olive oil
2 teaspoons ground cumin
1 teaspoon ground coriander
½ teaspoon cayenne pepper
1 teaspoon garlic powder
½ teaspoon freshly ground black pepper
½ teaspoon salt
6 whole-wheat pita breads, cut into 8 wedges each

SERVES 12
SERVING SIZE:
4 WEDGES

PER SERVING
CALORIES: 105;
TOTAL FAT: 6G
  MONO: 3.5G,
  POLY: 0.5 G;
  SAT: 0.5G,
PROTEIN: 2G;

CARB: 13G;
FIBER: 2G;
CHOL: 0MG;
SODIUM: 218MG

**EXCELLENT
SOURCE OF**
MANGANESE

GOOD SOURCE OF
SELENIUM

Preheat the oven to 375°F.
Combine the oil and spices in a large bowl. Add the pita wedges and toss to coat. Spread the wedges in a single layer on two baking sheets and bake, tossing once, until the pitas are brown and crisp, about 15 minutes. Let cool completely before serving. They will keep in an airtight container at room temperature for about 3 days.

Warm Spinach and Artichoke Dip

This is one of those indulgent treats on a restaurant menu that you have to splurge on every now and then. I came up with this equally decadent tasting version in my quest to guiltlessly eat it more often. This dip totally hits the spot. It is thick, creamy, warm, and cheesy proof that you can have what you crave in a healthful way.

1 tablespoon canola oil

1 medium onion, finely chopped (about 1½ cups)

3 cloves garlic, chopped (about 1 tablespoon)

One 9-ounce package frozen artichoke hearts, thawed, rinsed, and patted dry

One 10-ounce package frozen chopped spinach, thawed and excess liquid squeezed out

½ cup reduced-fat sour cream

2 tablespoons mayonnaise

½ cup (4 ounces) Neufchâtel cheese (reduced-fat cream cheese)

2 ounces part-skim mozzarella cheese, shredded (about ½ cup)

½ teaspoon salt

¼ teaspoon freshly ground black pepper

Cooking spray

SERVES 12
MAKES 3 CUPS;
SERVING SIZE:
¼ CUP

PER SERVING
CALORIES: 100;
TOTAL FAT: 7G
MONO: 1G,
POLY: 0.5G;
SAT: 3G,
PROTEIN: 4G;
CARB: 5G;

FIBER: 2G;
CHOL: 13MG;
SODIUM: 211MG

EXCELLENT SOURCE OF
VITAMIN A

GOOD SOURCE OF
VITAMIN C

Preheat the oven to 375°F.

Heat the oil in a medium skillet over medium-high heat. Add the onion and cook, stirring a few times, until softened, 3 to 5 minutes. Add the garlic and cook for 1 minute. Remove from the heat and let cool.

In a food processor, combine the artichoke hearts, spinach, sour cream, mayonnaise, Neufchâtel, mozzarella, salt, and pepper. Process until smooth. Add the cooled onion mixture and pulse a few times to combine. At this point, you can refrigerate the dip in an airtight container for up to 3 days before baking it.

Transfer the mixture into an 8-inch glass square baking dish or 9-inch glass pie plate that has been lightly coated with cooking spray. Bake until heated through, 20 to 25 minutes. Serve hot with pita wedges or crudités.

Roasted Red Pepper and Walnut Dip (Muhammara)

This dip shows off how well roasted red peppers and nuts pair up. Here the nuts are walnuts and the spicing is distinctly Middle Eastern, with tangy-sweet concentrated pomegranate juice, lemon, and cumin. Serve it as a dip with toasted pita wedges or vegetables, as a sandwich spread, or as a sauce for grilled chicken or fish.

¾ cup pomegranate juice or 4 teaspoons pomegranate molasses

½ cup walnuts

3 tablespoons plain dry bread crumbs

1 tablespoon fresh lemon juice

One 16-ounce jar roasted red peppers, drained and rinsed

¼ teaspoon cayenne pepper

¼ teaspoon ground cumin, plus more for garnish

1 tablespoon olive oil, plus 1 teaspoon for garnish

Salt to taste

SERVES 8
MAKES 2 CUPS;
SERVING SIZE:
¼ CUP

FIBER: 0.6G;
CHOL: 0MG;
SODIUM: 136MG

PER SERVING
CALORIES: 113;
TOTAL FAT: 7.4G
MONO: 2.5G;
POLY: 3.8G;
SAT: 0.8G;
PROTEIN: 1.6G;
CARB: 16G;

EXCELLENT SOURCE OF
VITAMIN A,
VITAMIN C

GOOD SOURCE OF
MANGANESE

Put the pomegranate juice, if using, into a small saucepan and bring to a boil. Reduce the heat to medium and simmer, uncovered, until the juice is reduced to about 2 tablespoons, about 6 minutes. Set aside to cool and thicken. If you're using pomegranate molasses, this step isn't necessary.

Toast the walnuts in a small dry skillet over medium-high heat until fragrant, 3 to 5 minutes, stirring frequently. Set aside to cool.

Put the walnuts and bread crumbs in a food processor and process until finely ground. Add the reduced pomegranate juice or pomegranate molasses, lemon juice, red peppers, cayenne, and cumin and process until smooth. With the processor running, add 1 tablespoon of the oil through the feed tube in a thin stream. Season with salt. This will keep in an airtight container in the refrigerator for up to 3 days.

Transfer the dip to a serving bowl. Sprinkle with cumin and the remaining 1 teaspoon oil and serve.

White Bean and Roasted Garlic Dip

This white bean purée, infused with lemon and sweet caramelized roasted garlic, is a Tuscan-inspired dip that can also be used, like hummus, as a sandwich filling or flavor-packed spread.

Two 15.5-ounce cans white beans, preferably low-sodium, rinsed and drained
2 tablespoons Whole Roasted Garlic (recipe follows)
3 tablespoons extra-virgin olive oil
¼ cup fresh lemon juice
Salt and white pepper to taste
¼ cup fresh flat-leaf parsley leaves for garnish

In a food processor, combine the beans, roasted garlic, oil, and lemon juice and process until smooth. Season with salt and pepper. This will keep in an airtight container in the refrigerator for up to 3 days.

Transfer to a serving bowl, garnish with the parsley leaves, and serve with your favorite vegetables for dipping.

SERVES 12
MAKES 3 CUPS;
SERVING SIZE:
¼ CUP

PER SERVING
CALORIES: 83;
TOTAL FAT: 4G
 MONO: 2.7G,
 POLY: 0G;
 SAT: 0.5G,
PROTEIN: 4G;
CARB: 12G;

FIBER: 3.5G;
CHOL: 0MG;
SODIUM:
265MG

EXCELLENT
SOURCE OF
VITAMIN K

GOOD
SOURCE OF
FIBER

Whole Roasted Garlic

Roasting mellows and sweetens garlic while softening it so it is spreadable. You can serve the stunning golden brown head whole and let your guests scoop the gems out with a knife, or mash it and serve it like butter.

1 head garlic
1 tablespoon olive oil

Preheat the oven to 375°F.

Cut the top third of the garlic head off so that the tops of the cloves are exposed. Place the garlic head, unpeeled, in a small ovenproof dish and drizzle with the oil. Cover with aluminum foil and bake for 30 minutes.

Uncover and bake until the garlic is soft and golden brown, another 30 to 40 minutes. If not using immediately, let cool, then store in an airtight container in the refrigerator for up to 5 days.

SERVES 4
MAKES ABOUT
3 TABLESPOONS
MASHED GARLIC,
OR ABOUT 16
WHOLE CLOVES;
SERVING SIZE:
ABOUT 2
TEASPOONS
MASHED OR
4 CLOVES

PER SERVING
CALORIES: 45;
TOTAL FAT: 3.5G
 MONO: 2.5G;
 POLY: 0G;
 SAT: 0.5G;
PROTEIN: 0.5G;
CARB: 3G;
FIBER: 0G;
CHOL: 0MG;
SODIUM: 1MG

soups & sandwiches

Tomato-Tortilla Soup

This tasty tomato soup packs a big flavor punch with just the right kick of spiciness. A quick whirl with a blender gives it body and thickness while preserving some lovely chunks of tomato. Topped with shards of crunchy corn tortillas, a bright spritz of lime juice, cool sour cream, and a confetti of cilantro, it's a fiesta in a bowl.

Two 6-inch corn tortillas
2 tablespoons canola oil
¼ teaspoon salt
1 small onion, chopped (about 1 cup)
3 cloves garlic, minced (about 1 tablespoon)
1 teaspoon ground cumin
4 cups low-sodium chicken broth
Two 14.5-ounce cans no-salt-added diced tomatoes, with their juices
1 small jalapeño pepper, seeded and thinly sliced
¾ teaspoon dried oregano
¼ cup fresh lime juice
¼ cup reduced-fat sour cream
2 tablespoons chopped fresh cilantro

SERVES 4
SERVING SIZE:
2 CUPS

PER SERVING
CALORIES: 220;
TOTAL FAT: 11G
  MONO: 5G;
  POLY: 2G;
  SAT: 2G,
PROTEIN: 8G;
CARB: 22G;
FIBER: 3G;
CHOL: 8MG;
SODIUM: 296MG

EXCELLENT SOURCE OF
IRON, VITAMIN A, VITAMIN C

GOOD SOURCE OF
FIBER, NIACIN, PHOSPHORUS, PROTEIN, POTASSIUM, VITAMIN K

Preheat the oven to 375°F.

Brush both sides of each tortilla with oil, using all but 2 teaspoons of the oil. Cut the tortillas in half, then cut each half into ¼-inch-wide strips. Arrange the strips on a baking sheet, sprinkle with the salt, and bake until crisp and golden, about 12 minutes. Remove from the oven and set aside.

Heat the remaining 2 teaspoons oil in a large heavy skillet over medium heat. Add the onion and cook, stirring, for 5 minutes, then add the garlic and cumin and cook, stirring, until the onion is soft and translucent but not browned, about another 3 minutes. Add the broth, tomatoes, jalapeño, and oregano, bring to a boil, then reduce the heat to low and simmer for about 10 minutes. Stir in the lime juice.

Remove the pan from the heat and purée with an immersion blender or in two batches in a regular blender until the soup lightens in color but chunks of tomato remain, about 30 seconds. Serve the soup topped with the tortilla strips, a dollop of sour cream, and a sprinkle of cilantro.

Sweet and Spicy Peanut Soup

This soup has exotic African origins but the ingredients are all comfortably familiar; chances are you already have everything on hand you need to make it. Its sweetness, from sweet potato and carrot, is heightened with honey and balanced with the clarity of ginger and hot pepper. Peanut butter brings it all together and makes it extra rich and satisfying. And don't forget the fresh scallions. Much more than a pretty garnish, they add an essential zingy freshness and crunch.

1 tablespoon canola oil

1 large onion, diced (about 2 cups)

1 medium red bell pepper, seeded and diced (about 1 cup)

2 medium carrots, diced (about 1 cup)

½ teaspoon cayenne pepper

½ teaspoon freshly ground black pepper

1 clove garlic, minced (about 1 teaspoon)

1 teaspoon peeled and grated fresh ginger

1 large sweet potato, peeled and cubed (2 cups)

6 cups low-sodium chicken or vegetable broth

One 14.5-ounce can no-salt-added diced tomatoes, with their juices

⅔ cup creamy natural peanut butter

2 teaspoons honey

½ cup chopped scallion greens (about 3 scallions)

SERVES 6
SERVING SIZE:
1½ CUPS

PER SERVING
CALORIES: 290;
TOTAL FAT: 18G
  MONO: 9G,
  POLY: 5G;
  SAT: 3.5G;
PROTEIN: 14G;
CARB: 23G;
FIBER: 5G;
CHOL: 0MG;
SODIUM: 260MG

EXCELLENT SOURCE OF
FIBER, NIACIN,
PROTEIN,
VITAMIN A,
VITAMIN C,
VITAMIN K

GOOD SOURCE OF
PHOSPHORUS,
POTASSIUM,
VITAMIN B$_6$

Heat the oil in a large soup pot over medium-high heat. Add the onion, bell pepper, and carrots and cook, stirring, until the vegetables soften, about 5 minutes. Add the cayenne, black pepper, garlic, and ginger and cook for 1 minute more. Stir in the sweet potato, broth, and tomatoes and bring to a boil. Reduce the heat to medium-low and simmer until the potatoes are tender, about 20 minutes.

Purée the soup in the pot using an immersion blender or in a regular blender in two batches and return the soup to the pot. Add the peanut butter and honey and stir, over low heat, until the peanut butter melts. Serve warm, garnished with the scallions.

Curried Butternut Squash Soup

Your senses of sight, smell, and taste will all be delighted by this soup. The butternut squash gives it a rich orange color and a natural sweetness that is the perfect counterpoint to the boldly fragrant curry spices. Full-bodied, creamy, and exotic, it tastes truly indulgent.

1 tablespoon canola oil

1 large onion, chopped (about 2 cups)

2 cloves garlic, minced (about 2 teaspoons)

One 2½-pound butternut squash, peeled, seeded, and cut into 1-inch cubes

6 cups low-sodium chicken or vegetable broth

1 tablespoon plus 2 teaspoons curry powder

½ teaspoon salt, plus more to taste

2 tablespoons honey

4 teaspoons plain nonfat yogurt, for garnish

SERVES 4
SERVING SIZE: 1½ CUPS

PER SERVING
CALORIES: 295;
TOTAL FAT: 6.5G
  MONO: 3G,
  POLY: 2G;
  SAT: 1G,
PROTEIN: 12G;
CARB: 56G;
FIBER: 7.5G;
CHOL: 0MG;
SODIUM: 415MG

EXCELLENT SOURCE OF
CALCIUM, FIBER, FOLATE, IRON, MAGNESIUM, MANGANESE, MOLYBDENUM, NIACIN, PHOSPHO-RUS, POTASSIUM, PROTEIN, THIAMIN, VITAMIN A, VITA-MIN B6, VITAMIN C, VITAMIN E

GOOD SOURCE OF
PANTOTHENIC ACID, RIBOFLAVIN, VITAMIN K

Heat the oil over medium heat in a large soup pot. Add the onion and garlic and cook, stirring, until softened, about 5 minutes. Add the squash, broth, curry powder, and salt and bring to a boil. Reduce the heat to medium-low and simmer until the squash is tender, about 15 minutes. Remove the soup from the heat, stir in the honey, and purée until smooth in the pot using an immersion blender or in two batches in a regular blender. Taste and season with salt, if necessary.

To serve, ladle the soup into serving bowls and drizzle with the yogurt.

Summer Corn and Vegetable Soup

This soup is inspired by summer farm stand visits when the corn is just picked, the tomatoes are deep red and kissed by the sun, the zucchini is plentiful, and fresh basil perfumes the air. The dish's simple flavorings allow the subtle essences of the vegetables to really come through. While it is the perfect showcase for fresh summer produce, you can make it anytime you need to be reminded of a warmer season.

4 cups fresh corn kernels or two 10-ounce packages frozen corn, thawed
2 cups nonfat milk
1 tablespoon olive oil
1 large onion, diced (about 2 cups)
1 medium red bell pepper, seeded and diced (about 1 cup)
1 small zucchini (about ½ pound), diced
2 cups low-sodium chicken or vegetable broth
2 plum tomatoes, seeded and diced
¾ teaspoon salt
Freshly ground black pepper to taste
½ cup fresh basil leaves, cut into ribbons

SERVES 6
SERVING SIZE:
1½ CUPS

PER SERVING
CALORIES: 180;
TOTAL FAT: 5G
  MONO: 2G,
  POLY: 0G;
  SAT: 1G,
PROTEIN: 9.5G;
CARB: 32G;
FIBER: 4G;
CHOL: 5MG;
SODIUM: 365MG

**EXCELLENT
SOURCE OF**
MANGANESE,
VITAMIN A,
VITAMIN K

**GOOD
SOURCE OF**
CALCIUM, FIBER,
MOLYBDENUM,
POTASSIUM,
VITAMIN B6

Put 2 cups of the corn and the milk into a blender or food processor and process until smooth. Set aside.

Heat the oil in a large soup pot over medium-high heat. Add the onion, bell pepper, and zucchini and cook, stirring, until the vegetables are tender, about 5 minutes. Add the remaining 2 cups corn and the broth and bring to a boil. Add the puréed corn and the tomatoes and cook until warmed through but not boiling. Add the salt and season with pepper. Serve garnished with the basil ribbons.

Creamy Soups Creamlessly

Who doesn't love a thick, creamy soup with lots of body to it? Luckily you don't need to add saturated-fat laden cream or butter to get a rich, velvety soup. A number of healthier additions do the trick remarkably well.

VEGETABLE PURÉES

Puréeing vegetable-based soups is a great way to create thick and lustrous dishes. If you want your soup ultrarich and creamy, purée the whole pot in batches in the blender, as with the Curried Butternut Squash Soup (page 78) and Green Pea Soup (page 84). If you just want to thicken it a little but retain a certain chunkiness, just purée some of it, as with the Summer Corn and Vegetable Soup (facing page) and Tomato-Tortilla Soup (page 76). For ease, you can use an immersion blender until the soup is the consistency you desire. But if you are aiming for something silky smooth, it's got to be done in a regular blender.

MASHED BEANS

Mash some white beans in a small bowl and stir the mash into your hot soup. There it will dissolve into the broth, thicken it, and provide body, not to mention vitamins, minerals, protein, and fiber. Kidney and black beans work too, but they will color the broth. If you want some whole beans in your soup as well, you can just mash half, as in the Tuscan Vegetable Soup (page 85).

EGGS

In my Lemon Chicken Soup with Orzo (page 86) I use a traditional Greek mixture of egg and lemon juice called avgolemono as a thickener. In it the egg and lemon juice are beaten together and tempered (meaning you gradually beat warm broth into the egg so it adjusts to the temperature and you don't wind up with scrambled eggs). Then you stir the mixture into the soup, which becomes luxuriously full-bodied.

BREAD

I use crustless white bread, moistened in a little water and puréed with the broth to make the White Gazpacho with Grapes and Toasted Almonds (page 83) thicker and more opaque. This technique works with most puréed cold soups.

White Gazpacho with Grapes and Toasted Almonds

A refreshingly updated version of the classic tomato-based cold Spanish soup, this gazpacho starts with a beautiful pale-green cucumber broth, light and cool, with just enough body to give it substance. Its surprising garnishes really bring it to life. Chopped scallions, toasted slivered almonds, cucumber chunks, and sweet-tart green grapes add an exciting mix of textures and flavors and keep it all elegantly green and white. This soup has so much visual and taste impact it's perfect for a dinner party where you really want to impress. It is also fun to serve half-portions in martini glasses at a cocktail party.

¼ cup plus 4 teaspoons slivered almonds

2 large English cucumbers or 3 large regular cucumbers, peeled, seeded, and roughly chopped

3 slices white bread, crusts removed

½ cup warm water

3 cloves garlic, peeled

6 scallions (whites only), thinly sliced (about ½ cup)

¼ cup white wine vinegar or sherry vinegar, plus more to taste

1 teaspoon fresh lemon juice, plus more to taste

½ teaspoon salt, plus more to taste

3 tablespoons olive oil

½ cup green grapes, cut in half

SERVES 4
SERVING SIZE:
1 CUP GAZPACHO
PLUS GARNISHES

EXCELLENT
SOURCE OF
VITAMIN C,
VITAMIN E,
VITAMIN K

PER SERVING
CALORIES: 245;
TOTAL FAT: 17G
    MONO: 12G;
    POLY: 2.5G;
    SAT: 2G,
PROTEIN: 5.5G;
CARB: 19G;
FIBER: 3G;
CHOL: 0MG;
SODIUM: 425MG

GOOD
SOURCE OF
COPPER, FIBER,
MAGNESIUM,
PROTEIN,
PHOSPHORUS,
RIBOFLAVIN,
THIAMIN

Toast the almonds in a small dry skillet over medium-high heat until fragrant, 3 to 5 minutes, stirring frequently; set aside.

Set aside 1 cup of the chopped cucumber for a garnish. Soak the bread in the water until soft, about 2 minutes. Place the soaked bread, the rest of the cucumber, the garlic, ¼ cup of the scallion whites, the vinegar, lemon juice, ¼ cup of the almonds, the salt, and oil in a food processor and process until the cucumbers are completely blended and the liquid and almonds are almost completely invisible, 1 to 2 minutes. Season with more salt and vinegar, if desired.

To serve, ladle 1 cup gazpacho into each serving bowl. Mound ¼ cup of the reserved chopped cucumber, 1 tablespoon of the remaining scallion whites, 2 tablespoons of the grapes, and 1 teaspoon of the almonds in the center of the soup and serve.

Green Pea Soup

This soup is so elegant in its emerald green, velvety splendor and so flavorful with savory, rich peas enhanced by a touch of tarragon that your friends and family will think you've secretly been attending French culinary school when you serve it to them. You never have to let on that you actually made it in less than 15 minutes with nothing fancier than a bag of frozen peas.

1 teaspoon olive oil
1 medium onion, chopped (about 1½ cups)
2½ cups low-sodium chicken broth
¾ teaspoon dried tarragon
½ teaspoon salt
Freshly ground black pepper to taste
One 10-ounce bag frozen peas
4 teaspoons plain nonfat yogurt (optional)

SERVES 4
SERVING SIZE:
1¼ CUPS

PER SERVING
CALORIES: 95;
TOTAL FAT: 2.5G
  MONO: 1.5G,
  POLY: 0G,
  SAT: 0G;
PROTEIN: 7G;
CARB: 12G;
FIBER: 3G;
CHOL: 0MG;
SODIUM: 415MG

EXCELLENT SOURCE OF
VITAMIN A,
VITAMIN C,
VITAMIN K

GOOD SOURCE OF
FIBER,
FOLATE, IRON,
MANGANESE,
NIACIN,
PHOSPHORUS,
PROTEIN, THIAMIN

In a large soup pot, heat the oil over medium-low heat. Add the onion, and cook, stirring a few times, until softened, about 5 minutes. Add the broth, tarragon, salt, and a few turns of black pepper and bring to a boil over high heat. Add the peas and cook just until heated through.

Purée the soup until very smooth in the pot using an immersion blender or in two batches in a regular blender. If serving hot, return the soup to the pot and bring just to a simmer. If serving cold, transfer to the refrigerator to chill.

To serve, ladle the soup into bowls and top each serving with a swirl of yogurt, if desired.

Tuscan Vegetable Soup

This soup is bursting with colorful vegetables, herbs, and white beans in a rich, tomatoy broth. It is a meal in a bowl with a long-cooked, hearty taste that can be made in about 30 minutes. Served with some crusty whole-grain bread, you have a perfect, ultrasatisfying meal.

One 15.5-ounce can cannellini or other small white beans, preferably
  low-sodium, drained and rinsed
1 tablespoon olive oil
½ large onion, diced (about 1 cup)
1 medium carrot, diced (about ½ cup)
2 stalks celery, diced (about ½ cup)
1 small zucchini (about ½ pound), diced (about 1½ cups)
1 clove garlic, minced (about 1 teaspoon)
1 tablespoon chopped fresh thyme or 1 teaspoon dried
2 teaspoons chopped fresh sage or ½ teaspoon dried
½ teaspoon salt, plus more to taste
¼ teaspoon freshly ground black pepper, plus more to taste
4 cups low-sodium chicken or vegetable broth
One 14.5-ounce can no-salt-added diced tomatoes, with their juices
2 ounces baby spinach leaves (2 cups lightly packed), chopped
⅓ cup freshly grated Parmesan cheese (optional)

SERVES 6
SERVING SIZE:
1½ CUPS

EXCELLENT
SOURCE OF
FIBER, VITAMIN A,
VITAMIN C

PER SERVING
CALORIES: 143;
TOTAL FAT: 4G
  MONO: 2G,
  POLY: 0.5G;
  SAT: 0.5G,
PROTEIN: 8G;
CARB: 20G;
FIBER: 5G;
CHOL: 0MG;
SODIUM: 323MG

GOOD
SOURCE OF
IRON,
MAGNESIUM,
NIACIN,
PHOSPHORUS,
PROTEIN

In a small bowl, mash half of the beans with a masher or the back of a spoon and set aside.

Heat the oil in a large soup pot over medium-high heat. Add the onion, carrot, celery, zucchini, garlic, thyme, sage, salt, and pepper, and cook, stirring occasionally, until the vegetables are tender, about 5 minutes.

Add the broth and tomatoes and bring to a boil. Add the mashed and whole beans and the spinach leaves and cook until the spinach is wilted, about 3 minutes more.

Serve topped with the Parmesan, if desired.

Lemon Chicken Soup with Orzo

I recently threw a soup party with huge pots of soup bubbling away on the stove and small serving cups so everyone could to taste each one. This is the soup no one could stop talking about. My guests all fell in love with its thyme-scented, thick, lemony broth, delicate orzo (a rice-shaped pasta), and meaty chunks of chicken. It's kind of like a girl-next-door chicken noodle soup that's traveled abroad and returned with an intriguing flair.

4 teaspoons olive oil

8 ounces skinless, boneless chicken breast halves, cut into small chunks

Pinch of salt, plus more to taste

1 medium onion, diced (about 1 ½ cups)

2 stalks celery, diced (about ½ cup)

1 medium carrot, diced (about ½ cup)

2 teaspoons chopped fresh thyme or ½ teaspoon dried

6 cups low-sodium chicken broth

1 cup orzo, preferably whole-wheat

2 large eggs

3 tablespoons fresh lemon juice

Freshly ground black pepper to taste

SERVES 4
SERVING SIZE: 1½ CUPS

PER SERVING
CALORIES: 280;
TOTAL FAT: 10G
  MONO: 6G;
  POLY: 1G;
  SAT: 2G,
PROTEIN: 26G;
CARB: 22G;
FIBER: 2G;
CHOL: 39MG;
SODIUM: 291MG

EXCELLENT SOURCE OF
NIACIN, PHOSPHORUS, POTASSIUM, PROTEIN, RIBOFLAVIN, SELENIUM, VITAMIN A, VITAMIN B6, VITAMIN C

GOOD SOURCE OF
COPPER, FOLATE, IODINE, IRON, MAGNESIUM, MOLYBDENUM, PANTOTHENIC ACID, THIAMIN, VITAMIN B12, VITAMIN K, ZINC

Heat 2 teaspoons of the oil in a soup pot over medium-high heat. Season the chicken with the salt, add it to the pot, and cook, stirring, a few times, until just cooked through, about 5 minutes. Transfer the chicken to a dish and set aside.

Add the remaining 2 teaspoons oil to the pot. Add the onion, celery, carrot, and thyme and cook, stirring, over medium-high heat until the vegetables are tender, about 5 minutes. Add 5 cups of the broth and bring to a boil. Add the orzo and let simmer until tender, about 8 minutes. Turn the heat down to low to keep the soup hot but not boiling.

Warm the remaining 1 cup broth in a small saucepan until it is hot but not boiling. In a medium bowl, beat the eggs. Gradually whisk the lemon juice into the eggs. Then gradually add the hot broth to the egg-lemon mixture, whisking all the while. Add the mixture to the soup, stirring well until the soup is thickened. Do not let the soup come to a boil. Add the cooked chicken to the soup. Season with salt and pepper and serve.

Rhode Island–Style Clam Chowder

It turns out not all New Englanders make their clam chowder with cream. Classic Rhode Island chowder is flavor-packed and distinctively creamless, as I discovered on my first-annual, all-sisters Newport weekend getaway with my sister and our friends. Whenever I make this hearty chowder, with its chunks of Red Bliss potato, tender plump clams, and briny broth doused with thyme, it takes me right back to the seaside with them. Use frozen clams packed in their own juice.

2 tablespoons olive oil
2 slices Canadian bacon (2 ounces), chopped
1 large onion, diced (about 2 cups)
4 stalks celery, diced (about 1 cup)
4 cups diced (½-inch) Red Bliss potatoes (about 1¼ pounds)
Two 1-pound containers of frozen clams packed in their own juice, thawed, juice reserved
1 teaspoons fresh thyme or ½ teaspoon dried
Salt and freshly ground black pepper to taste

SERVES 6
SERVING SIZE: 1½ CUPS

PER SERVING
CALORIES: 220;
TOTAL FAT: 7.5G
MONO: 4G,
POLY: 0.5G;
SAT: 1.5G;
PROTEIN: 15G;
CARB: 24G;
FIBER: 2.5G;
CHOL: 60.5MG;
SODIUM: 675MG

EXCELLENT SOURCE OF
IRON, PHOSPHO-RUS, POTASSIUM, PROTEIN, VITAMIN B12, VITAMIN C

GOOD SOURCE OF
CALCIUM, FIBER, FOLATE, MAG-NESIUM, MAN-GANESE, NIACIN, SELENIUM, THIA-MIN, VITAMIN B6, VITAMIN K

Heat the oil in a large soup pot over medium-high heat. Add the Canadian bacon, onion, and celery and cook, stirring a few times, until the vegetables soften, about 6 minutes. Add the potatoes, clams, clam juice, thyme, and water to cover. Bring to a boil, reduce the heat to medium-low, and simmer until the potatoes are soft, about 30 minutes. Season with salt and pepper.

＊ **EATING WELL TIP**
You need less food to feel satisfied when you eat from a smaller plate or bowl. That's because a lot of our sense of satiety is visual, and we can trick our eyes by piling a smaller plate with food.

Beef and Mushroom Barley Soup

Who says you can't have both beef and mushrooms in your barley soup? I have broken with the either/or tradition and put the two together for what I think is a perfect soup. Every spoonful has glorious chunks of tender meat, earthy, toothsome mushrooms, and buttery barley kernels. It is chock-full of other colorful vegetables too, including lots of chopped tomatoes. This soup is a meal in a bowl that will warm your belly and soul.

4 teaspoons olive oil
¾ pound beef stew meat (preferably from the shank),
    cut into ½-inch pieces
¼ teaspoon salt, plus more to taste
Pinch of freshly ground black pepper, plus more to taste
1 medium yellow onion, diced (about 1½ cups)
8 ounces button mushrooms, coarsely chopped
2 medium carrots, diced (about 1 cup)
2 stalks celery, diced (about ½ cup)
2 cloves garlic, minced (about 2 teaspoons)
6 cups low-sodium beef broth
One 14.5-ounce can no-salt-added diced tomatoes, with their juices
½ cup hulled or pearled barley
1 tablespoon coarsely chopped fresh thyme or 1 teaspoon dried
¼ cup chopped fresh flat-leaf parsley

SERVES 6
SERVING SIZE:
1½ CUPS

PER SERVING
CALORIES: 275;
TOTAL FAT: 10G
    MONO: 5G;
    POLY: 1G;
    SAT: 3G,
PROTEIN: 25G;
CARB: 22G;
FIBER: 5G;
CHOL: 26MG;
SODIUM: 255MG

EXCELLENT
SOURCE OF
COPPER, FIBER,
NIACIN, PHOSPHO-
RUS, POTASSIUM,
RIBOFLAVIN, PRO-
TEIN, SELENIUM,
VITAMIN A,
VITAMIN B$_6$,
VITAMIN B$_{12}$,
VITAMIN C,
VITAMIN K, ZINC

GOOD
SOURCE OF
IRON, MAGNESIUM,
MANGANESE,
PANTOTHENIC
ACID, THIAMIN

In a large soup pot, heat 2 teaspoons of the oil over medium-high heat. Sprinkle the meat with the salt and pepper. Add the meat to the pot and brown on all sides, about 5 minutes total. Transfer the meat to a paper towel–lined plate and set aside.

Add the remaining 2 teaspoons oil to the pot. Add the onion and mushrooms and cook over medium-high heat, stirring, until softened, about 5 minutes. Add the carrots, celery, and garlic and cook for 5 minutes more, stirring occasionally. Add the broth, tomatoes, browned meat, barley, and thyme and bring to a boil. Reduce the heat to low, cover, and simmer until the barley is cooked and the meat is tender, about 50 minutes. Taste and season with salt and pepper. Ladle into soup bowls and garnish each serving with a sprinkling of parsley.

✳ DID YOU KNOW?
Barley is rich in the same kind of soluble fiber as oats—the kind that's been shown to help lower cholesterol.

Sloppy Joes

These Sloppy Joes are everything you could wish for in this crowd-pleasing sandwich—a rich, meaty filling smothered in tangy-sweet, thick tomato sauce that just refuses to stay inside the bun. You definitely need a fork and a few napkins to eat this mouthwatering meal!

1 pound lean or extra-lean (90% lean or higher) ground beef
1 medium onion, diced (about 1½ cups)
4 cloves garlic, minced (about 4 teaspoons)
1 jalapeño pepper, seeded and minced
1 medium red bell pepper, seeded and diced (about 1 cup)
One 15.5-ounce can small red or pinto beans, preferably low-sodium, drained and rinsed
1½ cups no-salt-added tomato sauce
2 tablespoons tomato paste
1 tablespoon red wine vinegar
1 tablespoon unsulfured molasses
1 tablespoon Worcestershire sauce
1 teaspoon dry mustard
¾ teaspoon salt
Freshly ground black pepper to taste
8 whole-wheat burger buns

SERVES 8
SERVING SIZE:
1 SANDWICH

PER SERVING
CALORIES: 265;
TOTAL FAT: 4.5G
  MONO: 1.5G,
  POLY: 1.2G;
  SAT: 1.1G,
PROTEIN: 20G;
CARB: 40G;
FIBER: 8G;
CHOL: 30MG;
SODIUM: 535MG

EXCELLENT
SOURCE OF
FIBER, MANGA-
NESE, MOLYB-
DENUM, NIACIN,
PROTEIN,
SELENIUM,
VITAMIN B$_{12}$,
VITAMIN C, ZINC

GOOD
SOURCE OF
COPPER, FOLATE,
IRON, MAGNESIUM,
PHOSPHORUS,
THIAMIN,
VITAMIN A,
VITAMIN B$_6$

Brown the meat and onion in a large nonstick skillet over medium-high heat for 5 minutes, breaking up the meat into crumbles as it cooks. Pour the drippings out of the pan and discard. Add the garlic, jalapeño, and red pepper and cook 5 minutes more, stirring occasionally. Stir in the rest of the ingredients, except the buns, reduce the heat to low, and simmer for another 5 minutes.

Place a ½-cup scoop of the mixture onto each bun and serve.

Meatball and Pepper Hero

One of the foods highest on my personal crave list is an Italian meatball hero. How can anyone resist warm, saucy meatballs nestled in a hunk of crusty bread topped with oozy melted mozzarella cheese? Thankfully there is no need to resist mine because it is all that and better for you, thanks to savory turkey meatballs, lower fat (but still melt-a-licious) cheese, and the addition of luscious sautéed tricolor peppers and onions.

1 tablespoon olive oil
1 small onion, sliced
½ medium green bell pepper, seeded and sliced into thin strips
½ medium red bell pepper, seeded and sliced into thin strips
½ medium yellow bell pepper, seeded and sliced into thin strips
¼ teaspoon salt
One 12-ounce loaf Italian bread (preferably whole grain)
8 meatballs and 1 cup sauce from Spaghetti with Turkey Meatballs
    in Spicy Tomato Sauce (page 164)
½ cup shredded part-skim mozzarella cheese (2 ounces)

SERVES 4
SERVING SIZE: ONE-QUARTER OF THE HERO, CONTAINING 2 MEATBALLS, ¼ CUP SAUCE, ½ CUP PEPPER-AND-ONION MIXTURE, AND 2 TABLESPOONS CHEESE

PER SERVING
CALORIES: 415;
TOTAL FAT: 12G
    MONO: 4G,
    POLY: 1.7G;
    SAT: 3.6G,
PROTEIN: 25G;
CARB: 53G;
FIBER: 4.3G;

CHOL: 47MG;
SODIUM: 753MG

EXCELLENT SOURCE OF
CALCIUM, IRON, MANGANESE, NIACIN, PROTEIN, RIBOFLAVIN, SELENIUM, THIAMIN, VITAMIN A, VITAMIN C, VITAMIN K

GOOD SOURCE OF
COPPER, FIBER, FOLATE, MAGNESIUM, PHOSPHORUS

Preheat the broiler.

Heat the oil in a large skillet over medium heat. Add the onion, peppers, and salt and cook until the peppers are soft and the onions golden, about 15 minutes, stirring occasionally.

Cut the bread into quarters crosswise and cut each quarter in half, being careful not to cut all the way through, so the two halves stay connected. Scoop the soft center out of the bread and discard. Put the bread, open-faced, on a baking sheet. Place 2 of the meatballs and some of the sauce on one side of each piece of bread. Top with the pepper mixture. Moisten the other side of each sandwich with more of the sauce and sprinkle all over with the cheese. Broil until the cheese is melted, about 4 minutes. Serve hot.

A Well "Bread" Sandwich

I believe the day someone slapped a few edibles between two pieces of bread and called it a meal was a pivotal point in civilization. It's a shame so many people write sandwiches off their healthy menu because they are afraid of the bread. I am happy to report that you can enjoy your sandwiches guilt-free and healthfully, especially if you do the bread right.

TWO WILL DO (OUNCES, THAT IS)

You just need two pieces of bread to make a sandwich, but some of us make ours with the equivalent of 5 slices. For example, a large roll can weigh 5 ounces, which is the weight of 5 standard slices of bread! Even regular sliced bread can be monstrous these days, weighing in at almost 2 ounces a slice. When you whip up a sandwich, pay close attention to the weight of the bread (it's on the label) and try to keep it to 2 ounces per sandwich.

THE WRAP ADVANTAGE

Wrap bread and pita pocket bread are great sandwich choices because you can stuff them with piles of vegetables, which make a sandwich more healthful, more colorful, and extra satisfying. Wrap bread and pita don't have fewer calories than regular bread, though; each 9-inch-diameter wrap is about the equivalent of two bread slices.

GO WHOLE GRAIN

Whole grains are one of the food groups most of us need to eat more of, since they contain health-protective nutrients, antioxidants, and fiber. A sandwich is a great way to work them in. Just make sure you buy bread that is 100% whole grain (it will say so on the label). You can buy a huge variety of whole-grain breads now, from wraps and tortillas to dark ryes and burger buns.

Sweet and Spicy Grilled Cheese Sandwiches

This is what your basic childhood favorite wants to be when it grows up. Sweet-savory caramelized onion, two kinds of flavor-packed cheeses (one with a spicy kick!), and juicy slices of tomato on hearty sandwich bread, all toasted perfectly golden brown so the melted cheese oozes out. It reminds you why you loved grilled cheese as a kid, but makes you glad you're an adult.

2 teaspoons canola oil
1 large red onion, finely diced (about 2 cups)
Salt and freshly ground black pepper to taste
3 ounces sharp cheddar cheese, thinly sliced
8 slices whole-wheat bread
3 ounces pepper Jack cheese, thinly sliced
1 large or 2 medium ripe beefsteak or hothouse tomatoes, sliced
Cooking spray

SERVES 4
SERVING SIZE: 1 SANDWICH

PER SERVING
CALORIES: 350;
TOTAL FAT: 18G
   MONO: 2.5G,
   POLY: 1G;
   SAT: 8G,
PROTEIN: 16G;
CARB: 33G;
FIBER: 5G;
CHOL: 45MG;
SODIUM: 560MG

EXCELLENT SOURCE OF
CALCIUM, MANGANESE, PROTEIN, SELENIUM, VITAMIN A

GOOD SOURCE OF
FOLATE, IRON, MAGNESIUM, NIACIN, PHOSPHO-RUS, THIAMIN, VITAMIN B6, VITAMIN C, VITAMIN K

Heat the oil in a large nonstick skillet over medium heat. Add the onion and cook, stirring, until golden and the edges are browned, 10 to 12 minutes. Season with salt and pepper.

Divide the cheddar cheese between 4 slices of the bread. Spread 1 tablespoon of the caramelized onions on top of the cheddar, then top with the pepper Jack. Place 1 large or 2 medium slices of tomato and the other slice of bread on top.

Clean and dry the skillet, then coat with cooking spray and heat over medium-high heat until hot. Place one of the sandwiches in the skillet and weigh down with a heavy skillet or plate. Lower the heat to medium-low and grill until the underside is a deep brown but not burnt and the cheese is partially melted, 5 to 6 minutes. Flip the sandwich and grill the other side until it's nicely colored, another 4 to 5 minutes. Slice in half and serve hot. Repeat with the other sandwiches.

L.O.V.E. Wrap Sandwich
(Lettuce, Onion, Vegetable, Egg Salad)

I came up with this sandwich when I was trying to figure out what to make my husband for lunch on our anniversary one year. The idea is admittedly a little corny, but the sandwich is incredible: soft, creamy egg salad enlivened with Dijon mustard, nestled with crunchy red peppers, onion, and crisp lettuce in a hearty whole-grain wrap. Like most things, it tastes even better when you make it with love.

2 hard-boiled eggs
1 teaspoon mayonnaise
¼ teaspoon Dijon mustard
1 ½ teaspoons finely chopped fresh chives
Salt and freshly ground black pepper to taste
1 piece whole-wheat wrap bread (about 9 inches in diameter)
⅓ red bell pepper, seeded and cut into thin strips
3 thin slices red onion
2 leaves romaine lettuce, torn into pieces (about ½ cup)

SERVES 1

PER SERVING
CALORIES: 290;
TOTAL FAT: 12G
    MONO: 2G,
    POLY: 1G;
    SAT: 2G,
PROTEIN: 15G;
CARB: 27G;
FIBER: 3G;
CHOL: 215MG;
SODIUM: 350MG

EXCELLENT
SOURCE OF
IODINE, PROTEIN,
RIBOFLAVIN,
SELENIUM,
VITAMIN A,
VITAMIN C,
VITAMIN K

GOOD
SOURCE OF
FIBER, FOLATE,
IRON, MOLYB-
DENUM, PANTO-
THENIC ACID,
PHOSPHORUS,
VITAMIN B6,
VITAMIN B12

Discard the yolk from one of the hard-boiled eggs. Dice the remaining whole egg and egg white and put it into a small bowl. Add the mayonnaise and mustard and stir with a fork, mashing somewhat to your desired consistency. Stir in the chives and season with salt and pepper.

Place the wrap bread on a plate and spread the egg salad in the middle. Top with the pepper strips, onion slices, and lettuce. Roll into a wrap sandwich.

Hummus and Grilled Vegetable Wrap

It is amazing how a handful of inspired ingredients can turn a run-of-the-mill hummus wrap into a truly memorable meal. In this case, grilled zucchini adds a succulent charred-grilled flavor, plump roasted red peppers lend concentrated richness, pine nuts give a buttery crunch, and leaves of mint chime in with a burst of freshness. When it is all wrapped up with creamy hummus and tender spinach leaves, you have a real taste of the Mediterranean. Use plain hummus or jazz it up with some of the different flavors now available, like green olive, hot and spicy, or roasted red pepper.

2 medium zucchini, cut lengthwise into ¼-inch-thick slices
2 teaspoons olive oil
⅛ teaspoon salt
Pinch of freshly ground black pepper
1 cup store-bought hummus
4 pieces whole-wheat wrap bread (about 9 inches in diameter)
¼ cup pine nuts
2 jarred roasted red peppers, drained, rinsed, and quartered
2 ounces baby spinach leaves (2 cups lightly packed)
½ cup red onion thinly sliced into half-moons
¼ cup fresh mint leaves

SERVES 4
SERVING SIZE:
1 WRAP

PER SERVING
CALORIES: 320;
TOTAL FAT: 15G
  MONO: 6G;
  POLY: 6G;
  SAT: 2G;
PROTEIN: 12G;
CARB: 42G;
FIBER: 8G;
CHOL: 0MG;
SODIUM: 795MG

EXCELLENT
SOURCE OF
COPPER, FIBER,
FOLATE, IRON,
MAGNESIUM,
MANGANESE,
PHOSPHORUS,
PROTEIN, THIAMIN,
VITAMIN A, VITA-
MIN B6, VITAMIN C

GOOD
SOURCE OF
NIACIN, POTAS-
SIUM, RIBOFLAVIN,
VITAMIN K, ZINC

Preheat the grill or grill pan over medium heat. Brush both sides of the zucchini slices with the oil and sprinkle with the salt and pepper. Grill until tender and slightly browned, about 4 minutes per side.

Spread ¼ cup of the hummus over each piece of bread. Sprinkle 1 tablespoon of pine nuts on top. Top with 3 slices of zucchini, 2 pieces of red pepper, ½ cup of the spinach, a few sliced onions, and 1 tablespoon of the mint. Roll each of them up and cut in half on a diagonal.

Cornmeal-Crusted Roasted Ratatouille Tart

So often vegetables are an afterthought in a meal, but here they play the starring role they deserve. The vegetable trio that performs so well together in a classic French ratatouille—zucchini, eggplant, and tomato—is oven roasted to concentrate the flavors, then layered with mellow meltable mozzarella and intense Parmesan cheese in a tender golden cornmeal crust for a dish that is sure to get rave reviews at your table.

For the crust
⅔ cup yellow cornmeal
⅓ cup whole-grain pastry flour or whole-wheat flour
¼ teaspoons salt
2 tablespoons unsalted butter
2 tablespoons canola oil
3 tablespoons water

For the filling
2 tablespoons plus 1 teaspoon olive oil
2 shallots, thinly sliced (about ⅓ cup)
Cooking spray
1 small eggplant (about ½ pound), cut into ⅛-inch-thick rounds
1 small zucchini (about ½ pound), cut into ⅛-inch-thick rounds
3 medium ripe tomatoes, thinly sliced
¼ teaspoon salt
¼ teaspoon freshly ground black pepper
¾ cup shredded part-skim mozzarella cheese (about 3 ounces)
¼ cup shredded fresh basil
¼ cup freshly grated Parmesan cheese

SERVES 8
SERVING SIZE:
1 WEDGE

EXCELLENT
SOURCE OF
VITAMIN C

PER SERVING
CALORIES: 225;
TOTAL FAT: 14G
  MONO: 7G,
  POLY: 2G;
  SAT: 3.5G,
PROTEIN: 6.5G;
CARB: 20G;
FIBER: 3G;
CHOL: 8MG;
SODIUM: 230MG

GOOD
SOURCE OF
FIBER,
MANGANESE,
MOLYBDENUM,
POTASSIUM,
PROTEIN, THIAMIN,
VITAMIN A,
VITAMIN K

Preheat the oven to 350°F.

To make the crust, combine the cornmeal, flour, and salt in a food processor and pulse to incorporate. Add the butter and oil and pulse about 20 times, until the mixture resembles small pebbles. Add the water and pulse until the mixture forms a loose dough. Remove the dough from the processor and press into the bottom and about ⅛ inch up the sides of a 9-inch tart pan with a detachable rim. Press aluminum foil into the bottom and up the sides of the pan on top of the dough. Weight it down with uncooked rice or pie weights. Place the tart pan on a baking sheet and bake for 10 minutes. Remove the rice and foil and bake for another 5 minutes. Remove from the oven and let cool. Increase the oven temperature to 400°F.

To prepare the filling, heat 1 teaspoon of the oil in a small nonstick pan over medium heat; cook the shallots, stirring, until softened, 5 to 6 minutes.

Coat two baking sheets with cooking spray. Arrange the eggplant, zucchini, and tomato slices on the sheets in a single layer and brush with the remaining 2 tablespoons oil. Sprinkle with the salt and pepper, and roast the vegetables until soft but not browned, about 15 minutes. Remove from the oven and let cool.

Lower the oven temperature to 350°F. Lay the eggplant slices on the bottom of the tart, overlapping them if necessary; cover with one-third of the mozzarella and some of the shredded basil. Add the zucchini and shallots, top with another third of the mozzarella and the remaining basil, then the tomatoes. Top with rest of the mozzarella and all of the Parmesan. Bake until the cheese is melted and the vegetables have further wilted, 25 to 30 minutes. Remove from the oven, let cool for 5 minutes, and cut into 8 slices. Serve warm.

main &
side salads

Caesar Salad with Lemon Pepper Shrimp

This is what I call an ideal Caesar salad: Parmesan-packed Caesar dressing clinging to refreshing romaine lettuce, tossed with crunchy garlic-scented croutons, and made into an unforgettable meal with succulent lemon pepper shrimp. Not to mention it's completely guilt-free, with much less fat and fewer calories than the traditional version. If you don't like anchovies, don't let the anchovy paste scare you, it melts into the dressing so you don't recognize it—it just gives that classic Caesar taste.

¼ cup pasteurized egg substitute

1 clove garlic, minced (about 1 teaspoon)

1½ teaspoons anchovy paste

½ teaspoon Dijon mustard

¼ teaspoon Worcestershire sauce

2 tablespoons fresh lemon juice

2 tablespoons olive oil

¼ cup freshly grated Parmesan cheese

Salt and freshly ground black pepper to taste

8 cups coarsely torn romaine lettuce

Garlic-Scented Croutons (page 104)

Lemon Pepper Grilled Shrimp (page 104)

SERVES 4
SERVING SIZE: 2 CUPS LETTUCE, 5 TO 6 SHRIMP, AND ½ CUP CROUTONS

PER SERVING
CALORIES: 325;
TOTAL FAT: 17G
 MONO: 10G,
 POLY: 2G,
 SAT: 3G,
PROTEIN: 29G;
CARB: 14G;
FIBER: 3G;
CHOL: 174MG;
SODIUM: 821MG

EXCELLENT SOURCE OF
CALCIUM, COPPER, FOLATE, IRON, NIACIN, PROTEIN, PHOSPHORUS, SELENIUM, VITAMIN A, VITAMIN B_{12}, VITAMIN C, VITAMIN D, VITAMIN K

GOOD SOURCE OF
FIBER, MAGNESIUM, MANGANESE, POTASSIUM, RIBOFLAVIN, THIAMIN, VITAMIN B_6, ZINC

In a small bowl, whisk together the egg product, garlic, anchovy paste, mustard, Worcestershire, and lemon juice. Slowly add the oil in a steady stream, whisking the whole time. Stir in the Parmesan and season with salt and pepper.

In a large bowl, toss the dressing with the lettuce until well coated. Add the croutons and toss again to combine. Divide the salad between 4 plates and top each plate with the shrimp.

✱   EATING WELL TIP

Drizzling the oil into the other ingredients while whisking creates a rich and creamy dressing without mayonnaise, and using pasteurized egg substitute instead of the traditional raw egg eliminates the risk of salmonella.

Garlic-Scented Croutons

Whip these up whenever you have leftover bread. They will last about a week stored in an airtight container at room temperature.

Eight ½-inch-thick slices French bread or other crusty bread
   (about 2 ounces)
1 teaspoon olive oil or olive oil spray
1 clove garlic, peeled
¼ teaspoon salt

SERVES 4
MAKES 2 CUPS;
SERVING SIZE:
½ CUP

PER SERVING
CALORIES: 48
TOTAL FAT: 1.5G
   MONO: 1G,

POLY: 0G;
SAT: 0G,
PROTEIN: 1G;
CARB: 7G;
FIBER: 0G;
CHOL: 0MG;
SODIUM: 235MG

Preheat the oven to 325°F.

   Using a pastry brush, lightly brush both sides of the bread with the oil or spray the bread with the olive oil spray. Cut the garlic in half and rub it over both sides of the bread. Sprinkle both sides with the salt. Cut the bread into cubes and spread it in a single layer on a baking sheet. Bake until the bread is crispy and golden brown, stirring once or twice, about 10 minutes.

Lemon Pepper Grilled Shrimp

These shrimp make a delicious starter for a patio party or an easy everyday main course for lunch or dinner.

1 pound large shrimp, peeled and deveined
2 teaspoons olive oil
½ teaspoon salt
½ teaspoon coarsely ground black pepper
½ teaspoon finely grated lemon zest
3 tablespoons fresh lemon juice

SERVES 4
SERVING SIZE:
5 TO 6 SHRIMP

PER SERVING
CALORIES: 144;
TOTAL FAT: 4G
   MONO: 2G,
   POLY: 1G;
   SAT: 0.5G,
PROTEIN: 23G;
CARB: 2G;
FIBER: 0G;
CHOL: 72MG;
SODIUM: 460MG

EXCELLENT
SOURCE OF
PHOSPHORUS,
PROTEIN,
SELENIUM,
VITAMIN B$_{12}$,
VITAMIN D

GOOD
SOURCE OF
COPPER, IRON,
MAGNESIUM,
NIACIN, VITAMIN C

Preheat a grill pan over medium-high heat or prepare a grill. Toss the shrimp with the oil, add the salt, pepper, and lemon zest and toss again. Grill until just cooked through, 2 to 3 minutes per side.

   Transfer the shrimp to a plate and drizzle with the lemon juice. Enjoy hot or at room temperature.

Shrimp Salad with Cucumber and Mint

Banish boring mayonnaise-laden shrimp salad in favor of the bright, cool tastes of summer by tossing shrimp with a fresh mint pesto and crunchy cucumber. Serve it in lettuce or radicchio cups for a stunning presentation.

2 pounds medium shrimp, peeled and deveined
1 cup fresh mint leaves
2 tablespoon fresh lemon juice
3 tablespoons olive oil
½ large English cucumber, seeded and diced (about 1½ cups)
Finely grated zest of 1 lemon
Salt and freshly ground black pepper to taste

SERVES 6
SERVING SIZE:
1 CUP

PER SERVING
CALORIES: 230;
TOTAL FAT: 10G
  MONO: 6G;
  POLY: 1.5G;
  SAT: 1.5G;
PROTEIN: 31G;
CARB: 3.5G;
FIBER: 1G;
CHOL: 230MG;
SODIUM: 225MG

EXCELLENT
SOURCE OF
COPPER,
IRON, NIACIN,
PROTEIN,
PHOSPHORUS,
SELENIUM,
VITAMIN B$_{12}$,
VITAMIN D

GOOD
SOURCE OF
CALCIUM,
MAGNESIUM,
VITAMIN A,
VITAMIN C, ZINC

Bring a large saucepan of water to a boil. Add the shrimp and let cook for 3 minutes, then drain. Transfer the shrimp to a dish and set in the refrigerator to cool completely, at least 1 hour, or plunge into a bowl of ice water to cool quickly, then drain and pat dry.

Put the mint in a food processor and pulse to coarsely chop. Add the lemon juice, then, with the machine running, slowly pour the oil through the feed tube until incorporated.

In a large serving bowl, toss together the shrimp, cucumber, mint mixture, lemon zest, salt, and pepper until well combined. This will keep in the refrigerator in an airtight container for up to 2 days.

Grilled Thai Beef Salad

If you like full-frontal flavor, you are going to love this dish. The steak is marinated in a mixture that covers every angle—spicy, sweet, tangy, and salty—then it is grilled to caramelized perfection, sliced thin, and tossed with tender lettuce and fresh herbs. The robust marinade flavors are used in the dressing to give the salad a one-two punch. The result is so powerfully mouthwatering, it is sure to knock you out.

1 pound top-round London broil or flank steak, 1 to 1½ inches thick
3 tablespoons fresh lime juice
3 tablespoons low-sodium soy sauce
3 tablespoons canola oil
2 tablespoons firmly packed dark brown sugar
1 clove garlic, minced (about 1 teaspoon)
1½ teaspoons peeled and minced fresh ginger
1¼ teaspoons red curry paste or chili-garlic sauce
Cooking spray
½ head red-leaf lettuce, torn (about 5 cups lightly packed)
3 shallots, thinly sliced (about ½ cup)
½ cup coarsely chopped fresh cilantro leaves
1 cup fresh basil leaves, sliced into ribbons

SERVES 4
SERVING SIZE:
2½ CUPS

PER SERVING
CALORIES: 345;
TOTAL FAT: 18.5G
   MONO: 9G;
   POLY: 3G;
   SAT: 4.5G,
PROTEIN: 33G;
CARB: 12G;
FIBER: 1G;
CHOL: 1MG;
SODIUM: 440MG

EXCELLENT SOURCE OF
IRON, NIACIN, PHOSPHORUS, PROTEIN, SELENIUM, VITAMIN A, VITAMIN B$_6$, VITAMIN B$_{12}$

GOOD SOURCE OF
FOLATE, MAGNESIUM, MANGANESE, POTASSIUM, RIBOFLAVIN, THIAMIN, VITAMIN C, VITAMIN E

Rinse the meat and pat dry and place in a sealable plastic bag or small glass dish. In a medium bowl, combine 1 tablespoon of the lime juice, the soy sauce, oil, brown sugar, garlic, ginger, and red curry paste. Pour half the mixture into the bag with the meat. Add the remaining 2 tablespoons lime juice to the bag. Seal tightly and marinate the meat in the refrigerator for at least 4 hours or overnight, turning occasionally. Reserve the rest of the mixture to dress the salad.

Coat a grate or a grill pan with cooking spray and preheat over medium-high heat until hot. Grill the steak until medium-rare, about 5 minutes per side, or to your desired degree of doneness. Let it rest for 5 minutes until room temperature, then slice thinly against the grain.

Combine the lettuce, shallots (reserving a few slices for garnish), cilantro, basil, and beef in a large salad bowl. Add the reserved dressing and toss to coat. Divide the salad among 4 plates and garnish with the sliced shallots.

Buffalo Chicken Salad

I don't think I have ever been to a sports bar or college campus where fried chicken wings in spicy Buffalo sauce wasn't a staple. With blue cheese dressing, celery sticks, and a beer, it covers all the basic food groups, right? Well, not exactly. But this salad nearly does. And it really hits the Buffalo spot. In it chicken breast doused with hot sauce is served atop a cool, crispy salad chock-full of celery (of course) and coated in a tangy blue cheese dressing. You provide the beer.

1 pound boneless, skinless chicken breast halves

2 tablespoons cayenne pepper hot sauce (or other hot sauce),
   plus more to taste

2 teaspoons olive oil

1 heart of romaine, cut across into 1-inch-wide strips (about 8 cups)

4 stalks celery, thinly sliced (about 1 cup)

2 medium carrots, coarsely grated (about 1 cup)

2 scallions (green part only), thinly sliced

½ cup Blue Cheese Dressing (recipe follows)

SERVES 4

SERVING SIZE: ABOUT 2 CUPS SALAD, 5 STRIPS OF CHICKEN, AND 2 TABLESPOONS DRESSING

PER SERVING

CALORIES: 255; TOTAL FAT: 10G MONO: 2.5G, POLY: 1G; SAT: 3G, PROTEIN: 31G; CARB: 10G; FIBER: 4G; CHOL: 5MG; SODIUM: 475MG

EXCELLENT SOURCE OF

FOLATE, NIACIN, PHOSPHORUS, POTASSIUM, PROTEIN, SELENIUM, VITAMIN A, VITAMIN B6, VITAMIN C, VITAMIN K

GOOD SOURCE OF

CALCIUM, FIBER, IRON, MAGNESIUM, MOLYBDENUM, PANTOTHENIC ACID, RIBOFLAVIN, THIAMIN, VITAMIN B12, ZINC

Preheat the broiler.

Put the chicken between two sheets of waxed paper and pound with a mallet or hammer to an even thickness of about ¾ inch, then cut the chicken crosswise into ½-inch-thick strips. In a large bowl, combine the hot sauce and oil, add the chicken, and toss until it is well coated. Arrange the chicken on a baking sheet and broil until it is cooked through, 4 to 6 minutes total, turning once.

In a large bowl, combine the romaine, celery, carrots, and scallions and toss with the dressing. Divide the greens between 4 plates and top with the warm chicken. Serve with extra hot sauce on the side.

Blue Cheese Dressing

This is a full-flavored lighter version of a classic blue cheese dressing. Enjoy it as a dip or on any salad you like. It will keep in the fridge, tightly covered, for about 3 days.

¼ cup plain nonfat yogurt
¼ cup lowfat buttermilk
2 tablespoons mayonnaise
1 tablespoon white wine vinegar
½ teaspoon sugar
⅓ cup crumbled blue cheese
Salt and freshly ground black pepper to taste

SERVES 6
MAKES ¾ CUP
SERVING SIZE:
2 TABLESPOONS

PROTEIN: 2.5G;
CARB: 2G;
FIBER: 0G;
CHOL: 8MG;
SODIUM: 149MG

PER SERVING
CALORIES: 71;
TOTAL FAT: 6G
  MONO: 0.5G,
  POLY: 0G;
  SAT: 2G,

Fold a full sheet of paper towel into quarters and put it into a small strainer. Spoon the yogurt onto the paper towel and place over a bowl in the refrigerator for 20 minutes to drain and thicken.

In a medium bowl, whisk the buttermilk and thickened yogurt into the mayonnaise until smooth. Add the vinegar and sugar and continue to whisk until well combined. Stir in the blue cheese and season with salt and pepper.

✳ **EATING WELL TIP**
I use regular mayonnaise because I prefer the taste over light mayo, and I like that it is usually additive free. I just use it sparingly and I buy heart-healthier canola mayonnaise. Canola mayonnaise is real mayonnaise that is made with monounsaturated-rich canola oil instead of vegetable oils with less healthful fats. It tastes just like the mayonnaise you know and love, but it's better for you. While it used to be available only in health food stores, it is now being made by major national brands so it's easy to find in your local supermarket.

Savory Chinese Chicken Salad

My version of Chinese chicken salad is like an Asian slaw with ribbons of tender napa cabbage, a confetti of red cabbage, carrots, and scallions with crunchy water chestnuts and sweet mandarin oranges.

¼ cup sliced almonds

For the chicken

1 tablespoon low-sodium soy sauce
½ teaspoon toasted sesame oil
1 pound boneless, skinless chicken breast halves

For the salad

6 cups thinly shredded napa cabbage (about ½ head)
2 cups thinly shredded red cabbage
1 large carrot, shredded (about 1 cup)
3 scallions (white and green parts), thinly sliced (about ½ cup)
One 8-ounce can sliced water chestnuts, drained
One 11-ounce can mandarin oranges packed in water or light syrup, drained

For the dressing

⅓ cup rice vinegar
3 tablespoons low-sodium soy sauce
2 tablespoons canola oil
2 tablespoons firmly packed dark brown sugar
1½ teaspoons chili sauce, such as Sriracha
1½ teaspoons toasted sesame oil
1 clove garlic, minced (about 1 teaspoon)
1 teaspoon peeled and minced fresh ginger

SERVES 4
SERVING SIZE: 2½ CUPS SALAD AND 1 TABLESPOON ALMONDS

PER SERVING
CALORIES: 415;
TOTAL FAT: 14G
 MONO: 7.3G;
 POLY: 4.2G;
 SAT: 1.5G,
PROTEIN: 32G;
CARB: 41G;
FIBER: 9G;
CHOL: 66MG;
SODIUM: 930MG

EXCELLENT SOURCE OF
FIBER, MAGNE-SIUM, MANGA-NESE, NIACIN, PHOSPHORUS, POTASSIUM, PRO-TEIN, SELENIUM, VITAMIN A, VITAMIN B6, VITAMIN C, VITAMIN K

GOOD SOURCE OF
CALCIUM, FOLATE, IRON, MOLYBDENUM, PANTOTHENIC ACID, RIBOFLAVIN, THIAMIN, VITAMIN E, ZINC

Preheat the oven to 350°F.

Toast the almonds in a small dry skillet over medium-high heat until fragrant, stirring frequently, 2 to 3 minutes; set aside.

To make the chicken, combine the soy sauce and sesame oil in a small bowl and brush over the chicken on both sides. Arrange in a baking dish and bake until the juices run clear in the center, 13 to 15 minutes. Remove from the oven, let cool completely, and cut across into ¼-inch-thick slices.

In a large bowl, combine the salad ingredients and chicken. In a small bowl, whisk together the dressing in-gredients. Pour it over the salad and toss to combine. Divide among 4 plates and top each with the almonds. This salad will keep in the refrigerator in an airtight container for 1 day. Add the almonds when you serve.

Saffron Chicken, Lemon, and Green Bean Salad

This salad looks and tastes simply magical. The easy but unusual technique of boiling a whole lemon tenderizes the peel and mellows it, allowing it to be a main ingredient in this exotic salad. The saffron imparts a vibrant shade of yellow to the chicken and gives it a distinctive taste and aroma that contrasts beautifully with the crisp green beans and tangy lemon rind. Fresh thyme ties it all together and gives the dish an unmistakable earthiness.

1 lemon, preferably unwaxed or well scrubbed if waxed

1¼ teaspoons salt, plus more to taste

Pinch of saffron threads

2 tablespoons finely chopped fresh mint

1 clove garlic, minced (about 1 teaspoon)

3 tablespoons fresh lemon juice

¼ cup olive oil

1¼ pounds boneless, skinless chicken breast halves,
   pounded between 2 sheets of waxed paper to ½-inch thickness

1 pound fresh green beans, trimmed

Cooking spray

2 tablespoons finely chopped fresh thyme

1 tablespoon honey

Freshly ground black pepper to taste

SERVES 4
SERVING SIZE:
1½ CUPS

PER SERVING
CALORIES: 320;
TOTAL FAT: 14G
   MONO: 9G,
   POLY: 1.6G;
   SAT: 2G;
PROTEIN: 35G;
CARB: 14G;
FIBER: 5G;
CHOL: 82MG;
SODIUM: 320MG

EXCELLENT SOURCE OF
FIBER, NIACIN,
POTASSIUM,
PROTEIN,
VITAMIN A,
VITAMIN B6,
VITAMIN C,
VITAMIN K

GOOD SOURCE OF
IRON

Prick the lemon in three or four places with a fork and place in a small saucepan with 1 teaspoon of the salt and cover with water. Bring to a boil, cover, reduce the heat to low, and simmer until the lemon is very tender, about 50 minutes. Drain and set aside to cool.

Meanwhile, mix the saffron, mint, garlic, 1 tablespoon of the lemon juice, 1 tablespoon of the oil, and the remaining ¼ teaspoon of the salt together in a small bowl. Pour the marinade into a sealable plastic bag, add the chicken, and let it marinate at room temperature while you prepare the other ingredients.

Steam the green beans for 4 minutes and set aside to cool. Cut into ½-inch pieces.

Coat a large skillet or grill pan with cooking spray and preheat over medium-high heat. Cook the chicken until just cooked through, 3 to 4 minutes per side. Set aside to cool, then cut into bite-sized chunks.

Slice the ends off the lemon and slice it in half lengthwise. Scoop out the pulp and discard. Slice the peel thinly and then again into ¼-inch pieces.

In a large bowl, combine the chicken, lemon, green beans, and thyme. In a small bowl, combine the remaining 2 tablespoons lemon juice and the honey, then whisk in the remaining 3 tablespoons oil and season with salt and pepper. Pour the dressing over the salad and toss to combine. This salad will keep in the refrigerator in an airtight container for up to 3 days.

Eating By Color

Color plays a huge part in the pleasure we get from food. But besides making it enticing and enjoyable, color can also be a sign that what you're eating is good for you. Eating a rainbow of produce every day helps ensure you get the full range of nutrients for optimal health.

GET THE FULL SPECTRUM (PLUS WHITE)
Each color group of food has its own set of nutritional benefits. For example, red tomatoes and watermelon contain the antioxidant lycopene, which helps protect your skin, and spinach, arugula, and broccoli have lutein and zeaxanthin, which help keep your eyes healthy.

Some antioxidants actually impart color to food. Beta-carotene gives carrots, mangos, and winter squash their orange-yellow hue, while anthocyanins make berries and cherries red or blue. Generally, the more intense the color of the food, the more packed with nutrients it is. But don't neglect white foods like mushrooms and cauliflower; they are loaded with healthy properties too, including numerous cancer-preventing antioxidants, vitamin C, and potassium.

AMP UP YOUR SALADS
Salads naturally lend themselves to the multicolor principle. Make sure you take full advantage by kicking up their color as much as you can. Instead of adding green pepper to a green salad, amp up the color and nutrition by using a red one. Consider tossing orange segments or dried cherries onto your spinach salad. Use a richer colored lettuce like romaine instead of iceberg.

BUT DON'T STOP AT SALADS
I work colorful produce into almost every recipe I create. It is a core principle of healthful cooking. So golden peaches adorn my Peach French Toast Bake (page 35), I toss ribbon of deep green arugula in my Pasta Puttanesca (page 158), and stud my Ricotta Cheesecake (page 281) with ruby-red raspberries. These additions make the food more beautiful and crave-able, and make it more healthful. So next time you are whipping up your own invention, ask yourself: "Where's the color?"

Snow Pea, Scallion, and Radish Salad

Cutting the snow peas on a diagonal creates diamond-shaped pieces that give this salad an eye-catching look. That visual appeal and its lively flavors are testament to how much just a handful of ingredients can accomplish when they are put together with care.

2 cups (8 ounces) snow peas, trimmed

1 tablespoon water

2 scallions (white and green parts), thinly sliced

4 radishes, trimmed and cut into thin strips (about ½ cup)

¼ cup rice vinegar

2 teaspoons sugar

1 tablespoon walnut or canola oil

SERVES 4
SERVING SIZE:
¾ CUP

PER SERVING
CALORIES: 72;
TOTAL FAT: 3.5G
  MONO: 0.8G,
  POLY: 2.3G;
  SAT: 0.5G,
PROTEIN: 2G;
CARB: 9G;

FIBER: 1.5G;
CHOL: 0MG;
SODIUM: 147MG

EXCELLENT SOURCE OF
VITAMIN C,
VITAMIN K

Put the snow peas in a microwave-safe bowl with the water. Cover tightly and microwave for 1 minute. Drain and let cool. Cut the snow peas on the diagonal into ½-inch diamonds shapes, discarding the end pieces.

In a medium serving bowl, combine the snow peas, scallions, and radishes. In a small bowl, whisk together vinegar, sugar, and oil until the sugar dissolves. Pour over the salad and serve.

Five-Minute Salad of Goat Cheese, Herbs, and White Beans

Some days it just feels like too much effort even to chop a few veggies for a simple salad. Never fear. I created this salad for just those times. You can throw it together in five minutes and you don't even need a knife.

12 ounces mixed salad greens (about 8 cups lightly packed)

3 tablespoons olive oil

2 tablespoons balsamic vinegar

½ teaspoon Dijon mustard

Salt and freshly ground black pepper to taste

1½ cups cherry tomatoes (about 28)

1 cup canned cannellini or other white beans, preferably low-sodium, drained and rinsed

4 ounces fresh goat cheese, preferably reduced-fat, crumbled (about ½ cup)

2 tablespoons fresh basil leaves, torn, or 1 teaspoon dried basil

SERVES 4
SERVING SIZE: 2 CUPS GREENS, ¼ CUP BEANS, ABOUT 7 TOMATOES, AND 2 TABLESPOONS GOAT CHEESE

PER SERVING
CALORIES: 250;
TOTAL FAT: 17G
    MONO: 10G,
    POLY: 1G;
    SAT: 6G,
PROTEIN: 10G;
CARB: 17G;
FIBER: 5G;
CHOL: 13MG;
SODIUM: 274MG

EXCELLENT SOURCE OF FIBER, PROTEIN, VITAMIN A

GOOD SOURCE OF COPPER, IRON, VITAMIN C, VITAMIN K

Place the greens in a large bowl. Whisk together the oil, vinegar, and mustard, then season with salt and pepper. Drizzle the dressing over the greens and toss. Divide the greens between 4 plates, top each with about 7 tomatoes, ¼ cup of beans, and 2 tablespoons of goat cheese. Sprinkle with the basil and serve.

Chicory Salad with Walnuts and Parmesan

Chicory is a sturdy member of the endive family whose bold taste and texture really stand up to intense flavors. Here it is paired with rich walnuts and sharp Parmesan cheese in a sherry-mustard vinaigrette. You could use arugula instead of chicory here if you prefer. I like to serve this salad before a meaty, belly-warming stew or pasta entrée.

½ cup coarsely chopped walnuts

1 tablespoon sherry vinegar

3 tablespoons walnut or olive oil

½ teaspoon Dijon mustard

Salt and freshly ground black pepper to taste

½ pound chicory or other leafy green

¼ cup shaved Parmesan cheese (you can do this with a vegetable peeler)

SERVES 6
SERVING SIZE:
¾ CUP

PER SERVING
CALORIES: 146;
TOTAL FAT: 15G
  MONO: 2.4G,
  POLY: 9.2G;
  SAT: 2.3G,

PROTEIN: 3G;
CARB: 3G;
FIBER: 2G;
CHOL: 0.7MG;
SODIUM: 52MG

EXCELLENT
SOURCE OF
MANGANESE

In a small dry skillet, toast the nuts over medium-high heat until fragrant, shaking frequently, about 2 minutes; set aside.

In a small bowl, whisk together the vinegar, oil, mustard, salt, and pepper.

In a large bowl, toss the chicory with the dressing to coat evenly. Divide between 6 serving plates, top with the walnuts and shaved Parmesan, and serve.

*

Salad: The REAL Power Lunch

The right kind of salad for lunch can help you stay alert and prevent that sleepy feeling you sometimes get after you eat.

A carbohydrate-heavy meal (loaded with, say, bread or pasta) triggers the release of a brain chemical called serotonin, which gives a feeling of relaxation, well-being, and drowsiness. Basically, it makes you feel ready to kick back—not something you necessarily want in the middle of the day. So save the pasta for the evening when you are ready to relax.

For the afternoon, stick with protein and vegetables. Protein blocks the serotonin effect, helping you stay alert and on your game. That's why meals rich in protein without much concentrated carbohydrate, like most of the main course salads here, are the perfect power lunch.

Bibb Lettuce Wedges with De-Light-Ful Ranch Dressing

I have transformed the traditional wedge of iceberg lettuce slathered in creamy dressing, keeping the crunch and blue cheese pungency while swapping in a more nutrient-packed lettuce and a lighter dressing.

2 large heads Bibb or Boston lettuce or 4 heads baby Bibb lettuce
½ cup De-Light-Ful Ranch Dressing (recipe follows)

Remove and discard the outermost leaves of the lettuce. Trim the stem slightly to remove any tough or browned spots, but be sure to keep the head intact. Cut each head in half lengthwise so that each half is held together by a bit of stem.

Place the lettuce halves on a serving plate and drizzle with the ranch dressing. Serve immediately.

SERVES 4
SERVING SIZE:
½ LARGE
LETTUCE OR
2 HALVES BABY
LETTUCE AND
2 TABLESPOONS
DRESSING

PER SERVING
CALORIES: 60;
TOTAL FAT: 4.5G
  MONO: 0G,
  POLY: 0G;
  SAT: 0.7G,

PROTEIN: 2G;
CARB: 4G;
FIBER: 1G;
CHOL: 3MG;
SODIUM: 73MG

EXCELLENT
SOURCE OF
VITAMIN A,
VITAMIN K

GOOD
SOURCE OF
FOLATE

De-Light-Ful Ranch Dressing

Great as a dip or a sandwich spread as well as a salad dressing, this will last about 3 days in the refrigerator in an airtight container.

½ cup plain nonfat yogurt or ⅓ cup plain Greek-style nonfat yogurt
⅓ cup lowfat buttermilk
3 tablespoons mayonnaise
1½ teaspoons fresh lemon juice
1 teaspoon Dijon mustard
½ teaspoon onion powder
¼ teaspoon garlic powder
1 tablespoon finely chopped fresh chives
Salt to taste

SERVES 8
MAKES 1 CUP
SERVING SIZE:
2 TABLESPOONS

PER SERVING
CALORIES: 50;
TOTAL FAT: 4G
  MONO: 0G;
  POLY: 0G;
  SAT: 0.5G,

PROTEIN: 1G;
CARB: 2G;
FIBER: 0G;
CHOL: 2.5MG;
SODIUM: 69MG

If using regular yogurt, place it in a strainer lined with a paper towel and set the strainer over a bowl. Let the yogurt drain and thicken for 20 minutes. In a medium bowl, whisk together the strained or Greek-style yogurt with the remaining ingredients.

Chopped Niçoise Salad

Niçoise means "as prepared in Nice" on the French Riviera. This salad has the distinctive flavors of the classic: crisp green beans, hearty chunks of potato, olives, tomatoes, and tuna, all tossed with a lemon-mustard vinaigrette. But for a twist, it is all chopped so you get a little of everything in each bite.

4 small red potatoes (about ½ pound total)
⅓ pound fresh green beans, trimmed
One 12-ounce can chunk light tuna packed in water, drained
½ cup chopped pitted Greek or Spanish olives
¼ cup diced red onion
2 medium ripe tomatoes, seeded and diced (about 2 cups)
5 cups chopped romaine lettuce
2 tablespoons olive oil
¼ cup fresh lemon juice
½ teaspoon Dijon mustard
Salt and freshly ground black pepper to taste

SERVES 4
SERVING SIZE: 2 CUPS

PER SERVING
CALORIES: 270;
TOTAL FAT: 10G
  MONO: 7G;
  POLY: 1G;
  SAT: 1.5G,
PROTEIN: 25G;
CARB: 21G;
FIBER: 5G;
CHOL: 26MG;
SODIUM: 466MG

EXCELLENT SOURCE OF
FIBER,
FOLATE, IRON,
MANGANESE,
MOLYBDENUM,
NIACIN,
PHOSPHORUS,
POTASSIUM,
PROTEIN, SELE-
NIUM, VITAMIN A,
VITAMIN B6,
VITAMIN B12,
VITAMIN C,
VITAMIN K

GOOD SOURCE OF
COPPER,
MAGNESIUM,
RIBOFLAVIN,
THIAMIN

Boil a couple of inches of water in a large pot with a fitted steamer basket. Put the potatoes in the steamer, cover, and steam for 15 minutes. Add the green beans and steam for 5 minutes more, until the green beans are crisp tender and the potatoes are just tender all the way through. Transfer them to a dish and set in the refrigerator to cool, or plunge into a bowl of ice water to cool quickly.

Place the tuna, olives, onion, tomato, and lettuce in a large serving bowl. Dice the potatoes and green beans, add them to the bowl, and toss. In a small bowl, whisk together the oil, lemon juice, and mustard, then season with salt and pepper. Pour the dressing over the salad, toss well, and serve.

Spinach Salad with Warm Bacon Dressing

You don't normally think of salad as comfort food, but this one definitely qualifies. The warm bacon and cider dressing wilts the spinach, softening it just enough while it douses the earthy mushrooms and onions with its smoky meatiness. This is the kind of salad that fills up your body and soul.

10 ounces baby spinach leaves (about 10 cups lightly packed)

2 slices bacon, finely chopped

4 slices Canadian bacon (4 ounces), finely chopped

2 teaspoons olive oil

½ large red onion, thinly sliced into half-moons

1 pound white mushrooms, coarsely chopped (about 6 cups)

1 cup apple cider

2 tablespoons cider vinegar

1 teaspoon Dijon mustard

Salt and freshly ground black pepper to taste

SERVES 4
SERVING SIZE: 2½ CUPS

PER SERVING:
CALORIES: 220;
TOTAL FAT: 10G
  MONO: 5G,
  POLY: 1G;
  SAT: 3G,
PROTEIN: 13G;
CARB: 23G;
FIBER: 5G;
CHOL: 22MG;
SODIUM: 650MG

EXCELLENT SOURCE OF
COPPER, FIBER, NIACIN, PANTOTHENIC ACID, PHOSPHORUS, PROTEIN, RIBOFLAVIN, SELENIUM, THIAMIN, VITAMIN A, VITAMIN C, VITAMIN D

GOOD SOURCE OF
IRON, MOLYBDENUM, POTASSIUM, VITAMIN B6

Place the spinach in a large bowl.

Cook the bacon in a large skillet over medium heat until it is just crispy. Add the Canadian bacon to the skillet and cook for 2 more minutes, stirring frequently. Remove the meat from the pan and place on a plate lined with paper towels. Drain any remaining fat from the skillet. Add the oil and onion to the skillet and cook over medium heat until they soften slightly, about 2 minutes. Add the mushrooms to the pan and cook, stirring occasionally, until their liquid has evaporated and they begin to brown, about another 10 minutes. Spoon the mushroom mixture over the spinach.

Add cider and vinegar to the skillet and turn the heat up to medium-high. Stir to scrape up any browned bits that are stuck to the bottom of the pan and cook until the cider is reduced to about ½ cup, 8 to 10 minutes. Whisk in the mustard and season with salt and pepper. Pour the warm cider dressing over the mushrooms and spinach and toss well until the spinach is well coated and wilted slightly. Sprinkle the meat on top and serve immediately.

✳ DID YOU KNOW?
Canadian bacon has all the rich, smoky flavor of regular bacon, but calorie for calorie gives you more than double the protein while containing nearly half the fat.

Dress for Success

Just because a food is a salad doesn't mean it's good for you. Case in point: that goopy macaroni salad at the deli counter. But sometimes even the most healthful-looking salads are unsuspectingly packed with fat and calories. The culprit is usually the dressing. Happily there are ways to make it better.

TAKE A DRESSING REALITY CHECK
Most traditional dressing recipes are shockingly high in fat and calories, turning your otherwise low-cal salad into the energy equivalent of a fast-food meal. Add 2 tablespoons of creamy dressing (upward of 150 calories and 15 grams of fat) to your well-meaning salad with grilled chicken and it could actually tote up to be more fat and calories than a cheeseburger! So much for good intentions.

BUY IT BETTER
At a restaurant:
• Get dressing on the side, so you control the amount
• Request "light" or lowfat dressing
• Choose vinaigrettes, which typically have more healthful fat and fewer calories
• Ask for oil and vinegar, or oil and a wedge of lemon.

At the store:
• Look for dressings made with healthful oils like canola or olive oil
• Buy reduced-fat dressings that have a short list of additives
• Avoid fat-free dressings. You need some fat to absorb the fat-soluble nutrients in the salad.

MAKE IT BETTER
The recipes in this chapter employ a few key tactics for making divine dressings that are good for you:
• Use yogurt and/or buttermilk or avocado as a base for more healthful creamy dressings
• Whisk oil gradually into herb purées and use mustard to make more full-bodied dressings
• Use less oil in vinaigrettes than traditional recipes and balance the acidity with juices or other flavor elements.

Tomatoes with Green Goddess Dressing

Use only the best tomatoes you can find for this dish—ideally homegrown or heirloom varieties. A great tomato speaks for itself, but it really sings when it is covered in a creamy herby Green Goddess Dressing.

4 large ripe tomatoes (about 2½ pounds total)
½ cup Green Goddess Dressing (recipe follows)

Core, then cut the tomatoes into wedges and put them into a large bowl. Toss with the dressing and serve.

SERVES 4
SERVING SIZE:
1½ CUPS
TOMATOES AND
2 TABLESPOONS
DRESSING

EXCELLENT SOURCE OF
VITAMIN A,
VITAMIN C,
VITAMIN K

GOOD SOURCE OF
COPPER, FIBER,
MANGANESE,
MOLYBDENUM,
PANTOTHENIC
ACID, PHOSPHO-
RUS, POTASSIUM,
THIAMIN,
VITAMIN B6

PER SERVING
CALORIES: 81;
TOTAL FAT: 2G
   MONO: 1G,
   POLY: 0G;
   SAT: 0G,
PROTEIN: 4G;
CARB: 14G;
FIBER: 3G;
CHOL: 1MG;
SODIUM: 200MG

Green Goddess Dressing

Buttery avocado and thick buttermilk make a silky green base for this tangy dressing laced with the light anise flavor of fresh tarragon. It is an ideal dressing for delicately flavored lettuces like Bibb, red leaf, or romaine.

½ ripe avocado, peeled
¾ cup lowfat buttermilk
3 tablespoons white wine vinegar
2 tablespoons coarsely chopped fresh tarragon
1 scallion (white and green parts), coarsely chopped
½ teaspoon salt
¼ teaspoon freshly ground black pepper

Put all the ingredients in a blender and blend until smooth. Any leftover dressing will keep well in the refrigerator for 2 to 3 days in an airtight container.

SERVES 8
MAKES 1 CUP;
SERVING SIZE:
2 TABLESPOONS

PROTEIN: 1G;
CARB: 2G;
FIBER: 1G;
CHOL: MG;
SODIUM: 170MG

PER SERVING
CALORIES: 30;
TOTAL FAT: 2G
   MONO: 1.29G,
   POLY: 0.24G;
   SAT: 0G,

Arugula Salad with Pesto Vinaigrette

This is the perfect rush-hour dinner salad made fabulous with a couple of pantry staples: artichoke hearts and pesto. Effortless never tasted so good!

1 medium ripe tomato, cored and chopped (about 1 cup)
1 cup jarred artichoke hearts packed in water, drained, rinsed, and quartered
5 ounces baby arugula (about 5 cups lightly packed)
2 tablespoons red wine vinegar
2 tablespoons Basil Pesto (page 144) or store-bought basil pesto

SERVES 4
SERVING SIZE:
1¼ CUP
ARUGULA,
¼ CUP EACH
TOMATO AND
ARTICHOKE
HEARTS, AND
1 TABLESPOON
DRESSING

PER SERVING
CALORIES: 60;
TOTAL FAT: 4G
    MONO: 2G,
    POLY: 0.5G;
    SAT: 1G,

PROTEIN: 3G;
CARB: 4G;
FIBER: 1.5G;
CHOL: 2.5MG;
SODIUM: 73MG

**EXCELLENT
SOURCE OF**
VITAMIN A,
VITAMIN C,
VITAMIN K

**GOOD
SOURCE OF**
FOLATE,
MANGANESE

Arrange the tomato and artichoke hearts over a bed of arugula. Whisk together the vinegar and pesto, drizzle over the salad, and serve.

✳ **EATING WELL TIP**
Ready-to-eat packaged greens and salad mixes mean you can always have a salad at your fingertips; all you need is the time it takes to open up a bag. I almost always use prewashed packed versions of baby spinach, arugula, and mixed baby lettuces. True, they cost extra, but they really pay off in convenience and nutrition. Thanks to the high-tech bags, which control the air exchange, they are actually just as nutritious as their unpackaged counterparts. Just make sure you keep the greens refrigerated, rewash them before using, and abide by the sell-by date on the label.

Chopped Salad with Lemon and Dill

They serve a version of this delightful salad at one of my favorite Greek restaurants in New York, Molyvos. The first time I tried it, I enjoyed its fresh, simple flavors so much that I just had to whip up my own the next day. I have been making it regularly ever since.

1 head romaine lettuce, shredded (about 6 cups)
½ head radicchio, shredded (about 2 cups)
2 scallions (white and green parts), chopped
3 tablespoons olive oil
2 tablespoons fresh lemon juice
1 tablespoon chopped fresh dill or 1 teaspoon dried
Salt and freshly ground black pepper to taste

SERVES 4
SERVING SIZE:
1½ CUPS

PER SERVING
CALORIES: 115;
TOTAL FAT: 11G
  MONO: 8G,
  POLY: 1G;
  SAT: 1.5G,
PROTEIN: 1G;

CARB: 4G;
FIBER: 1G;
CHOL: 0MG;
SODIUM: 12MG

**EXCELLENT
SOURCE OF**
VITAMIN A,
VITAMIN C,
VITAMIN K

In a large bowl, toss together the romaine, radicchio, and scallions.

In a small bowl, whisk together the oil, lemon juice, dill, salt, and pepper. Pour the dressing over the salad, toss to coat evenly, and serve.

Beet Salad with Watercress Drizzle

With sweet ruby-red beets covered in a tangy emerald green dressing topped with crunchy golden walnuts, this salad boasts all the colors of the finest jewels, and tastes just as lustrous.

4 medium beets, with root and about 1 inch of the green attached, if possible
¼ cup walnut pieces
4 cups watercress, trimmed of thick stems
3 ounces fresh goat cheese, preferably reduced-fat
½ cup lowfat buttermilk
1½ teaspoons white wine vinegar
¼ teaspoon salt, plus more to taste
Freshly ground black pepper to taste

SERVES 4
SERVING SIZE:
1 CUP BEETS,
3 TABLESPOONS
SAUCE, AND
1 TABLESPOON
WALNUTS

PER SERVING
CALORIES: 140;
TOTAL FAT: 8G
  MONO: 0.8G,
  POLY: 3.5G;
  SAT: 2G,
PROTEIN: 6G;

CARB: 12G;
FIBER: 3G;
CHOL: 5MG;
SODIUM: 350MG

**EXCELLENT
SOURCE OF**
FOLATE,
VITAMIN A,
VITAMIN C,
VITAMIN K

**GOOD
SOURCE OF**
PROTEIN

Put the beets in a steamer basket over a large pot of boiling water. Cover and steam until the beets are tender, about 45 minutes. Or rub them with a little olive oil, wrap them in aluminum foil, and roast in a roasting pan at 400°F for about 1½ hours. Either way, let the beets cool until you can handle them. Cut the ends off and peel them (the peel should rub off easily with a little help from a paring knife) and cut them into a large dice.

Toast the walnuts in a small dry skillet over medium-high heat until fragrant, 3 to 5 minutes, stirring frequently, and set aside.

Put the watercress, goat cheese, buttermilk, vinegar, and salt in a food processor and process until smooth and creamy.

Put the beets on a serving dish, drizzle the watercress sauce on top, and sprinkle with walnuts. Season with salt and pepper and serve immediately.

Orange, Radish, and Mint Salad

Each of the four elements in this unique salad contributes its own distinctive taste: the orange sections are sweet and juicy, the red onion provides a lively bite, the radishes a peppery crunch, and mint keeps it all cool and bright. Together they make an incredibly refreshing treat that perfectly complements rich, deeply spiced foods, like my Spice-Rubbed Lamb Pops (page 192).

4 navel oranges
½ red onion, thinly sliced into half-moons
8 radishes, cut in half, then thinly sliced into half-moons
¼ cup torn fresh mint leaves
2 tablespoons olive oil
Salt and freshly ground black pepper to taste

SERVES 4
SERVING SIZE:
1 CUP

EXCELLENT
SOURCE OF
VITAMIN C

PER SERVING
CALORIES: 145;
TOTAL FAT: 7G
  MONO: 5G,
  POLY: 0.5G;
  SAT: 1G,
PROTEIN: 2G;
CARB: 20G;
FIBER: 3G;
CHOL: 0MG;
SODIUM: 155MG

GOOD
SOURCE OF
FIBER,
FOLATE

Cut the top and bottom off each orange. Stand the orange on one end on a cutting board and, following the curve of the fruit, cut away the skin and woolly white pith of the orange. Cut each orange section away from the membrane.

In a medium bowl, toss together the orange sections, onion, radishes, and mint. Drizzle with the oil and season with salt and pepper. This salad will keep in the refrigerator in an airtight container for about a day.

Asian-Style Three-Bean Salad

Here an all-time favorite, three-bean salad, gets an exciting Asian twist. It's made with a trio of legumes all commonly used in the Far East: green beans, edamame, and black beans. The dressing is sweet and tangy, just like in the traditional recipe, but this one, inspired by Chinese duck sauce, gets its sweetness from apricot preserves and has a zingy hint of fresh ginger.

1 pound fresh green beans, trimmed and cut into 1-inch pieces
One 10-ounce bag frozen shelled edamame
3 tablespoons canola oil
3 tablespoons rice vinegar
¼ cup 100% fruit apricot preserves
1 tablespoon sugar
1 teaspoon peeled and grated fresh ginger
One 15-ounce can black beans, preferably low-sodium, drained and rinsed
2 scallions (white and green parts), thinly sliced
Salt to taste

SERVES 8
SERVING SIZE:
¾ CUP

PER SERVING
CALORIES: 180;
TOTAL FAT: 7G
   MONO: 3G,
   POLY: 1.5G;
   SAT: 0G,
PROTEIN: 7G;
CARB: 25G;
FIBER: 6G;

CHOL: 0MG;
SODIUM: 72MG

EXCELLENT
SOURCE OF
FIBER

GOOD
SOURCE OF
IRON, PROTEIN,
VITAMIN C,
VITAMIN K

Put the green beans and frozen edamame in a steamer basket over several inches of boiling water and steam them for 4 minutes. Drain well, then transfer the beans to a large bowl and put them into the refrigerator to cool for 15 minutes or longer.

In a small bowl, whisk together the oil, vinegar, apricot preserves, sugar, and ginger.

Add the black beans and scallions to the green beans and edamame, drizzle with the dressing, and toss to coat. Season with salt and serve at room temperature or chilled. This salad will keep in the refrigerator in an airtight container for about 3 days.

Green Bean and Walnut Salad

This salad has become a well-loved holiday staple on my family's holiday table. It is a satisfying, fresh alternative to soggy green bean casseroles, and it has a truly festive look and taste.

¾ pound fresh green beans, trimmed

¼ cup walnuts pieces

3 tablespoons finely chopped fresh flat-leaf parsley

3 tablespoons finely chopped red onion

1 tablespoon walnut or olive oil

1½ teaspoons red wine vinegar

1 teaspoon Dijon mustard

Salt and freshly ground black pepper to taste

SERVES 4
SERVING SIZE: ¾ CUP

PER SERVING
CALORIES: 91;
TOTAL FAT: 6G
MONO: 1G;
POLY: 4G;
SAT: 0.5G,
PROTEIN: 3G;
CARB: 8G;
FIBER: 3.5G;

CHOL: 0MG;
SODIUM: 39MG

EXCELLENT SOURCE OF
MANGANESE, VITAMIN C, VITAMIN K

GOOD SOURCE OF
COPPER, FIBER, FOLATE, VITAMIN A

Put the green beans in a steamer basket and steam over several inches of boiling water for 4 minutes. Transfer to a medium serving bowl.

Toast the walnuts in a small dry skillet over medium heat, stirring frequently until fragrant, 3 to 5 minutes, then chop them finely and transfer them to a small bowl. Add the parsley and onion and stir to combine.

In another small bowl, whisk together the oil, vinegar, and mustard. Toss the dressing with the green beans, top with the walnut mixture, and season with salt and pepper. Serve warm or at room temperature.

✳ **EATING WELL TIP**
Walnut oil has a delightful nutty flavor and rich texture, and it emulsifies beautifully, which means it integrates well with other dressing ingredients. It is also rich in protective omega-3 fats. While it's wonderful to use on salads and as a finishing oil, don't cook with walnut oil because it can't take the heat. Unfortunately, it is pretty expensive and can be hard to find, so when I call for walnut oil in my recipes, I always offer an acceptable alternative, like olive oil or canola.

Black-Eyed Pea and Spinach Salad

Here black-eyed peas, greens, and buttermilk—staples of Southern cooking—are combined in a refreshing new way. The hearty peas and tender ribbons of spinach are tossed with crunchy red onion and celery in a tangy buttermilk dressing. It makes a perfect side dish with grilled meat or fish or an outstanding part of a buffet or picnic.

¾ cup lowfat buttermilk

3 tablespoons mayonnaise

1½ teaspoons spicy brown mustard

¼ cup cider vinegar

⅛ teaspoon hot pepper sauce, plus more to taste

½ teaspoon salt, plus more to taste

⅛ teaspoon freshly ground black pepper, plus more to taste

Two 15.5-ounce cans black-eyed peas (about 3 cups), preferably low-sodium, drained and rinsed

½ cup diced red onion

3 stalks celery, thinly sliced (about ¾ cup)

2 tablespoons chopped fresh chives

4 ounces baby spinach leaves (about 4 cups lightly packed), cut into wide ribbons

SERVES 6
SERVING SIZE:
1⅓ CUPS

PER SERVING
CALORIES: 205;
TOTAL FAT: 8G
    MONO: 0.5G,
    POLY: 0G;
    SAT: 1G,
PROTEIN: 5G;
CARB: 26G;
FIBER: 5.5G;
CHOL: 3.5MG;
SODIUM: 415MG

EXCELLENT SOURCE OF
FIBER, PHOSPHO-RUS, THIAMIN

GOOD SOURCE OF
CALCIUM, FOLATE, IRON, MAGNESIUM, NIACIN, POTAS-SIUM, PROTEIN, RIBOFLAVIN, VITAMIN A, VITAMIN C, ZINC

In a small bowl, whisk together the buttermilk, mayonnaise, mustard, vinegar, hot sauce, salt, and pepper.

In a large salad bowl, combine the black-eyed peas, onion, celery, and chives. Pour the dressing over the mixture and gently stir to incorporate, being careful not to break up too many of the beans. Add the spinach and toss to coat. Season with more salt, pepper, and hot sauce to taste. Serve immediately.

Whole-Wheat Pasta Salad with Walnuts and Feta Cheese

This takes pasta salad off the sidelines and turns it into an elegant main course. The bold-flavored feta cheese and bright vinaigrette dressing really stand up to the flavor of the whole-wheat pasta, while the walnuts bring out its nuttiness. It's the easy-to-bring salad that everyone will be fawning over at your next potluck.

½ pound whole-wheat fusilli or other spiral-shaped pasta
½ cup walnut pieces
½ cup crumbled feta cheese
½ cup diced red onion
1½ cups chopped baby spinach leaves
2 tablespoons walnut or olive oil
2 tablespoons red wine vinegar
1 clove garlic, minced (about 1 teaspoon)
½ teaspoon Dijon mustard
Salt and freshly ground black pepper to taste

SERVES 4
SERVING SIZE: ABOUT 2 CUPS

PER SERVING
CALORIES: 420;
TOTAL FAT: 21.5G
  MONO: 4G,
  POLY: 12G;
  SAT: 4.5G,
PROTEIN: 13.5G;
CARB: 49G;
FIBER: 9G;
CHOL: 16.5MG;
SODIUM: 245MG

EXCELLENT SOURCE OF
COPPER, FIBER, MAGNESIUM, MANGANESE, PHOSPHORUS, PROTEIN, SELENIUM, THIAMIN

GOOD SOURCE OF
CALCIUM, FOLATE, IRON, NIACIN, VITAMIN B6, ZINC

Cook the pasta according to the package directions. Drain the pasta, rinse under cold running water, and put it in the refrigerator to chill.

In a small dry skillet, toast the walnuts over medium-high heat, stirring frequently until fragrant, 3 to 5 minutes. Set aside to cool, then chop coarsely.

In a large bowl, toss together the pasta, walnuts, feta, onion, and spinach. In a small bowl, whisk together the oil, vinegar, garlic, and mustard. Pour the dressing over the pasta salad and toss to combine. Season with salt and pepper. This salad will keep in the refrigerator in an airtight container for about a day.

Soba Noodle–Vegetable Salad

Ribbons of colorful vegetables and fresh herbs intertwine with tender noodles in this delicately flavored salad. It is a perfect accompaniment for spicy Asian dishes like the Chicken Saté with Spicy Peanut Dipping Sauce (page 54).

For the salad

4 ounces soba noodles or whole-wheat spaghetti

1 large shallot, very thinly sliced

1 large carrot, shredded (about 1 cup)

1 medium red bell pepper, seeded and cut into thin strips

⅓ cup shredded fresh basil

⅓ cup shredded fresh mint

1 tablespoon chopped fresh cilantro

For the dressing

¼ cup rice vinegar

1 teaspoon sugar

1 tablespoon walnut or canola oil

½ teaspoon toasted sesame oil

1 clove garlic, finely minced (about 1 teaspoon)

½ teaspoon red pepper flakes

½ teaspoon finely grated lime zest

1 teaspoon fresh lime juice

½ teaspoon Asian fish sauce or 1 teaspoon low-sodium soy sauce

Salt to taste

To serve

12 large Bibb lettuce leaves

SERVES 6
SERVING SIZE:
¾ CUP AND
2 LETTUCE LEAVES

PER SERVING
CALORIES: 124;
TOTAL FAT: 3G
  MONO: 0.5G,
  POLY: 1.7G;
  SAT: 0.5G,
PROTEIN: 4.5G;
CARB: 22G;
FIBER: 2G;
CHOL: 0MG;
SODIUM: 212MG

EXCELLENT
SOURCE OF
MANGANESE,
VITAMIN A,
VITAMIN C,
VITAMIN K

GOOD
SOURCE OF
FOLATE, IRON,
POTASSIUM,
THIAMIN

Bring a large saucepan of water to a boil and cook the noodles according to the package directions. Drain and let cool.

In a medium to large bowl, combine the noodles and the remaining salad ingredients. In a small bowl, whisk together the dressing ingredients, add to the noodle salad, and toss lightly to coat.

To serve, scoop spoonfuls of the noodle salad into the lettuce leaves and eat out of hand.

Tabbouleh

In this traditional Middle Eastern salad, parsley isn't just a bit player; it has a starring role, along with fresh mint, balancing the hearty bulgur wheat with green freshness. This is one of those dishes that gets even better after it sits for a few hours and the flavors meld.

1 cup bulgur wheat
1½ cups boiling water
2 medium ripe tomatoes, seeded and diced (about 2 cups)
1 medium English cucumber, peeled, seeded, and diced (about 2 cups)
½ cup diced red onion
2 cups finely chopped fresh flat-leaf parsley
⅓ cup finely chopped fresh mint
3 tablespoons olive oil
¼ cup fresh lemon juice
1 teaspoon finely grated lemon zest
1 teaspoon ground cumin
Salt and freshly ground black pepper to taste

SERVES 6
SERVING SIZE:
1¼ CUPS

PER SERVING
CALORIES: 175;
TOTAL FAT: 8G
   MONO: 5G,
   POLY: 1G;
   SAT 1G,
PROTEIN: 4G;
CARB: 25G;
FIBER: 6G;
CHOL: 0MG;
SODIUM: 20MG

EXCELLENT
SOURCE OF
FIBER,
MANGANESE,
VITAMIN A,
VITAMIN C,
VITAMIN K

GOOD
SOURCE OF
FOLATE, IRON,
MAGNESIUM,
PHOSPHORUS,
POTASSIUM

Place the bulgur in a large heatproof bowl. Pour the boiling water over it, stir, and cover tightly with plastic wrap. Let it sit for about 15 minutes, until the water is absorbed and the bulgur is tender. Drain any excess water from the bulgur. Stir in the tomatoes, cucumber, onion, parsley, and mint.

In a small bowl, whisk together the oil, lemon juice and zest, cumin, salt, and pepper. Pour the dressing over the bulgur mixture and toss well to combine. Cover and place in the refrigerator for 1 hour or up to a day stored in an airtight container. Serve chilled.

All-Day Breakfast Salad

You know those late weekend mornings when you just can't decide if you want breakfast or lunch? This salad is the perfect solution: a bacon and egg breakfast atop a satisfying spinach salad. It's the best of both meals.

4 slices Canadian bacon (4 ounces)
3 tablespoons extra-virgin olive oil
2 tablespoons balsamic vinegar
½ teaspoon Dijon mustard
Salt and freshly ground black pepper to taste
8 ounces baby spinach leaves (about 8 cups lightly packed)
2 cups cherry or grape tomatoes, cut in half
4 hard-boiled eggs, peeled and chopped
½ cup chopped fresh flat-leaf parsley

SERVES 4
SERVING SIZE:
2 CUPS SALAD,
½ CUP
TOMATOES,
ABOUT 5 STRIPS
CANADIAN BACON,
AND ⅓ CUP
CHOPPED EGG

PER SERVING
CALORIES: 260;
TOTAL FAT: 18G
  MONO: 11G;
  POLY: 2G;
  SAT: 4G;
PROTEIN: 14G;
CARB: 11G;
FIBER: 4G;
CHOL: 226MG;
SODIUM: 575MG

EXCELLENT SOURCE OF
PROTEIN,
VITAMIN A,
VITAMIN C,
VITAMIN K

GOOD SOURCE OF
FIBER, FOLATE,
IODINE, IRON,
MOLYBDENUM,
NIACIN, PANTO-
THENIC ACID,
PHOSPHORUS,
RIBOFLAVIN,
SELENIUM,
THIAMIN,
VITAMIN B_6,
VITAMIN B_{12}

Cook the Canadian bacon in a medium nonstick skillet over medium heat until golden brown, about 5 minutes, turning once. Remove from the skillet and cut into ½-inch strips. Set aside.

In a small bowl, whisk together the oil, vinegar, and mustard. Season with salt and pepper. Place the spinach in a large serving bowl. Add the dressing and toss to coat evenly. Top with the tomatoes, eggs, Canadian bacon, and parsley, and serve.

✳ **DID YOU KNOW?**
Extra-virgin olive oil is unrefined so it is higher in health protective antioxidants and other nutrients than more refined or "pure" olive oil. However, it can't take heat as well so it is best for dressings or moderate-heat cooking. For high heat, use refined canola oil or pure olive oil.

Toasted Pita and Herb Salad

Shards of toasted pita yield just a touch of their crunchy edge when they meet the lemony dressing in this salad. Loaded with fresh herbs and crisp lettuce, this salad ups the ante for crouton lovers everywhere.

One 6-inch whole-wheat pita bread with pocket

2 tablespoons fresh lemon juice

½ teaspoon finely grated lemon zest

Salt and freshly ground black pepper to taste

2 tablespoons extra-virgin olive oil

½ large head romaine lettuce, leaves torn into bite-size pieces
   (about 5 cups lightly packed)

½ cup chopped fresh flat-leaf parsley

1 scallion (white and green parts), thinly sliced

¼ cup chopped fresh mint

½ large English cucumber, cut in half lengthwise, seeded,
   and thinly sliced into half-moons

½ pint grape tomatoes, cut in half

SERVES 4
SERVING SIZE:
1½ CUPS

PER SERVING
CALORIES: 144;
TOTAL FAT: 8G
   MONO: 5.5G,
   POLY: 1G;
   SAT: 1G,
PROTEIN: 4G;
CARB: 17G;
FIBER: 5G;
CHOL: 0MG;
SODIUM: 100MG

**EXCELLENT
SOURCE OF**
FIBER, FOLATE,
MANGANESE,
VITAMIN A,
VITAMIN C,
VITAMIN K

**GOOD
SOURCE OF**
IRON,
MOLYBDENUM,
POTASSIUM,
SELENIUM,
THIAMIN

Preheat the oven to 375°F.

Split the pita into 2 rounds and toast on a baking sheet on the middle rack of the oven until golden brown, about 10 minutes. Allow the pita to cool and break into bite-size pieces. Set aside.

In a small bowl, whisk together the lemon juice, lemon zest, salt, and pepper. Add the oil and whisk to incorporate.

Toss the lettuce, parsley, scallion, mint, cucumber, and tomatoes together in a large serving bowl. Right before serving, add the pita and dressing to the salad. Toss well to coat and serve.

*   DID YOU KNOW?
Herbs like the parsley, basil, mint, and dill offer more than taste; they are rich in antioxidants and other healing compounds. Many herbs also have a substantial amount of vitamin A.

Pesto Potato Salad

With its hearty red potatoes and sweet red and yellow bell peppers tossed in an aromatic basil pesto, this dish is a definite crowd pleaser.

1½ pounds small red potatoes
1 medium yellow bell pepper, seeded and coarsely chopped (about 1 cup)
1 medium red bell pepper, seeded and coarsely chopped (about 1 cup)
⅓ cup Basil Pesto (recipe follows) or store-bought basil pesto
Salt and freshly ground black pepper to taste

SERVES 8
SERVING SIZE:
¾ CUP

PER SERVING
CALORIES: 115;
TOTAL FAT: 5G
  MONO: 2.5G,
  POLY: 1G;
  SAT: 1G;
PROTEIN: 3G;
CARB: 16G;
FIBER: 2G;

CHOL: 0MG;
SODIUM: 20MG

**EXCELLENT
SOURCE OF**
MANGANESE,
VITAMIN C,
VITAMIN K

**GOOD
SOURCE OF**
POTASSIUM,
VITAMIN A,
VITAMIN B$_6$

Put the potatoes in a large steamer basket over boiling water and steam until cooked through but the skins remain intact, about 20 minutes. Set aside until cool enough to handle, then quarter and put in a large bowl. Add the peppers and pesto and toss gently to combine. Season with salt and pepper. Refrigerate until completely cooled. This salad will keep in the refrigerator in an airtight container for about 3 days.

Basil Pesto

Make a big batch of this when the basil is fresh and plentiful. You can freeze it in ice cube trays, bag up the cubes, and have it year-round to use as a pasta sauce or to enhance the flavor of one. It is also excellent as a sandwich spread or as a base for salad dressing.

¼ cup pine nuts
1 clove garlic, peeled
3 cups lightly packed fresh basil leaves
¼ cup freshly grated Parmesan cheese
1 tablespoon fresh lemon juice
¼ cup olive oil
Salt and freshly ground black pepper to taste

MAKES ¾ CUP
SERVING SIZE:
3 TABLESPOONS

PER SERVING
CALORIES: 207;
TOTAL FAT: 21G
  MONO: 12G,
  POLY: 4G;
  SAT: 3G;
 PROTEIN: 4G;
CARB: 3G;
FIBER: 1.5G;

CHOL: 1MG;
SODIUM: 62MG

**EXCELLENT
SOURCE OF**
MANGANESE,
VITAMIN A,
VITAMIN K

GOOD SOURCE OF
CALCIUM,
COPPER,
MAGNESIUM,
VITAMIN C

Toast the pine nuts in a small, dry skillet over medium heat until fragrant and golden brown, shaking the pan frequently, about 3 minutes

In a food processor, process the pine nuts and garlic together until minced. Add the basil, Parmesan, and lemon juice and process until finely minced. With the machine running, slowly pour the oil in a steady stream through the feed tube and process until well blended. Season with salt and pepper.

Southwestern Slaw

Jicama is a large Mexican root vegetable that tastes like a sweet, juicy water chestnut. Its refreshing crispness lends itself perfectly to a slaw like this one, which is accented with the quintessentially Southwestern tastes of cilantro and lime, all covered in a creamy buttermilk dressing.

1 medium jicama, peeled and sliced into thin strips (about 3 cups)
¼ head red cabbage, cored and thinly sliced (about 5 cups)
1 small red onion, cut in half and thinly sliced into half-moons
½ cup chopped fresh cilantro leaves
¼ cup mayonnaise
½ cup lowfat buttermilk
1 tablespoon fresh lime juice
Salt and freshly ground black pepper to taste

SERVES 12
SERVING SIZE:
ABOUT ¾ CUP

PER SERVING
CALORIES: 75;
TOTAL FAT: 4G
    MONO: 0G,
    POLY: 0G;
    SAT: 0.5G,
PROTEIN: 1.5G;
CARB: 9G;
FIBER: 4G;

CHOL: 2MG;
SODIUM: 54MG

EXCELLENT
SOURCE OF
VITAMIN C,
VITAMIN K

GOOD
SOURCE OF
FIBER,
VITAMIN A

In a large serving bowl, toss together the jicama, cabbage, onion, and cilantro.

In a small bowl, whisk together the mayonnaise, buttermilk, and lime juice and season with salt and pepper. Pour the dressing over the vegetables and toss to coat. This will keep in the refrigerator in an airtight container for about 3 days.

Orange-Pistachio Wild Rice Salad

A mix of toothsome brown and wild rice is enlivened here with succulent bits of orange, ribbons of fresh basil, and buttery nuggets of pistachio nuts for a memorable taste of the Mediterranean.

For the salad

⅔ cup brown rice

⅔ cup wild rice

3 cups low-sodium chicken broth

3 tablespoons chopped unsalted pistachios

1 orange

10 large fresh basil leaves, sliced into ribbons

¼ cup minced red onion

For the dressing

⅓ cup red wine vinegar

¼ cup olive oil

1 tablespoon orange juice

1½ teaspoons Dijon mustard

1 teaspoon honey

¼ teaspoon salt

SERVES 6
SERVING SIZE: ABOUT ¾ CUP

PER SERVING
CALORIES: 280;
TOTAL FAT: 13G
    MONO: 8G,
    POLY: 2G;
    SAT: 2G,
PROTEIN: 8G;
CARB: 36G;
FIBER: 3G;
CHOL: 0MG;
SODIUM: 150MG

EXCELLENT SOURCE OF
MANGANESE,
NIACIN,
PHOSPHORUS,
VITAMIN C

GOOD SOURCE OF
COPPER, FIBER,
PROTEIN, THIAMIN,
VITAMIN B₆,
VITAMIN C,
VITAMIN K, ZINC

Combine the brown rice, wild rice, and broth in a medium saucepan and bring to a boil. Cover, reduce the heat to a slow simmer, and cook until all water is evaporated and the rice is fully cooked, 45 to 55 minutes. Remove from the heat and let cool completely.

Toast the pistachios in a small dry skillet over medium-high heat until fragrant, about 3 minutes, stirring frequently; cool.

Grate the zest from the orange; measure 1 teaspoon and set aside. Cut the top and bottom off the orange. Stand it on one end and remove the rest of the peel and the woolly white pith by cutting down the orange, following its curve with your knife. Then remove each orange segment from the membrane.

When the rice is cool, add the orange sections, the basil, onion, pistachios, and orange zest, and mix to incorporate.

To make the dressing, whisk together the vinegar, oil, orange juice, mustard, honey, and salt in a small bowl. Pour over the rice mixture and toss to incorporate. This salad will keep in the refrigerator in an airtight container for a day or two.

pasta, pizza & grains

Portobello Lasagna Rollups with Easy Tomato Sauce

Meaty, earthy mushrooms are the perfect complement for hearty whole-wheat noodles. Smothered in tomato sauce and prepared with three cheeses, this updated lasagna dish is old-fashioned delicious.

12 whole-wheat lasagna noodles (about ¾ pound)

2 teaspoons olive oil

12 ounces portobello mushrooms, chopped

½ teaspoon salt

4 cups Easy Tomato Sauce (recipe follows) or store-bought marinara sauce

One 15-ounce container part-skim ricotta cheese

One 10-ounce package frozen chopped spinach, thawed, drained, and squeezed dry

1 large egg, lightly beaten

Freshly ground black pepper

Pinch of ground nutmeg

¼ cup freshly grated Parmesan cheese

¾ cup grated part-skim mozzarella cheese (3 ounces)

SERVES 6
SERVING SIZE: 2 ROLLS

PER SERVING
CALORIES: 500;
TOTAL FAT: 18G
  MONO: 4.3G,
  POLY: 1.2G;
  SAT: 7.5G,
PROTEIN: 26G;
CARB: 56G;
FIBER: 12G;
CHOL: 76MG;
SODIUM: 1110MG

EXCELLENT SOURCE OF
CALCIUM, FIBER, IRON, NIACIN, POTASSIUM, PROTEIN, RIBOFLAVIN, THIAMIN, VITAMIN A, VITAMIN C

GOOD SOURCE OF
COPPER, PANTOTHENIC ACID, SELENIUM

Preheat the oven to 375°F.

Cook the noodles according to the package directions. Drain well and spread them out on a sheet of aluminum foil or waxed paper to prevent them from sticking.

Heat the oil in a large skillet over medium-high heat. Add the mushrooms and cook, stirring occasionally, until browned and all the liquid has evaporated, about 5 minutes. Season with ¼ teaspoon of the salt, stir in 1½ cups of the tomato sauce, and simmer for 2 minutes.

In a medium bowl, combine the ricotta, spinach, egg, the remaining ¼ teaspoon salt, a few turns of pepper, and the nutmeg.

Spread 1 cup of the remaining tomato sauce on the bottom of a 9 x 13-inch baking dish. Spread about 2 tablespoons of the ricotta mixture onto a lasagna noodle. Top with about 1½ tablespoons of the mushroom mixture, then roll the noodle and stand it up or lay it down in the baking dish. Repeat with the remaining noodles, ricotta mixture, and mushroom mixture. Spread the remaining 1½ cups tomato sauce over the lasagna rolls. Top with the Parmesan and mozzarella, cover loosely with foil, and bake for 45 minutes. Uncover and bake for 15 minutes more.

Easy Tomato Sauce

You don't need to cook all day to get a great homemade tomato sauce. This sauce has that robust long-cooked taste but takes just a little more than 30 minutes. I have a hard time finding no-salt-added whole tomatoes, so I call for regular here.

1 tablespoon olive oil
1 medium onion, finely chopped (about 1½ cups)
2 cloves garlic, minced (about 2 teaspoons)
Two 28-ounce cans whole tomatoes, drained and the tomatoes chopped
3 tablespoons tomato paste
1 teaspoon dried oregano
1 bay leaf
Salt and freshly ground black pepper to taste

In a large saucepan, heat the oil over medium heat. Add the onion and cook, stirring a few times, until softened, about 5 minutes. Add the garlic and cook for 1 minute more. Add the remaining ingredients and cook, uncovered, stirring occasionally, until thickened, about 30 minutes. Season with salt and pepper.

SERVES 6
MAKES 3 CUPS;
SERVING SIZE:
½ CUP

PER SERVING
CALORIES: 94;
TOTAL FAT: 3G
  MONO: 2G
  POLY: 0G;
  SAT: 0.3G,
PROTEIN: 2.5G;
CARB: 14G;

FIBER: 3G;
CHOL: 0MG;
SODIUM: 476MG

**EXCELLENT
SOURCE OF**
IRON, VITAMIN A,
VITAMIN C

**GOOD
SOURCE OF**
FIBER

Pasta with Escarole, White Beans, and Chicken Sausage

Sausage, white beans, and escarole with pasta in a garlicky sauce is a classic Italian combination. Here chicken sausage and chicken broth lighten the dish while keeping it meaty, moist, and flavorful.

¾ box (12 ounces) whole-wheat bowtie (or other shape) pasta
1 tablespoon olive oil
½ medium onion, chopped (about ¾ cup)
3 cloves garlic, minced (about 1 tablespoon)
6 ounces uncooked lowfat Italian-style chicken sausage, casings removed and crumbled
1 medium head escarole, chopped (about 8 cups)
One 15.5-ounce can cannellini or other white beans, preferably low-sodium, drained and rinsed
1½ cups low-sodium chicken broth
1 tablespoon chopped fresh sage
½ teaspoon red pepper flakes
Salt and freshly ground black pepper to taste
¼ cup freshly grated Parmesan cheese

SERVES 4
SERVING SIZE: 2 CUPS

PER SERVING
CALORIES: 595;
TOTAL FAT: 13.5G
  MONO: 3G,
  POLY: 0.5G;
  SAT: 3G,
PROTEIN: 30G;
CARB: 90G;
FIBER: 19G;
CHOL: 39MG;
SODIUM: 442MG

EXCELLENT SOURCE OF
CALCIUM, FIBER, FOLATE, IRON, MANGANESE, PHOSPHORUS, POTASSIUM, PROTEIN, THIAMIN, VITAMIN A, VITAMIN C, VITAMIN K, ZINC

GOOD SOURCE OF
MAGNESIUM, NIACIN, RIBOFLAVIN

Cook the pasta according to the package directions.

Meanwhile, heat the oil over medium heat in a large, deep sauté pan. Add the onion and cook, stirring a few times, until softened, 3 to 5 minutes. Add the garlic and cook an additional minute. Stir in the sausage and cook until heated through and browned, about 4 minutes. Add the escarole and cook until wilted, 3 to 4 minutes. Add the beans, 1 cup of the broth, the sage, and red pepper and simmer until the mixture is heated through and liquid is slightly reduced.

Drain the pasta, add it to the sausage-bean mixture, and toss well, loosening with the remaining ½ cup broth if necessary. Season with salt and black pepper. Divide between 4 pasta bowls, top with the Parmesan, and serve.

Fettuccine with Walnuts and Parsley

This is a hearty, out-of-the-ordinary, absolutely scrumptious meal.

¾ box (12 ounces) whole-wheat fettuccine

⅔ cup chopped walnuts

¼ cup olive oil

5 cloves garlic, minced (about 1⅔ tablespoons)

½ cup low-sodium chicken broth

½ cup chopped fresh flat-leaf parsley, plus more for garnish

½ teaspoon salt

½ teaspoon freshly ground black pepper

¾ cup freshly grated Parmesan cheese

SERVES 4
SERVING SIZE:
2 CUPS

PER SERVING
CALORIES: 640;
TOTAL FAT: 34G
  MONO: 13G,
  POLY: 12G;
  SAT: 5G,
PROTEIN: 18G;
CARB: 69G;
FIBER: 10G;
CHOL: 1MG;
SODIUM: 405MG

EXCELLENT
SOURCE OF
COPPER, FIBER,
IRON, MANGA-
NESE, PROTEIN,
VITAMIN C,
VITAMIN K

GOOD
SOURCE OF
CALCIUM,
MAGNESIUM,
MOLYBDENUM,
POTASSIUM,
VITAMIN A,
VITAMIN B6

Cook the pasta according to the package directions, then drain in a colander.

Meanwhile, toast the walnuts in a small dry skillet over medium-high heat until fragrant, stirring frequently, 3 to 5 minutes.

In the pot the pasta was cooked in, heat the oil with the garlic over low heat, stirring until the garlic is soft and fragrant, 3 to 4 minutes (be careful not to burn it). Return the pasta to the pot, add the broth, all but 2 tablespoons of the walnuts, the parsley, salt, and pepper and toss to combine, cooking over low heat for 1 to 2 minutes. Add ½ cup of the Parmesan and toss to combine. Divide among 4 bowls. Top with the remaining ¼ cup cheese, the reserved walnuts, and more parsley and serve.

*
The Whole Story

Whole grains have not been stripped of their germ and endosperm, like refined grains have. Thanks to these intact parts, whole grains contain a unique balance of vitamins and minerals plus fiber and anti-oxidants. People who eat whole grains regularly are less likely to get heart disease and cancer and are more likely to have healthy blood sugar levels. Whole grains also help you feel fuller on fewer calories.

Most Americans don't get even a single serving of whole grain a day, when we should all be aiming for at least three daily. This book can help you get there easily, since I almost always use whole grains in my recipes, including whole-wheat pasta, except when its nutty taste and heavier texture isn't right for a recipe.

Penne with Roasted Tomatoes, Garlic, and White Beans

Roasting the tomatoes concentrates their flavor and gives them an almost melted quality. When you toss them with the roasted garlic, lemon, white beans, and basil, you wind up with a wonderfully flavored dish you barely had to lift a finger to make.

3 large ripe tomatoes (about 2 pounds)
6 large cloves garlic, papery outermost skin removed, but left unpeeled
3 tablespoons olive oil
½ teaspoon salt, plus more to taste
Freshly ground black pepper
One 15.5-ounce can cannellini or other white beans, preferably low-sodium
½ box (8 ounces) penne pasta
2 tablespoons fresh lemon juice
⅓ cup fresh basil leaves, cut into ribbons
¼ cup freshly grated Parmesan cheese

SERVES 4
SERVING SIZE: 1½ CUPS

PER SERVING
CALORIES: 476;
TOTAL FAT: 14.5G
  MONO: 8G,
  POLY: 2G;
  SAT: 2.5G;
PROTEIN: 16.5G;
CARB: 70.5G;
FIBER: 9.5G;
CHOL: 1MG;
SODIUM: 602MG

EXCELLENT SOURCE OF
FIBER, IRON, MANGANESE, PROTEIN, VITAMIN A, VITAMIN C, VITAMIN K

GOOD SOURCE OF
CALCIUM, COPPER, FOLATE, MAGNESIUM, MOLYBDENUM, POTASSIUM, THIAMIN, VITAMIN B6

Preheat the oven to 450°F.

Slice each tomato into 8 wedges and discard the seeds. Put the tomato wedges and garlic in a 9 x 13-inch roasting pan, toss with 2 tablespoons of the oil, and sprinkle with ¼ teaspoon of the salt and a few turns of pepper. Roast, uncovered, until the tomatoes lose their shape and become slightly charred, 35 to 40 minutes.

Drain the beans in a large colander in the sink.

Cook the pasta according to the package directions. Drain the pasta in the colander containing the beans, so the hot pasta water warms the beans. Return the drained pasta and beans to the pasta pot.

When the tomatoes are done, carefully pick out the garlic cloves, squeeze the garlic out of the skin into a small bowl, and mash with a fork. Add the lemon juice, the remaining 1 tablespoon oil and ¼ teaspoon salt, and a pinch of pepper, and stir to combine. Transfer the roasted tomatoes to the pasta pot, add the garlic-lemon mixture and basil and season with salt and pepper to taste. Toss to combine. Serve topped with the Parmesan.

* **DID YOU KNOW?**
Rinsing canned beans removes about 40% of their sodium.

Pasta Puttanesca

This lusty tomato sauce is laden with bold flavors—olives, capers, red pepper flakes, and garlic. Chopped arugula tossed in at the final stage of cooking brings in a fresh green dimension and a peppery taste that can hold its own.

One 16-ounce box whole-wheat thin spaghetti, vermicelli, or angel hair pasta
2 tablespoons extra-virgin olive oil
4 cloves garlic, minced (about 4 teaspoons)
½ cup chopped fresh flat-leaf parsley
½ cup pitted Spanish or Greek olives, drained and chopped
¼ cup capers, drained
2 teaspoons anchovy paste
2 teaspoons dried oregano
¼ teaspoon red pepper flakes
Two 14.5-ounce cans no-salt-added diced tomatoes, with their juices
1½ cups chopped fresh arugula
¼ cup freshly grated Parmesan cheese

SERVES 6
SERVING SIZE:
ABOUT 2 CUPS

PER SERVING
CALORIES: 372;
TOTAL FAT: 8G
  MONO: 4.5G,
  POLY: 1G;
  SAT: 2G,
PROTEIN: 15G;
CARB: 64G;
FIBER: 12G;
CHOL: 2MG;
SODIUM: 733MG

EXCELLENT SOURCE OF
COPPER, FIBER, IRON, MAGNESIUM, MANGANESE, NIACIN, PHOSPHORUS, PROTEIN, SELENIUM, THIAMIN, VITAMIN A, VITAMIN C, VITAMIN K

GOOD SOURCE OF
CALCIUM, FOLATE, VITAMIN B6, ZINC

Cook the spaghetti according to the package directions.

While the pasta is cooking, heat the oil in a large skillet over medium heat. Add the garlic and cook until fragrant, about 1 minute. Add the parsley, olives, capers, anchovy paste, oregano, and red pepper and cook for another 2 minutes. Add the tomatoes and simmer for about 5 minutes. Stir in the arugula and simmer for another minute, just until the greens wilt slightly.

When the pasta is done, drain and add it to the skillet, tossing it with the sauce to combine. Divide between 6 plates, sprinkle with the Parmesan, and serve.

Canned and Frozen: Healthy Convenience

While I believe in using fresh food whenever possible, I also believe in taking advantage of the convenience of canned and frozen. A well-stocked pantry and freezer means you can have a healthful meal at your fingertips any time. The key is to stock smartly.

IT'S NUTRITIOUS

Many people are surprised to find that canned and frozen food is comparable in nutrition to its cooked fresh counterpart. Most canned and frozen produce is picked at the peak of ripeness and packaged within hours. Canning and freezing are remarkably effective means of preserving nutrients and quality, and they require no preservatives.

In some cases canned or frozen food is even more nutritious than fresh. This is especially true if the fresh food has traveled thousands of miles to get to your store and then sits for days before you eat it, losing nutrients all the while. The canning process also concentrates some nutrients like lycopene in tomatoes and beta-carotene in pumpkin.

THE PRICE IS RIGHT

Frozen and canned produce and fish are usually considerably cheaper than fresh. Plus, since frozen foods keep at peak quality for about six months and canned for two years, they are naturals for buying in bulk. Frozen produce in bags is especially thrifty if you are cooking for one or two as you can take what you need and wrap up the rest.

BUY SMART

The downside of canned and frozen food is that they are often packaged with a lot of sugar and salt. So my rule of thumb is to buy them as close to their farm-fresh state as possible. That means getting low-sodium or no-salt-added canned broths, beans, and vegetables, and fruit packed in natural juice instead of syrup. And it means buying frozen fruit without added sugar and vegetables without added sauces. There are plenty of these options available at markets these days, and I find "natural" or organic brands are often lower in salt and sugar although they may not be advertised that way.

You may wind up adding add salt or sugar to flavor your food, but this way you, not the food manufacturer, are in control of how much you get.

Linguine with Shrimp and Vegetables

Tender asparagus, bright cherry tomatoes, and big succulent shrimp tossed with linguine in a lemon and white wine sauce—a perfect meal to celebrate spring.

¾ box (12 ounces) linguine

2 tablespoons olive oil

1 bunch (about 1 pound) asparagus, woody bottoms removed
    and cut into 1-inch pieces

2 cloves garlic, minced (about 2 teaspoons)

1 pound large shrimp, peeled and deveined

⅓ cup fresh lemon juice

½ cup dry white wine

1 cup chopped fresh flat-leaf parsley

1 pint cherry tomatoes, cut in half

¼ cup freshly grated Parmesan cheese

Salt and freshly ground black pepper to taste

SERVES 4
SERVING SIZE:
2 ¼ CUPS

PER SERVING
CALORIES: 579;
TOTAL FAT: 12G
  MONO: 6G,
  POLY: 1.5G;
  SAT: 2G,
PROTEIN: 39G;
CARB: 71.5G;
FIBER: 5G;
CHOL: 173MG;
SODIUM: 242MG

**EXCELLENT
SOURCE OF**
COPPER, FIBER,
FOLATE, IRON,
MANGANESE,
NIACIN,
PHOSPHORUS,
PROTEIN,
SELENIUM,
VITAMIN A,
VITAMIN B$_{12}$,
VITAMIN C,
VITAMIN D,
VITAMIN K

**GOOD
SOURCE OF**
CALCIUM,
MAGNESIUM,
MOLYBDENUM,
POTASSIUM,
RIBOFLAVIN,
THIAMIN,
VITAMIN B$_6$,
ZINC

Cook the linguine according to the package directions. Drain, reserving 1 cup of the pasta water.

Meanwhile, heat the oil in a large skillet over medium-high heat. Add the asparagus and garlic and cook for 2 minutes. Add the shrimp and cook until they turn pink and the asparagus is tender but firm, 3 to 4 minutes more. Remove the shrimp mixture from the pan and set aside.

Combine the lemon juice, wine, and reserved pasta water in the skillet over medium-high heat. Let simmer until the liquid is reduced by about half. Return the shrimp and asparagus to the pan and stir in the parsley. Add the drained linguine, tossing to combine. Add the tomatoes and toss. Sprinkle with cheese, season with salt and pepper, and serve.

Tricolore Penne with Chicken

This dish is inspired by my favorite Italian salad, the tricolore: dark green arugula, red radicchio, and white endive in a balsamic vinaigrette. It is amazing how the tricolored vegetables' flavors are transformed and intensified when warmed. They are gently wilted here and tossed with chewy sun-dried tomatoes, fresh basil, whole-wheat penne, and sliced chicken to make an exceptional, deeply flavorful meal.

¾ box (12 ounces) whole-wheat penne

¼ cup olive oil

4 large cloves garlic, thinly sliced

½ cup sun-dried tomatoes (not oil-packed), sliced into strips

½ pound skinless, boneless chicken breast halves, thinly sliced

2 cups roughly chopped arugula leaves

1 medium head radicchio, thinly sliced

1 large head Belgian endive, bottom ½ inch removed, then sliced into thin strips

¾ cup low-sodium chicken broth

½ teaspoon salt

½ teaspoon freshly ground black pepper

1½ cups fresh basil leaves, thinly sliced, plus more for garnish

SERVES 4
SERVING SIZE: 2½ CUPS

PER SERVING
CALORIES: 575;
TOTAL FAT: 18G
MONO: 11G,
POLY: 2G;
SAT: 2G,
PROTEIN: 28G;
CARB: 76G;
FIBER: 13G;
CHOL: 33MG;
SODIUM: 538MG

EXCELLENT SOURCE OF
COPPER, FIBER, FOLATE, IRON, MANGANESE, NIACIN, PANTOTHENIC ACID, PHOSPHORUS, PROTEIN, POTASSIUM, VITAMIN A, VITAMIN B6, VITAMIN C, VITAMIN K

GOOD SOURCE OF
CALCIUM, MAGNESIUM, MOLYBDENUM, RIBOFLAVIN, SELENIUM, THIAMIN, ZINC

Cook the pasta according to the package directions. Drain, reserving ½ cup of the pasta water.

While the pasta is cooking, heat the oil over medium heat in a large, heavy skillet. Cook the garlic and tomatoes, stirring, until the garlic is soft but not browned, about 2 minutes. Add the chicken and cook, stirring a few times, until just cooked through, about 5 minutes. Add the arugula, radicchio, endive, broth, salt, and pepper, and cook until the greens are wilted, 1 to 2 minutes. Add pasta water as necessary for a wetter sauce.

Combine the pasta and vegetable mixture in the pasta pot and toss to combine. Add the basil just before serving.

*   **EATING WELL TIP**
    If you haven't tried whole-wheat pasta in a while, it is worth sampling again. Pasta makers have really improved it, making it more tender and mild tasting, in contrast to the cardboard versions available not too long ago. Whole-wheat pasta's softly nutty taste works best with deeply flavored, earthy sauces. For light sauces, I stick with regular pasta for a better flavor balance.

Fettuccine Bolognese

Pasta with creamy meat sauce is something you would think would be off the menu when you are trying to eat healthy. Now you can welcome its satisfying goodness back into your life. My bolognese is beefy and rich but better for you, thanks to lean beef amped up with meaty mushrooms, fresh herbs, tomatoes, and a touch of milk for creaminess.

¾ box (12 ounces) whole-wheat fettuccine

1 tablespoon olive oil

1 small onion finely chopped (about 1 cup)

1 medium carrot, finely chopped (about ½ cup)

2 stalks celery, finely chopped (about ½ cup)

8 ounces white mushrooms, finely chopped

3 cloves garlic, minced (about 1 tablespoon)

1 pound lean or extra-lean (90% lean or higher) ground beef

2 tablespoons chopped fresh thyme or 2 teaspoons dried

Two 14.5-ounce cans no-salt-added diced tomatoes, with their juices

½ cup low-sodium chicken broth

¼ cup fat-free evaporated milk or regular whole milk

Salt and freshly ground black pepper to taste

¼ cup freshly grated Parmesan cheese

SERVES 4
SERVING SIZE: 2½ CUPS

PER SERVING
CALORIES: 580;
TOTAL FAT: 11G
  MONO: 5G,
  POLY: 1.5G;
  SAT: 3G,
PROTEIN: 42.5G;
CARB: 82G;
FIBER: 14.5G;
CHOL: 62MG;
SODIUM: 265MG

EXCELLENT SOURCE OF
COPPER, FIBER, FOLATE, IRON, MAGNESIUM, MANGANESE, NIACIN, PHOSPHORUS, PROTEIN, RIBOFLAVIN, SELENIUM, THIAMIN, VITAMIN B6, VITAMIN B12, VITAMIN C, ZINC

GOOD SOURCE OF
CALCIUM, MOLYBDENUM, PANTOTHENIC ACID, POTASSIUM, VITAMIN D, VITAMIN K

Cook the fettuccine according to the package directions.

In the meantime, heat the oil in a large skillet over medium-high heat. Add the onion, carrot, and celery and cook, stirring a few times, until softened, about 5 minutes. Add the mushrooms and cook until the water they release has evaporated, another 5 to 7 minutes, stirring a few times. Add the garlic, ground beef, and thyme and cook until the meat is browned, breaking it up into small pieces as it cooks, about 5 minutes. Stir in the tomatoes and broth and cook until the sauce is thickened, about another 5 minutes. Stir in the milk and cook for 1 minute more. Season with salt and pepper.

When the pasta is done, drain it, put it back in the pasta pot, add the sauce, and stir the sauce and pasta together. Divide between 4 serving bowls, sprinkle with the Parmesan, and serve.

* EATING WELL TIP
Evaporated milk is milk with 60% of its water removed. It is usually found canned and is free of added sodium or preservatives. Because it is thickened, it has a creamlike texture and can replace cream in many recipes. But because it has a high protein content, it should be added at the end of cooking and heated only slightly, or it will curdle.

Spaghetti with Turkey Meatballs in Spicy Tomato Sauce

A little chipotle kick and the multiple herbs in this sauce lend layers of flavor without fat. The carrot, onion, and Parmesan in the meatballs make them luxuriously plump and moist. Together, over spaghetti, you have a comfort-food classic that satisfies on every level.

For the sauce

1 tablespoon olive oil
1 medium onion, chopped (about 1½ cups)
4 cloves garlic, minced (about 4 teaspoons)
3 tablespoons tomato paste
One 28-ounce can crushed fire-roasted tomatoes, with their juices
1 teaspoon finely minced canned chipotle chile in adobo sauce,
   or more to taste
2 teaspoons dried oregano
1 sprig fresh rosemary
Salt and freshly ground black pepper to taste
¼ cup torn fresh basil

For the meatballs

Cooking spray
1 pound lean ground turkey meat
1 slice whole-wheat bread, crusts removed and pulsed into crumbs
   in a food processor
¼ cup freshly grated Parmesan
½ cup finely grated carrot
½ cup finely chopped onion
2 large cloves garlic, minced (about 2 teaspoons)
2 tablespoons minced fresh flat-leaf parsley
2 teaspoons minced fresh thyme
1 large egg, lightly beaten
½ teaspoon salt
Freshly ground black pepper

For the spaghetti

One 16-ounce box whole-wheat spaghetti
⅓ cup freshly grated Parmesan cheese
Minced fresh flat-leaf parsley for garnish

SERVES 6
SERVING SIZE: 1⅓ CUPS PASTA AND SAUCE, PLUS 2 MEATBALLS

PER SERVING
CALORIES: 330;
TOTAL FAT: 10.5G;
   MONO: 4.3G,
   POLY: 2G;
   SAT: 3G;
PROTEIN: 23G;
CARB: 38G;
FIBER: 7.5G;
CHOL: 60MG;
SODIUM: 625MG

EXCELLENT SOURCE OF
FIBER, IRON, MANGANESE, NIACIN, PHOSPHORUS, POTASSIUM, PROTEIN, SELENIUM, VITAMIN A, VITAMIN B6, VITAMIN C, VITAMIN K

GOOD SOURCE OF
CALCIUM, COPPER, MAGNESIUM, PANTOTHENIC ACID, RIBOFLAVIN, THIAMIN, ZINC

To make the sauce, in a 4-quart saucepan heat the oil over medium heat. Add the onion and cook, stirring a few times, until translucent, about 3 minutes, then add the garlic and cook for 1 minute. Add the tomato paste, tomatoes, chipotle, oregano, and rosemary, bring to a low boil, reduce the heat to low, and cook until the liquid has evaporated slightly, about 15 minutes. Season with salt and pepper.

While the sauce is cooking, make the meatballs. Preheat the broiler. Spray a baking sheet with cooking spray. Combine the ingredients for the meatballs in a large bowl. Form into 2½-inch balls and place on a baking sheet. Broil until browned and almost entirely cooked through, about 10 minutes.

Meanwhile, remove the rosemary sprig from the sauce and stir in the basil. Add the meatballs to the sauce, cover, and cook until the sauce has slightly thickened and the meatballs have absorbed some of the sauce, about another 10 minutes.

While the meatballs are cooking, cook the spaghetti according to the package directions. Drain the pasta and return it to the pot. Add the sauce and meatballs, toss together, and heat through over medium heat. Divide evenly among 6 pasta bowls, sprinkle with the Parmesan, garnish with parsley, and serve.

Aromatic Noodles with Lime-Peanut Sauce

This crisp green vegetable medley is the refreshing yin to the yang of the rich, spicy peanut sauce. Served over tender noodles, this decadent dish gives a whole new meaning to balanced eating.

¾ box (12 ounces) spinach linguine or whole-wheat spaghetti

2 cups (about 9 ounces) broccoli florets

2 cups (about 6 ounces) snow peas, trimmed

2 cups (about 6 ounces) sugar snap peas, trimmed

½ cup unsalted peanuts

½ cup creamy natural peanut butter

¼ cup low-sodium soy sauce

¼ cup water

2 tablespoons rice vinegar

2 tablespoons fresh lime juice

1 scallion (white and green parts), cut into pieces

One ¾-inch piece fresh ginger, peeled and finely grated

2 tablespoons firmly packed dark brown sugar

¼ teaspoon red pepper flakes, plus more to taste

SERVES 6

SERVING SIZE: 1 CUP PASTA, 1 CUP VEGETABLES, AND 2½ TABLESPOONS SAUCE

PER SERVING
CALORIES: 450;
TOTAL FAT: 18G
   MONO: 8G,
   POLY: 3G;
   SAT: 3G;
PROTEIN: 19G;
CARB: 61G;
FIBER: 11G;
CHOL: 0MG;
SODIUM: 390MG

EXCELLENT SOURCE OF COPPER, FIBER, FOLATE, IRON, MAGNESIUM, MANGANESE, NIACIN, PHOSPHORUS, PROTEIN, RIBOFLAVIN, THIAMIN, VITAMIN A, VITAMIN C

GOOD SOURCE OF CALCIUM, POTASSIUM, VITAMIN B6, ZINC

Cook the pasta according to the package directions. Drain and rinse under cold running water.

While the pasta is cooking, put the broccoli in a steamer basket over a large pot of boiling water and steam it for 3 minutes. Add the snow peas and sugar snap peas and steam for 2 minutes more, until all the vegetables are crisp-tender.

Toast the peanuts in a small dry skillet over medium-high heat until fragrant, 3 to 5 minutes, stirring frequently. Set aside to cool.

Make the sauce by puréeing the peanut butter, soy sauce, water, vinegar, lime juice, scallion, ginger, brown sugar, and red pepper in a food processor or blender until smooth.

Right before serving, toss the pasta with ¾ cup of the peanut sauce. Divide between 6 serving bowls and top each serving with the vegetables. Drizzle the remaining sauce over the vegetables. Coarsely chop the peanuts, sprinkle them on top, and serve.

Macaroni and Four Cheeses

This creamy, crumb-topped macaroni-and-cheese gets is bright orange color and a big nutritional boost from puréed winter squash. Don't tell and no one will ever know. They'll just thank you for making their favorite cheesy comfort meal.

Cooking spray

One 16-ounce box elbow macaroni

Two 10-ounce packages frozen puréed winter squash

2 cups lowfat milk

1⅓ cups grated extra-sharp cheddar cheese (4 ounces)

⅔ cup grated Monterey Jack cheese (2 ounces)

½ cup part-skim ricotta cheese

1 teaspoon salt

1 teaspoon dry mustard

⅛ teaspoon cayenne pepper

2 tablespoons plain dry bread crumbs

2 tablespoons freshly grated Parmesan cheese

1 teaspoon olive oil

SERVES 8
SERVING SIZE:
2 CUPS

PER SERVING
CALORIES: 390;
TOTAL FAT: 11G
  MONO: 1G;
  POLY: 0.5G;
  SAT: 6G,
PROTEIN: 18G;
CARB: 56G;
FIBER: 3.5G;
CHOL: 35MG;
SODIUM: 547MG

EXCELLENT SOURCE OF
CALCIUM, FOLATE, MANGANESE, NIACIN, PROTEIN, SELENIUM, THIAMIN, VITAMIN A

GOOD SOURCE OF
FIBER, IRON, PHOSPHORUS, RIBOFLAVIN

Preheat the oven to 375°F. Coat a 9 x 13-inch baking dish with cooking spray.

Cook the macaroni according the package directions. Drain and transfer to the prepared baking dish.

Meanwhile, place the frozen squash and milk in a large saucepan and cook over low heat, stirring occasionally and breaking up the squash with a spoon until it is defrosted. Turn the heat up to medium and cook until the mixture is almost simmering, stirring occasionally. Remove the pan from the heat and stir in the cheddar, Jack cheese, ricotta, salt, mustard, and cayenne. Pour this mixture over the macaroni and stir to combine.

Combine the bread crumbs, Parmesan, and oil in a small bowl. Sprinkle over the top of the macaroni and cheese. Bake until the cheeses are bubbling around the edges, about 20 minutes, then broil for 3 minutes so the top is crisp and nicely browned.

Mushroom, Onion, and Basil Pizza

Why order in a pizza when you can have this sumptuous, fresh-out-of-the-oven mushroom pizza on your table in less time? Besides, you can't get one this good delivered, with its sun-dried tomatoes, sweet red onion, fresh basil, and two cheese toppings.

¼ cup sun-dried tomatoes (not oil-packed)
Boiling water
1 tablespoon olive oil
8 ounces white mushrooms, sliced (about 3 cups)
½ medium red onion, sliced into half-moons
2 cloves garlic, minced (about 2 teaspoons)
One 10-ounce store-bought baked thin pizza crust
1 cup Easy Tomato Sauce (page 153) or store-bought marinara sauce
1 cup shredded part-skim mozzarella cheese (4 ounces)
¼ cup freshly grated Parmesan cheese
¼ cup thinly sliced fresh basil

SERVES 4
SERVING SIZE:
2 SLICES

EXCELLENT SOURCE OF
FOLATE, PROTEIN

PER SERVING
CALORIES: 350;
TOTAL FAT: 14G
  MONO: 5.3G,
  POLY: 2.5G;
  SAT: 3G,
PROTEIN: 17G;
CARB: 41G;
FIBER: 3G;
CHOL: 1MG;
SODIUM: 750MG

GOOD SOURCE OF
CALCIUM, COPPER, FIBER, IRON, NIA-CIN, PANTOTHENIC ACID, POTASSIUM, RIBOFLAVIN, SELE-NIUM, VITAMIN A, VITAMIN B6, VITA-MIN C, VITAMIN D

Preheat the oven to 450°F.

Reconstitute the sun-dried tomatoes by soaking them in boiling water for 10 minutes. Pat dry and slice thinly.

Heat the oil in a large skillet over medium heat. Add the mushrooms and onion and cook until tender and the mushroom liquid evaporates and they begin to brown, 5 to 7 minutes. Stir in the garlic and remove from the heat.

Place the pizza crust on a baking sheet. Spread the tomato sauce over the crust, leaving a 1-inch border. Top with the mushroom mixture and sun-dried tomatoes. Sprinkle with the mozzarella and Parmesan. Bake until the crust is crisp and the cheese is nicely melted, about 13 minutes. Sprinkle with the basil, cut into 8 slices, and serve.

Tomato, Olive, and Parmesan Pizza

I love the simplicity and crystal clear flavors of this pizza. When a dish has this few ingredients, each one needs to bring a lot to the table, so make sure you use the freshest, highest quality products.

Four 6-inch-diameter whole-wheat tortillas
2 medium ripe tomatoes, seeded and chopped
¼ cup pitted and coarsely chopped calamata olives
2 teaspoons olive oil
¼ cup freshly grated Parmesan cheese
2 tablespoons torn fresh basil leaves
Freshly ground black pepper to taste

Preheat the oven to 400°F.

Put the tortillas on a baking sheet and top each with the tomatoes and olives. Drizzle with the oil, sprinkle with the cheese and bake until crisp and the cheese is slightly melted, about 10 minutes. Garnish with the basil and season with pepper. Let cool for a few minutes, then slice each into 4 wedges and serve.

SERVES 4
SERVING SIZE:
4 WEDGES

PER SERVING
CALORIES: 150;
TOTAL FAT: 7G
  MONO: 1.5G,
  POLY: 0G;
  SAT: 1G,
PROTEIN: 6G;
CARB: 17G;
FIBER: 1G;

CHOL: 1MG;
SODIUM: 409MG

**EXCELLENT
SOURCE OF**
VITAMIN C

**GOOD
SOURCE OF**
CALCIUM,
PROTEIN,
VITAMIN A,
VITAMIN K

* Cheese Rules!

While cheese is high in calcium and protein, much of it is also packed with saturated fat and calories. What's a health-conscious cheese lover to do?

CHOOSE CHEESES NATURALLY LOWER IN FAT
Softer cheeses like feta, fresh goat cheese (chèvre), and Neufchâtel (which is like cream cheese) naturally have about a third less fat than hard cheeses such as cheddar.

SKIP NONFAT AND USE REDUCED-FAT CHEESE WHERE IT WORKS
Taking all the fat out of cheese usually leaves it rubbery and tasteless. So I say, don't bother with nonfat. But lower fat cheeses like part-skim ricotta and mozzarella, reduced-fat cheddar, and lowfat cottage cheese have enough fat so taste isn't compromised.

A LITTLE GOES A LONG WAY
Sometimes only the full-fat version will cut it. In that case, a little of a strong-flavored cheese—Parmesan, blue, Gorgonzola, and extra-sharp cheddar—goes a long way, just use them sparingly.

Arugula, Caramelized Onion, and Goat Cheese Pizza

The key to this pizza is cooking the onions very slowly over low heat so the sugars develop and caramelize. Their sweet flavor and purple color is the perfect foil for the peppery ribbons of arugula and tangy, creamy goat cheese.

1 tablespoon olive oil
1 medium red onion, cut in half and thinly sliced into half-moons
4 cups arugula, washed, dried, and coarsely chopped
Salt and freshly ground black pepper to taste
Four 6-inch-diameter whole-wheat tortillas
2 ounces fresh goat cheese, preferably reduced-fat

SERVES 4
SERVING SIZE:
4 WEDGES

**EXCELLENT
SOURCE OF**
VITAMIN K

PER SERVING
CALORIES: 141;
TOTAL FAT: 5.5G
    MONO: 3G;
    POLY: 0.5G;
    SAT: 1.5G,
PROTEIN: 5G;
CARB: 24G;
FIBER: 2.5G;
CHOL: 2.5MG;
SODIUM: 242MG

**GOOD
SOURCE OF**
FIBER,
MAGNESIUM,
MANGANESE,
PHOSPHORUS,
PROTEIN,
VITAMIN A

Preheat the oven to 400°F.

Heat the oil in a large nonstick skillet over medium heat. Add the onion and cook, stirring, until golden and the edges are browned, 10 to 12 minutes. Add the arugula and cook until it is wilted, about 1 minute. Season with salt and pepper.

Place the tortillas on a baking sheet and top each one with the arugula mixture. Crumble the goat cheese over each and bake until the tortillas are crisp and the cheese is slightly melted, about 10 minutes. Let cool for a few minutes, then cut each pizza into 4 wedges and serve.

Black Bean Mexican-Style Pizza

It is sort of a stretch to call this a pizza, but whatever you want to call it, I know you'll call it delicious. Here the tortilla is spread with spicy black bean dip and crowned with cabbage that softens slightly when cooked while still retaining a nice crunch. A sprinkle of fresh cilantro adds color and a bright citrusy flavor.

Four 6-inch-diameter corn or whole-wheat tortillas
½ cup Black Bean Dip (recipe follows)
1 medium ripe tomato, seeded and diced
1 cup shredded green cabbage
¼ cup chopped fresh cilantro

Preheat the oven to 400°F.

Place the tortillas on a baking sheet and spread 2 tablespoons of the black bean dip on top of each. Top with the tomato and cabbage and bake until the tortillas are crisp and the cabbage is lightly browned, about 10 minutes. Remove the pizzas from the oven and sprinkle with the cilantro. Let cool slightly, then cut each one into 4 wedges and serve.

SERVES 4
SERVING SIZE: 4 WEDGES

PER SERVING
CALORIES: 130;
TOTAL FAT: 2G
MONO: 1G,
POLY: 0G;
SAT: 0G,
PROTEIN: 4G;
CARB: 24G;
FIBER: 4G;

CHOL: 0MG;
SODIUM: 88MG

EXCELLENT SOURCE OF
VITAMIN C

GOOD SOURCE OF
FIBER,
VITAMIN A,
VITAMIN K

Black Bean Dip

This is a fantastically versatile dip. Besides making a flavorful base for the Mexican pizza, it is great for dipping raw veggies and baked tortilla chips, and it makes a satisfying sandwich used like hummus in a pita or wrap stuffed with vegetables.

2 teaspoons olive oil
½ medium onion, diced (about ¾ cup)
1 clove garlic, minced (about 1 teaspoon)
1 tablespoon seeded and minced jalapeño pepper
One 15.5-ounce can black beans, preferably low-sodium, drained and rinsed
2 tablespoons fresh lime juice
¼ teaspoon ground cumin
2 tablespoons coarsely chopped fresh cilantro
1 tablespoon water
Salt and freshly ground black pepper to taste

SERVES 4
MAKES 1 CUP;
SERVING SIZE: ¼ CUP

PER SERVING
CALORIES: 97;
TOTAL FAT: 2.5G
MONO: 2G;
POLY: 0G;
SAT: 0G,

PROTEIN: 4G;
CARB: 15G;
FIBER: 3.5G;
CHOL: 0MG;
SODIUM: 93MG

GOOD SOURCE OF
FIBER

Heat the oil in a medium skillet over medium-high heat. Add the onion and cook, stirring, until softened, about 5 minutes. Stir in the garlic and jalapeño and cook for 1 minute.

Place the beans in a food processor. Add the onion mixture and the remaining ingredients and process until smooth.

Mushroom-Barley "Risotto"

This richly flavored dish, loaded with wild mushrooms, gives you the thick, creamy feel of risotto, but instead of rice it uses tender barley. And instead of having to attentively add broth as you do with most risottos, you just let this one simmer on the stove untouched while it thickens and all the flavors meld.

4 teaspoons canola oil
½ pound skinless, boneless chicken breast, cut into ½-inch cubes
1 medium onion, diced (about 1½ cups)
2 cloves garlic, minced (about 2 teaspoons)
5 cups low-sodium chicken broth
1¼ cups pearl barley
¾ ounce dried porcini or other wild mushrooms
One 4-ounce package (about 2 cups) fresh wild mushroom assortment, roughly chopped
2 teaspoons low-sodium soy sauce
¼ cup freshly grated Parmesan cheese
Salt and freshly ground black pepper to taste
¼ cup minced fresh flat-leaf parsley

SERVES 4
SERVING SIZE: ABOUT 2 CUPS

PER SERVING
CALORIES: 433;
TOTAL FAT: 10G;
    MONO: 4G;
    POLY: 2G;
    SAT: 2G;
PROTEIN: 30G;
CARB: 60G;
FIBER: 11G;
CHOL: 34MG;
SODIUM: 288MG

EXCELLENT
SOURCE OF
COPPER,
FIBER, IRON,

MANGANESE,
NIACIN,
PHOSPHORUS,
POTASSIUM,
PROTEIN,
RIBOFLAVIN,
SELENIUM,
VITAMIN B6,
VITAMIN K

GOOD
SOURCE OF
CALCIUM,
MAGNESIUM,
PANTOTHENIC
ACID, THIAMIN,
VITAMIN C, ZINC

Heat 2 teaspoons of the oil in a Dutch oven over medium-high heat. Add the chicken and cook on all sides until almost cooked through, 4 to 5 minutes. Transfer the chicken to a small bowl.

Heat the remaining 2 teaspoons oil. Add the onion and cook, stirring occasionally, until softened and beginning to brown, 3 to 5 minutes. Add the garlic and cook another 1 minute. Add the broth, barley, porcini, fresh mushrooms, and soy sauce and bring to a boil. Reduce the heat to a simmer, cover, and cook until most of the liquid is absorbed and mixture is thickened, 40 to 45 minutes. In the last 2 minutes of cooking, stir in the cheese and season with salt and pepper. Ladle into bowls, garnish with parsley, and serve.

Fried Rice with Scallions, Edamame, and Tofu

This is my lip-smacking take on the Chinese favorite, bejeweled with colorful vegetables: red peppers, green scallions, golden corn, and emerald edamame. What's more, a steaming, fragrant bowl of it is packed with soy protein, so it's a meal in itself.

1 tablespoon plus 1 teaspoon canola oil

2 large cloves garlic, minced (about 2 teaspoons)

4 scallions (white and green parts), thinly sliced

1 tablespoon peeled and minced fresh ginger

4 cups cooked brown rice

¾ cup seeded and finely diced red bell pepper

¾ cup frozen shelled edamame, cooked according to package directions and drained

½ cup fresh or frozen (thawed) corn kernels

6 ounces firm tofu, cut into ¼-inch cubes

2 large eggs, beaten

3 tablespoons low-sodium soy sauce

SERVES 4
SERVING SIZE:
ABOUT 1½ CUPS

PER SERVING
CALORIES: 400;
TOTAL FAT: 12.5G
  MONO: 4.5G,
  POLY: 2.5G;
  SAT: 2G,
PROTEIN: 16.5G;
CARB: 56G;
FIBER: 7G;
CHOL: 106MG;
SODIUM: 465MG

EXCELLENT SOURCE OF
IRON,
MAGNESIUM,
MANGANESE,
NIACIN,
PHOSPHORUS,
PROTEIN,
SELENIUM,
VITAMIN A,
VITAMIN B6,
VITAMIN C,
VITAMIN K

GOOD SOURCE OF
CALCIUM, FOLATE,
PANTOTHENIC
ACID, RIBOFLAVIN,
THIAMIN, ZINC

Heat 1 tablespoon of the oil in a wok or large skillet over high heat until very hot but not smoking. Add the garlic, scallions, and ginger and cook, stirring, until softened and aromatic, 1 to 2 minutes. Add the rice, red pepper, edamame, corn, and tofu and cook, stirring, until heated through, about 5 minutes.

Make a 3-inch well in the center of the rice mixture. Add the remaining 1 teaspoon oil, then add the eggs and cook until nearly fully scrambled. Stir the eggs into the rice mixture, then add the soy sauce and incorporate thoroughly. Serve hot.

the
main course

Beef Tenderloin with Rosemary and Chocolate

This dish is based on a classic Italian recipe that calls for a touch of grated chocolate or cocoa to add complexity to a red wine sauce. The sauce doesn't taste chocolatey; rather, it has a full-bodied, extraordinary flavor that you just can't pin down. You can make this with any cut of roast beef or steak and the sauce can be prepared a day ahead.

One 2-pound beef tenderloin roast

¼ teaspoon salt, plus more to taste

¼ teaspoon freshly ground black pepper, plus more to taste

4 teaspoons olive oil

½ cup chopped shallots

1 small carrot, finely chopped

1 stalk celery, finely chopped (about ¼ cup)

1 clove garlic, minced (about 1 teaspoon)

2 cups dry red wine

2 cups low-sodium beef broth

2 tablespoons tomato paste

1 bay leaf

1 sprig fresh thyme

1 tablespoon unsweetened natural cocoa powder

1 teaspoon chopped fresh rosemary

SERVES 6
SERVING SIZE:
3 SLICES OF MEAT
AND ABOUT
2 TABLESPOONS
SAUCE

PER SERVING
CALORIES: 270;
TOTAL FAT: 9G;
  MONO: 4G;
  POLY: 0G;
  SAT: 3G;
PROTEIN: 31G;
CARB: 6G;

FIBER: 1G;
CHOL: 82MG;
SODIUM: 375MG

EXCELLENT SOURCE OF
IRON,
MANGANESE,
NIACIN,
PROTEIN,
VITAMIN B$_{12}$,
ZINC

Preheat the oven to 425°F.

Season the meat with the salt and pepper. In a large skillet, heat the 2 teaspoons of the oil over medium-high heat until good and hot, then add the meat and sear until well browned on all sides, about 10 minutes total.

Transfer the meat to a rack set on a baking sheet. Roast until an instant-read thermometer inserted in the thickest part registers 140°F for medium-rare, about 30 minutes, or to your desired degree of doneness. Remove it from the oven, cover with aluminum foil, and let rest until the sauce is nearly done before slicing.

While the meat cooks, make the sauce. Heat the remaining 2 teaspoons oil in a large saucepan over medium-high heat. Add the shallots, carrot, and celery and cook, stirring a few times, until softened, about 5 minutes. Add the garlic and cook for 2 minutes more. Add the wine and broth and stir in the tomato paste. Add the bay leaf and thyme and bring to a boil. Simmer until the liquid is reduced to about ½ cup, about 40 minutes. Strain through a fine mesh strainer into a small saucepan. Stir in the cocoa and rosemary and season with salt and pepper. Serve on the side with the sliced tenderloin.

Beef Tenderloin with Rosemary and Chocolate with Green Beans with Mushrooms and Shallots (page 246)

The Skinny on Meat

Meat is not only crave-ably delicious, it can also be quite healthful if you do it right. Red meats like beef, lamb, and pork are loaded with essential nutrients like protein, zinc, iron, and B-vitamins. The trick is to get all that good stuff without overdoing calories and saturated fat. My advice: Think cut, trim, and portion.

CUT

Choose cuts that make the "Under 10" cutoff, that is, 10 grams of fat or less per 3-ounce portion. Such cuts qualify as lean, whereas less than 5 grams of fat means they're extra-lean. To put that in perspective, a 3-ounce portion of skinless chicken breast has 3 grams of fat while a skinless chicken thigh has 9.2 grams. All of the meats I use here make the grade. Here's a list of a dozen lean or extra-lean cuts with their fat content. Remember; when in doubt, go for cuts with the word "loin" or "round" in their names.

EXTRA LEAN	GRAMS OF FAT/ 3 OUNCES COOKED	LEAN	GRAMS OF FAT/ 3 OUNCES COOKED
Beef top round	3.4	Lamb leg, top round	6.0
Beef eye round	3.5	Beef flank steak	6.3
Pork tenderloin	4.1	Beef top loin (strip) steak	6.5
Ham, extra lean	4.2	Pork loin	7.7
Beef top sirloin	4.7	Beef tenderloin	7.8
		Lamb loin chop	8.0
		Ground beef, 90% lean	9.8

TRIM

To make sure your lean cut is truly lean, trim off all visible fat before cooking.

PORTION

When it's the norm for a piece of meat to fill nearly your entire plate these days, it is hard to wrap your head around what a healthful-sized portion of meat is. Although everyone has different protein needs, a good starting place for most when it comes to meat is 3 to 4 ounces cooked (that's 4 to 5 ounces uncooked). Size-wise, 3 to 4 ounces of cooked meat is about the dimensions of a deck of cards.

Cowboy Steak with Coffee and Ancho Rub

Cowboys are known for cooking resourcefully, using whatever they have with them out on the range to make a great meal. Legend has it that coffee was one of the staples that often found its way into the preparation of their steaks. It gives a deep flavor that brings out the best in beef. Coffee, along with smoky ancho chile powder, dry mustard, and a hint of sweetness from molasses-laced brown sugar, make a steak rub that will knock your boots off.

Cooking spray
1½ teaspoons ground ancho chile or regular chili powder
1½ teaspoons finely ground espresso coffee
½ teaspoon dark brown sugar
¼ teaspoon dry mustard
¼ teaspoon ground coriander
¼ teaspoon salt
¼ teaspoon freshly ground black pepper
One 1¼-pound shoulder center steak (ranch steak) or top sirloin,
   about 1¼ inches thick

SERVES 4
SERVING SIZE: ABOUT 7 SLICES

PER SERVING
CALORIES: 205;
TOTAL FAT: 10G
   MONO: 3.8G,
   POLY: 0.7G;
   SAT: 3.8G,
PROTEIN: 25G;

CARB: 1G;
FIBER: 0.5G;
CHOL: 69MG;
SODIUM: 230MG

EXCELLENT SOURCE OF IRON, NIACIN, PROTEIN, VITAMIN B$_{12}$, ZINC

Coat a large nonstick skillet with cooking spray and preheat it over medium-high heat or preheat the grill.

In a small bowl, combine all the ingredients except the meat and rub it well into both sides of the steak.

Cook the steak for 5 minutes per side, turning once, for medium-rare or to your desired degree of doneness. Allow the steak to sit for 5 minutes before slicing thinly.

Steak Tacos with Cucumber-Avocado Salsa

This is an updated version of everyone's favorite make-your-own taco dinner. Here you fill warm corn tortillas with slices of succulent spice-rubbed steak, crunchy red cabbage, and cool, creamy avocado salsa.

1 tablespoon chili powder
2 cloves garlic, minced (about 2 teaspoons)
¼ teaspoon ground cinnamon
¼ teaspoon salt
Pinch of cayenne pepper
1¼ pounds top sirloin steaks (about 1¼ inches thick)
Twelve 6-inch-diameter corn tortillas
3 cups shredded red cabbage
½ cup chopped fresh cilantro
1 lime, cut into wedges
Cucumber-Avocado Salsa (recipe follows)

SERVES 6
SERVING SIZE:
2 TACOS AND
⅓ CUP SALSA

PER SERVING
CALORIES: 410;
TOTAL FAT: 18G
 MONO: 8G;
 POLY: 2G;
 SAT: 4G,
PROTEIN: 21G;
CARB: 42G;
FIBER: 8G;
CHOL: 46MG;
SODIUM: 250MG

EXCELLENT SOURCE OF
FIBER, FOLATE,
IRON, NIACIN,
PROTEIN,
VITAMIN A,
VITAMIN B6,
VITAMIN B12,
VITAMIN C,
VITAMIN K, ZINC

GOOD SOURCE OF
MANGANESE,
PANTOTHENIC
ACID,
POTASSIUM

Coat a large nonstick skillet with cooking spray and preheat it over medium-high heat or preheat the grill.

In a small bowl, stir together the chili powder, garlic, cinnamon, salt, and cayenne. Rub the spice mixture into both sides of the steaks.

Grill or broil the steaks for 5 minutes per side, turning once, for medium rare or to your desired degree of doneness. Remove from the grill and let the meat sit for 5 minutes. Carve into thin slices.

Warm the tortillas by placing them on the grill for about 30 seconds, turning once. Or place 6 tortillas at a time between two moist paper towels and microwave for 45 seconds. Wrap in a cloth napkin or place in a tortilla warmer to keep warm.

Place the carved steak, warm tortillas, cabbage, cilantro, lime wedges, and salsa in serving dishes and let diners make their own tacos at the table.

✳ DID YOU KNOW?
Slicing the meat thinly makes the portion of meat appear more plentiful, making it more satisfying.

Cucumber-Avocado Salsa

Chunks of cucumber add a cool crunch to this guacamole-like salsa.
It makes a great chip dip, too.

1 medium English cucumber, seeded and diced (about 2 cups)
2 medium firm-ripe avocados, peeled, pitted, and diced
½ red onion, diced
Juice of 2 limes (about ¼ cup)
Salt to taste
¼ cup chopped fresh cilantro
3 jalapeño peppers, seeded and finely chopped, or to taste

Combine all the ingredients in a medium bowl and toss gently to combine.
Serve within an hour of preparing.

SERVES 6
MAKES 2 CUPS;
SERVING SIZE:
⅓ CUP

PER SERVING
CALORIES: 111;
TOTAL FAT: 9G
    MONO: 5.5G;
    POLY: 1G;
    SAT: 1G;
PROTEIN: 1.5G;
CARB: 8G;
FIBER: 4.5G;

CHOL: 0MG;
SODIUM: 6.5MG

**EXCELLENT
SOURCE OF**
VITAMIN C,
VITAMIN K

GOOD SOURCE OF
FIBER, FOLATE,
PANTOTHENIC
ACID, POTASSIUM,
VITAMIN B6

Sweet-and-Sour Brisket

This dish takes pot roast, one of my all-time-favorite comfort foods, to new heights with a sweet-and-sour tomato sauce usually found in an Old World stuffed cabbage recipe. The brisket is meltingly tender and the familiar tangy-sweet, raisin-studded sauce makes you want to lick your plate clean. Growing up, we always had pot roast on special occasions. While this recipe is festive and makes enough to serve company, don't wait for a holiday to make it. You'll be glad for the leftovers any day of the week.

One 3-pound beef brisket, first-cut or flat-half cut, trimmed of any excess fat

1 teaspoon salt

½ teaspoon freshly ground black pepper

2 tablespoons canola oil

1 medium onion, cut in half, then thinly sliced into half-moons

3 cloves garlic, chopped (about 1 tablespoon)

One 15-ounce can tomato sauce, preferably no-salt-added

¼ cup low-sodium chicken broth or water

3 tablespoons firmly packed dark brown sugar

⅓ cup plus 1 tablespoon cider vinegar

⅓ cup raisins

5 black peppercorns

1 allspice berry

SERVES 10
SERVING SIZE:
4 OUNCES
BRISKET PLUS
3 TABLESPOONS
SAUCE

PER SERVING
CALORIES: 360;
TOTAL FAT: 12G
  MONO: 6G,
  POLY: 1G;
  SAT: 4G,
PROTEIN: 46G;
CARB: 14G;
FIBER: 1G;
CHOL: 94MG;
SODIUM: 330MG

EXCELLENT SOURCE OF
IRON, NIACIN,
PHOSPHORUS,
PROTEIN,
 SELENIUM,
VITAMIN B6,
VITAMIN B12,
ZINC

GOOD SOURCE OF
COPPER,
POTASSIUM,
PANTOTHENIC
ACID,
RIBOFLAVIN

Preheat the oven to 300°F.

Pat the brisket dry and sprinkle with the salt and pepper. Heat 1 tablespoon of the oil over medium-high heat in a Dutch oven or braising pot. Sear the brisket until it is browned, 4 to 5 minutes per side. Transfer the brisket to a plate.

Add the remaining 1 tablespoon oil to the pot and cook the onion, stirring a few times, until softened, 3 to 5 minutes. Add the garlic and cook, stirring, for 1 minute. Add the tomato sauce, broth, brown sugar, ⅓ cup of the vinegar, the raisins, peppercorns, and allspice and stir to combine well. Bring the mixture to a boil, return the brisket and any accumulated juices to the pot, spoon some of the tomato-vinegar mixture over the brisket, cover tightly, and transfer to the oven. Cook until the brisket is fork-tender, 2½ to 3 hours.

Remove the brisket from the oven, transfer the meat to a cutting board, and let rest for 10 to 20 minutes or, if serving later, cover and refrigerate the meat and sauce for several hours or overnight. When you are ready to serve, cut the meat against the grain into ¼-inch-thick slices. Stir the remaining 1 tablespoon vinegar into the warm sauce. Return the sliced brisket to the sauce until heated through, then serve.

Confetti Chili

I call this confetti chili because it is flecked with multicolored vegetables: golden corn, red peppers, orange carrots, and black and red beans. Together they add excitement and texture to the beefy flavor-packed base, while chipotle chile in adobo gives it a spicy, smoky kick.

1 tablespoon olive oil

1 small onion, diced (1 cup)

1 medium red bell pepper, seeded and diced (1 cup)

1 medium carrot, diced ($\frac{1}{2}$ cup)

2 teaspoons ground cumin

1 teaspoon ground coriander

1 pound lean or extra-lean (90% lean or higher) ground beef

One 28-ounce can no-salt-added crushed tomatoes, with their juices

2 cups water

1 canned chipotle chile in adobo sauce, seeded and minced,
  plus 2 teaspoons of the sauce

$\frac{1}{2}$ teaspoon dried oregano

One 15.5-ounce can black beans, preferably low-sodium, drained and rinsed

One 15.5-ounce can kidney beans, preferably low-sodium, drained and rinsed

$1\frac{1}{2}$ cups frozen corn kernels

Salt and freshly ground black pepper to taste

SERVES 8
SERVING SIZE:
1¼ CUPS

PER SERVING
CALORIES: 225;
TOTAL FAT: 5G
  MONO: 2G,
  POLY: 0G;
  SAT: 1G,
PROTEIN: 20G;
CARB: 27G;
FIBER: 9G;
CHOL: 20MG;
SODIUM: 115MG

EXCELLENT
SOURCE OF
FIBER, IRON,
PROTEIN,
VITAMIN A,
VITAMIN B$_{12}$,
VITAMIN C,
ZINC

GOOD
SOURCE OF
MAGNESIUM,
NIACIN,
PHOSPHORUS,
POTASSIUM

Heat the oil in a large pot or Dutch oven over medium heat. Add the onion, bell pepper, and carrot, cover, and cook, stirring occasionally, until softened, about 10 minutes. Add the cumin and coriander and cook, stirring, for 1 minute. Add the ground beef; raise the heat to high and cook, breaking up the meat with a spoon, until the meat is no longer pink. Stir in the tomatoes, water, chipotle and adobo sauce, and oregano and bring to a boil. Reduce the heat to medium-low and cook, partially covered, stirring from time to time, for 30 minutes.

Stir in the beans and continue cooking, partially covered, 20 minutes longer, until the chili is nicely thickened. Stir in the corn and cook until heated through. Season with salt and pepper and serve.

✳ **EATING WELL TIP**
Chipotles are dried, smoked jalapeños, usually found canned in adobo sauce, which is made from dried chiles, herbs, and vinegar. Chipotles in adobo add a punch of intense, smoky, hot flavor to stews and sauces. It is so powerful you only need a little. Chop the leftovers and freeze them in sealable snack bags with about 2 tablespoons in each. Then you can throw it, still frozen, right into a stew or sauce and you don't have to worry about waste.

Greek-Style Stuffed Peppers

Hearty bulgur wheat, flecks of spinach and zucchini, and a crowning sprinkle of feta cheese give these gorgeous, beefy stuffed peppers their Mediterranean flair.

1 pound lean or extra-lean ground beef (90% lean or higher)
One 10-ounce package frozen chopped spinach, thawed and squeezed dry
1 medium zucchini, coarsely grated (about 1½ cups)
1 small onion, minced (about 1 cup)
½ cup bulgur
1 large egg, lightly beaten
½ teaspoon dried oregano
½ teaspoon salt
Freshly ground black pepper to taste
3 medium red bell peppers, cut in half lengthwise, core and ribs removed
Two 14.5-ounce cans no-salt-added stewed tomatoes,
    finely chopped and juices reserved
⅓ cup crumbled feta cheese

SERVES 6
SERVING SIZE:
1 STUFFED HALF
PEPPER

PER SERVING
CALORIES: 200;
TOTAL FAT: 6G
    MONO: 2G,
    POLY: 0.5G;
    SAT: 2.5G,
PROTEIN: 21G;
CARB: 17G;
FIBER: 6G;
CHOL: 83MG;
SODIUM: 445MG

EXCELLENT SOURCE OF
FIBER, IRON,
NIACIN, PROTEIN,
VITAMIN A,
VITAMIN B$_{12}$,
VITAMIN C, ZINC

GOOD SOURCE OF
CALCIUM, FOLATE,
MAGNESIUM,
MANGANESE,
MOLYBDENUM,
PHOSPHORUS,
POTASSIUM,
RIBOFLAVIN,
VITAMIN B$_6$

Preheat the oven to 350°F.

In a large bowl, combine the beef, spinach, zucchini, onion, bulgur, egg, oregano, salt, and a few grinds of pepper. Mix until thoroughly combined.

Arrange the pepper halves cut side up in a 9 x 13-inch baking dish and fill each pepper half with the meat mixture. Pour the tomatoes with their juices over the peppers and sprinkle with the feta. Cover with aluminum foil and bake for 30 minutes.

Uncover and bake the peppers until the filling is completely cooked and the peppers are tender, about 45 minutes longer.

*

DID YOU KNOW?
Bulgur is whole-wheat that has been parboiled so it cooks up fast. It is higher in fiber than most other grains. It has twice the fiber of brown rice!

Lamb Stew with Orange

This aromatic dish delightfully shakes up the common notion of what lamb stew tastes like. Here warm, earthy cumin, refreshing orange and mint, and sweet carrots and parsnips balance the rich taste of lamb perfectly.

2 tablespoons olive oil
1 pound lamb cubes (lean, from the leg and shoulder)
¼ teaspoon salt, plus more to taste
Pinch of freshly ground black pepper, plus more to taste
1 medium onion, diced (about 1½ cups)
2 large cloves garlic, minced (about 2 teaspoons)
2 tablespoons tomato paste
2 stalks celery, diced (about ½ cup)
2 large carrots, cut into ¼-inch-thick rounds
2 large parsnips, roughly chopped (about 2 cups)
One 15.5-ounce can chickpeas, preferably low-sodium, drained and rinsed
¾ cup dry red wine
3 cups low-sodium chicken broth or water
One 15-ounce can no-salt-added tomato sauce
1 teaspoon finely grated orange zest
1 large orange, segmented and any juice reserved
1½ teaspoons ground cumin
2 tablespoons chopped fresh mint

SERVES 4
SERVING SIZE: 2 CUPS

PER SERVING
CALORIES: 485;
TOTAL FAT: 16G
  MONO: 8.4G;
  POLY: 1.5G;
  SAT: 3.5G,
PROTEIN: 36G;
CARB: 47G;
FIBER: 11G;
CHOL: 74MG;
SODIUM: 382MG

EXCELLENT SOURCE OF
FIBER, IRON, MAGNESIUM,
MANGANESE, NIACIN, PHOSPHORUS, POTASSIUM, PROTEIN, RIBOFLAVIN, SELENIUM, THIAMIN, VITAMIN A, VITAMIN B6, VITAMIN B12, VITAMIN C, VITAMIN K, ZINC

GOOD SOURCE OF
CALCIUM, FOLATE, VITAMIN E

Heat the oil in an 8-quart Dutch oven or other large pot over high heat until hot but not smoking. Season the meat with the salt and pepper and sear in the oil until browned on all sides, about 5 minutes total. Add the onion and cook until softened, 3 to 5 minutes, add the garlic and cook for 1 minute, stirring a few times. Add the tomato paste and stir to incorporate. Add the celery, carrots, parsnips, chickpeas, wine, broth, tomato sauce, orange zest, segments, and juice, and cumin. Bring to a boil, then the reduce heat to low, cover, and simmer until the lamb is tender, about 1½ hours. Season with salt and pepper. Remove from heat, let cool slightly, and ladle into bowls. Top with the mint and serve.

* **EATING WELL TIP**
Replacing some of the meat in stews and chili with hearty, protein-rich beans gives you a more healthful, satisfying dish that still has meat in every bite.

Lemon-Garlic Marinated Lamb Chops

A simple Greek-inspired marinade of lemon, garlic, and oregano, with a touch of oil, brings out the absolute best in these tender, tasty lamb chops.

1 tablespoon olive oil
2 tablespoons fresh lemon juice
½ teaspoon finely grated lemon zest
2 tablespoons chopped fresh oregano or 2 teaspoons dried
6 cloves garlic, minced (about 2 tablespoons)
½ teaspoon salt
¼ teaspoon freshly ground black pepper
Eight 4-ounce lamb loin chops, trimmed of all visible fat

SERVES 4
SERVING SIZE: 2 LAMB CHOPS

PER SERVING
CALORIES: 285;
TOTAL FAT: 15G
  MONO: 7G,
  POLY: 1G;
  SAT: 5G,
PROTEIN: 31G;
CARB: 3G;
FIBER: 0G;
CHOL: 95MG;
SODIUM: 240MG

EXCELLENT SOURCE OF
NIACIN, PHOSPHORUS, PROTEIN, RIBOFLAVIN, VITAMIN B_6, VITAMIN B_{12}, ZINC

GOOD SOURCE OF
COPPER, MAGNESIUM, PANTOTHENIC ACID, POTASSIUM, SELENIUM, THIAMIN

Preheat the broiler, grill, or grill pan over medium heat.

In a small bowl, stir together the oil, lemon juice and zest, oregano, garlic, salt, and pepper. Put the lamb chops in a sealable plastic bag and pour the marinade over them. Move the chops around in the bag so the marinade coats them well. Seal the bag and marinate for 20 minutes to 1 hour at room temperature.

Remove the chops from the marinade and discard the marinade. Grill or broil the chops for 4 to 5 minutes per side for medium rare or to your desired degree of doneness.

Lemon-Garlic Marinated Lamb Chops
with Grilled Romaine Hearts (page 258)

Spice-Rubbed Lamb Pops

I was served this modern take on shish kebab at a hot New York restaurant, and I couldn't stop thinking about how fun and delicious they were. In my version, each skewer is adorned with one rectangular slice of spice-dusted lamb steak, making for a seriously luscious lollipop.

1 teaspoon ground cumin
1 teaspoon ground coriander
½ teaspoon ground cinnamon
½ teaspoon freshly ground black pepper
½ teaspoon salt
1¼ pounds boneless lamb (top round), trimmed of all visible fat
    and cut into ½ x 2½-inch strips
12 skewers, soaked in water for 20 minutes if wooden

SERVES 4
SERVING SIZE:
3 SKEWERS

PER SERVING
CALORIES: 195;
TOTAL FAT: 8G
    MONO: 3G,
    POLY: 0.7G;
    SAT: 2.7G,
PROTEIN: 29G;
CARB: 0.5G;
FIBER: 0G;
CHOL: 385MG;
SODIUM: 92MG

EXCELLENT SOURCE OF
NIACIN, PHOS-PHORUS, PROTEIN, RIBOFLAVIN, SELENIUM, VITAMIN B$_{12}$, ZINC

GOOD SOURCE OF
IRON, MAGNESIUM, PANTOTHENIC ACID, POTASSIUM, THIAMIN, VITAMIN B$_6$

Preheat the grill or a grill pan.

In a small bowl, combine the cumin, coriander, cinnamon, pepper, and salt. In a large bowl, sprinkle the spice mixture over the lamb strips and toss to coat evenly.

Thread 1 piece of lamb onto each skewer and grill over medium-high heat for 4 to 5 minutes, turning once.

✳ **EATING WELL TIP**
A dry spice rub is a perfect solution when you want to eat lean, fast, and flavorful food.
It adds a punch of flavor without any of the oil or soaking time of a marinade. Just rub and grill.

Pork Medallions with Cherry Sauce

One of my favorite cooking techniques is highlighted here: browning meat in a skillet, then removing it from the pan and using wine, broth, vinegar, or juice to dissolve the caramelized, flavorful bits stuck to the pan to make a fabulous sauce. The flavor combinations are limitless. Here the meat is tender pork medallions and the sauce is balsamic vinegar and chicken broth studded with plump tart cherries. The key is to not use a nonstick pan. You want the meat to leave some golden brown bits behind for the sauce.

One 1¼-pound pork tenderloin, trimmed of all visible fat
    and silverskin, then cut into ½-inch-thick medallions
½ teaspoon salt, plus more to taste
¼ teaspoon freshly ground black pepper, plus more to taste
3 teaspoons olive oil
2 tablespoons chopped shallot
¾ cup low-sodium chicken broth
2 tablespoons balsamic vinegar
¼ cup dried tart cherries

SERVES 4
SERVING SIZE:
4 MEDALLIONS
AND 2
TABLESPOONS
SAUCE

PER SERVING
CALORIES: 245;
TOTAL FAT: 9G
    MONO: 5G;
    POLY: 1G;
    SAT: 2G;
PROTEIN: 31G;
CARB: 8.5G;
FIBER: 0G;
CHOL: 92MG;
SODIUM: 380MG

EXCELLENT
SOURCE OF
NIACIN,
PHOSPHORUS,
PROTEIN,
RIBOFLAVIN,
SELENIUM,
THIAMIN,
VITAMIN B6,
VITAMIN B12,
ZINC

GOOD
SOURCE OF
IRON,
MAGNESIUM,
POTASSIUM

Season the pork medallions with ¼ teaspoon of the salt and the pepper. Heat 2 teaspoons of the oil in a large skillet over a medium-high heat and cook the meat until there is just a slight blush in the center about 3 minutes per side. Transfer the meat to a plate and tent with aluminum foil.

Add the remaining 1 teaspoon oil and the shallot to the pan and cook, stirring, until it begins to soften, about 1 minute. Add the broth, vinegar, the remaining ¼ teaspoon salt, and the cherries and cook until the liquid is reduced by half, about 4 minutes. Taste and correct the seasonings with salt and pepper, if necessary. Pour the sauce over the pork medallions and serve.

Sage-Rubbed Pork Chops with Warm Apple Slaw

Here juicy pork chops are served with their match-made-in-heaven accompaniments, apple, sage, and cabbage. But I spin them in a fresh new way, by amping up the color with carrot and turning them into a warm sage-scented apple slaw to nestle the chops into. To make this recipe quicker and even easier, you can use one 16-ounce bag of preshredded carrots and cabbage, called "slaw mix," instead of starting with a whole cabbage and carrots.

For the chops

1 tablespoon chopped fresh sage or 1 teaspoon dried
1 large clove garlic, minced (about 1 teaspoon)
½ teaspoon salt
Freshly ground black pepper
Four ¾-inch-thick bone-in pork loin chops (about 8 ounces each)
2 teaspoons olive oil

For the slaw

2 teaspoons olive oil
1 large onion, cut in half, then thinly sliced into half-moons
1 large Granny Smith apple, cut in half, cored, and coarsely shredded
1 teaspoon chopped fresh sage or ½ teaspoon dried
½ head green cabbage, cored and coarsely shredded (about 9 cups)
3 large carrots, coarsely shredded (about 3 cups)
2 tablespoons cider vinegar
½ teaspoon salt
¾ cup low-sodium chicken broth

SERVES 4
SERVING SIZE:
1 PORK CHOP AND
1¼ CUPS SLAW

PER SERVING
CALORIES: 330;
TOTAL FAT: 13G
    MONO: 7G,
    POLY: 1.6G;
    SAT: 3.5G,
PROTEIN: 32G;
CARB: 22G;
FIBER: 6G;
CHOL: 70MG;
SODIUM: 720MG

EXCELLENT
SOURCE OF
FIBER,
PHOSPHORUS,
POTASSIUM,
NIACIN,
PROTEIN,
RIBOFLAVIN,
SELENIUM,
THIAMIN,
VITAMIN A,
VITAMIN B$_6$,
VITAMIN C, ZINC

GOOD
SOURCE OF
CALCIUM, IRON,
MAGNESIUM,
MANGANESE,
MOLYBDENUM,
VITAMIN B$_{12}$

To make the chops, combine the sage, garlic, salt, and a few grinds of pepper in a small bowl. Rub this mixture all over the pork chops and let them sit at room temperature for 10 minutes.

Heat the oil in a large nonstick skillet over medium-high heat until good and hot. Add the chops and brown well on both sides, 1 to 2 minutes per side. Transfer the chops to a plate.

To make the slaw, carefully wipe out the pan. Heat the oil over medium heat and add the onion, apple, and sage. Cook, stirring a few times, until softened and golden brown, 4 to 5 minutes. Add the cabbage, carrots, vinegar, and salt and continue cooking until the cabbage and carrots begin to soften, about 5 minutes. Add the broth and return the pork chops to the pan, burying them in the vegetable mixture. Cover and cook just until the pork chops have just a slight blush in the center, 5 to 7 minutes longer.

To serve, arrange the warm slaw on individual plates and top with a pork chop and some pan juices.

Peppercorn Pork with Wine Sauce

I knew I had a winner with this dish when my father-in-law (whose picture could be in the dictionary next to the definition of "meat-and-potatoes man") declared this one of his favorites. Serve it with Parmesan Mashed Potatoes (page 262) for a home-run hungry-man pleaser.

One 1¼-pound pork tenderloin, trimmed of all visible fat and silverskin
1 teaspoon Dijon mustard
1 tablespoon black peppercorns, coarsely ground or crushed
2 teaspoons olive oil
½ cup low-sodium chicken broth
½ cup dry red or dry white wine
Salt to taste

SERVES 4
SERVING SIZE:
1 PIECE OF
PORK AND
2 TABLESPOONS
SAUCE

PER SERVING
CALORIES: 235;
TOTAL FAT: 10G
  MONO: 5.5G,
  POLY: 1G;
  SAT: 3G,
PROTEIN: 30G;
CARB: 2G;
FIBER: 0G;
CHOL: 94MG;
SODIUM: 111MG

EXCELLENT SOURCE OF
NIACIN,
PHOSPHORUS,
PROTEIN,
RIBOFLAVIN,
SELENIUM,
THIAMIN,
VITAMIN B6,
VITAMIN B12,
ZINC

GOOD SOURCE OF
IRON,
MAGNESIUM,
MANGANESE,
PANTOTHENIC
ACID

Slice the tenderloin open lengthwise, being careful not to cut through to the other side. You want to split the meat into one large, flat piece. Spread the mustard over both sides of the meat and rub in the pepper, pressing gently so it adheres well. Cut the meat across into 4 even portions.

In a large skillet, heat the oil over medium heat until hot. Put the tenderloin in the hot pan and cook, turning once, until an instant-read thermometer inserted in the thickest part registers 155°F, about 10 minutes total. Transfer the meat to a plate and tent with aluminum foil to keep it warm.

Add the broth and wine to the pan and cook over medium-high heat, scraping up any browned bits that have stuck to the bottom. Continue to cook until the sauce has reduced to about ½ cup, 8 to 10 minutes. Pour the sauce over the meat, season with salt, and serve.

✳ **EATING WELL TIP**
The key to succulent lean pork is not overcooking it—that will make it tough and dry. Perfectly cooked pork loin and tenderloin shouldn't be cooked beyond medium, when it still has a slight blush in the center.

Teriyaki Pork Tenderloin

Sure you could prepare this dish with store-bought teriyaki sauce, but it just doesn't compare to home-made, which is easy to make. You will thank yourself with each bite of this succulent inside, crusty and flavorful outside, pork tenderloin. While you're at it, double the recipe for the sauce and use the rest for Sesame-Teriyaki Chicken Thighs (page 209).

½ cup Teriyaki Sauce (recipe follows)
One 1¼-pound pork tenderloin, trimmed of all visible fat and silverskin

Put the teriyaki sauce and pork in a sealable plastic bag. Seal the bag and marinate the pork in the refrigerator, turning once, for at least 30 minutes or up to 4 hours.
   Preheat the broiler. Remove the pork from the marinade and discard the marinade. Place the pork on a roasting pan and broil until an instant-read meat thermometer inserted into the thickest part registers 155°F, about 15 minutes, turning once. Let rest for 10 minutes before slicing.

SERVES 4
SERVING SIZE: ABOUT 4 SLICES

PER SERVING
CALORIES: 212;
TOTAL FAT: 8G
   MONO: 3.5G,
   POLY: 1G;
   SAT: 2.5G,
PROTEIN: 30G;
CARB: 4G;
FIBER: 0G;
CHOL: 94MG;
SODIUM: 337MG

EXCELLENT SOURCE OF
NIACIN, PHOSPHORUS, PROTEIN, RIBOFLAVIN, SELENIUM, THIAMIN, VITAMIN B$_6$, VITAMIN B$_{12}$, ZINC

GOOD SOURCE OF
IRON, MAGNESIUM, POTASSIUM

Teriyaki Sauce

This sauce will keep for about a week in the refrigerator.

¼ cup low-sodium soy sauce
2 tablespoons firmly packed dark brown sugar
2 tablespoons dry sherry
2 tablespoons rice vinegar
2 garlic cloves, crushed with a garlic press or minced (about 2 teaspoons)
1 teaspoon peeled and finely grated fresh ginger
¼ teaspoon red pepper flakes

Combine all the ingredients in a small bowl, stirring until the sugar dissolves.

SERVES 4
MAKES ABOUT ½ CUP;
SERVING SIZE: 2 TABLESPOONS

PER SERVING
CALORIES: 40;
TOTAL FAT: 0G

PROTEIN: 1G;
CARB: 8G;
FIBER: 0G;
CHOL: 0MG;
SODIUM: 535MG

Roasted Pork Loin with Parsley-Shallot Sauce

This dish is so simple to make, yet it looks and tastes incredibly impressive. The slices of rich, juicy pork are fragrant with herbs, and the accompanying emerald-green sauce adds a perfect zesty freshness.

2 cloves garlic, minced
½ teaspoon salt
2 teaspoons olive oil
1 tablespoon finely chopped fresh sage or 1 teaspoon dried, crumbled
1 tablespoon finely chopped fresh rosemary or 1 teaspoon dried, crumbled
1 tablespoon finely chopped fresh thyme or 1 teaspoon dried
½ teaspoon freshly ground black pepper
One 2½-pound center-cut boneless pork loin, trimmed of all visible fat
Parsley-Shallot Sauce (recipe follows)

Preheat the oven to 350°F.

Mash the garlic and salt together with the flat side of a knife blade on a cutting board until it forms a coarse paste. Transfer to a small bowl and stir in the oil, herbs, and pepper. Rub the paste all over the pork. Transfer the pork to a roasting pan and roast until an instant-read meat thermometer inserted into the thickest part registers 155°F, about 1¼ hours. Transfer the roast to a carving board and let rest for 15 minutes. Carve the pork into slices and serve with the sauce on the side.

SERVES 8
SERVING SIZE:
TWO ½-INCH
SLICES OF
MEAT AND
1 TABLESPOON
SAUCE

PER SERVING
CALORIES: 265;
TOTAL FAT: 16G;
  MONO: 9G,
  POLY: 1.5G;
  SAT: 5G;
PROTEIN: 28G;
CARB: 3G;
FIBER: 1G;

CHOL: 70MG;
SODIUM: 875MG

EXCELLENT SOURCE OF
PROTEIN,
VITAMIN A,
VITAMIN C,
VITAMIN K

GOOD SOURCE OF
IRON,
MAGNESIUM,
POTASSIUM,
ZINC

Parsley-Shallot Sauce

This brightly flavored sauce will enliven any grilled or roasted meat.

1½ cups lightly packed fresh flat-leaf parsley
2 tablespoons coarsely chopped shallot
3 tablespoons Dijon mustard
2 tablespoons extra-virgin olive oil
2 tablespoons water
2 teaspoons fresh lemon juice
¼ teaspoon salt
Freshly ground black pepper to taste

Combine all the ingredients in a blender and purée.

SERVES 8
MAKES ½ CUP;
SERVING SIZE:
1 TABLESPOON

PER SERVING
CALORIES: 45;
TOTAL FAT: 4G;
  MONO: 3G,
  POLY: 0.5G;
  SAT: 0.5G;
PROTEIN: 1G;

CARB: 2G;
FIBER: 0.5G;
CHOL: 0MG;
SODIUM: 221MG

EXCELLENT SOURCE OF
VITAMIN A,
VITAMIN C,
VITAMIN K

Pork Loin with Parsley-Shallot Sauce with
Roasted Nutmeg Cauliflower (page 250)

Crispy Chicken Fingers

Why feed your kids those fried mystery-meat chicken nuggets when it is so simple to make these? They are baked crisp on the outside and tender on the inside and have a lovely mild flavor.

1¼ pounds boneless, skinless chicken breast halves,
    cut across into ½-inch-thick slices
½ cup lowfat buttermilk
Cooking spray
4 cups whole-grain corn cereal such as Corn Chex® or corn flakes
¼ teaspoon salt
Pinch of freshly ground black pepper
Honey-Mustard Sauce (recipe follows)

Preheat the oven to 400°F.

Combine the chicken and buttermilk in a shallow dish, turning the chicken to coat it with the buttermilk. Cover and chill for 15 minutes. Coat two baking sheets with cooking spray.

Put the cereal in a sealable plastic bag and crush with a rolling pin. Transfer the crumbs to a shallow dish and season them with the salt and pepper. Dip each piece of chicken in the cereal to fully coat and arrange on the prepared baking sheets. Bake until cooked through, about 8 minutes. Leave the chicken on the baking sheets to cool slightly. It will become crispier.

Serve with the mustard sauce on the side.

SERVES 4
SERVING SIZE: 10 CHICKEN FINGERS

PER SERVING
CALORIES: 262;
TOTAL FAT: 2G
    MONO: 0.5G;
    POLY: 0.5G;
    SAT: 1G,
PROTEIN: 35G;
CARB: 23G;
FIBER: 0.5G
CHOL: 83MG;
SODIUM: 502MG

EXCELLENT SOURCE OF
FOLATE, IRON, NIACIN, PHOSPHORUS, PROTEIN, RIBOFLAVIN, SELENIUM, THIAMIN, VITAMIN B6, VITAMIN B12, ZINC

GOOD SOURCE OF
CALCIUM, COPPER, MAGNESIUM, MANGANESE, PANTOTHENIC ACID, POTASSIUM, VITAMIN A, VITAMIN C

Honey-Mustard Sauce

This sauce also makes an incredible sandwich spread. It will keep about a week in the refrigerator.

⅓ cup Dijon mustard
2 teaspoons mayonnaise
2 tablespoons honey

In a small bowl, stir together the mustard and mayonnaise until smooth. Stir in the honey.

SERVES 5
MAKES ABOUT ⅔ CUP;
SERVING SIZE: 2 TABLESPOONS

PER SERVING
CALORIES: 97;
TOTAL FAT: 3G

MONO: 0.5G,
POLY: 0.5G;
SAT: 0G,
PROTEIN: 1G;
CARB: 19G;
FIBER: 0G;
CHOL: 0.5MG;
SODIUM: 413MG

Safe at the Plate

The starting point for preparing healthful food is making sure it's safe to eat. Raw meats can contain harmful bacteria that are killed with cooking. That's why it is critical to avoid contact between raw meats and foods that are ready to eat, and to cook meats to the proper degree of doneness. Here are three simple safety steps to take in your kitchen:

1. SEPARATE RAW FROM READY-TO-EAT
- Store raw meats, poultry, and seafood in a dish on the bottom shelf of the refrigerator so the juices won't drip onto other foods.
- Designate separate cutting boards, one for cutting raw meat, poultry, and seafood, and another for vegetables, bread, and the like.

2. WASH, WASH, WASH
- Wash your hands after handling raw meat
- Wash surfaces, cutting boards, and utensils with hot soapy water
- Wash and replace sponges frequently (hint: smelly=dirty)

3. GET A MEAT THERMOMETER
The surest way to cook meats until they are done but not overcooked is to use an instant-read meat thermometer. Just put the thermometer in the thickest part of the meat, not touching any bone. I have listed appropriate cooking temperatures in recipes wherever practical. Keep in mind that the temperature of a roast will rise by about 5 degrees as it rests after cooking. If you take it out of the oven or pan at the temperature I suggest, it will be done perfectly after resting.

Chicken Pot Pie with Phyllo Crust

My life is full of wonderful chicken pot-pie moments. I even have fond memories of the frozen TV-dinner pies my mom would heat for me after she worked all day. Embarrassingly, my sister and I composed a silly chicken-pot-pie song long ago—a kind of ode to our favorite dinner—that we will still croon today if you get us going.

This version of the dish satisfies my most intense pot-pie yearnings in a way that's a step up from the familiar food of my childhood. I make it a bit more sophisticated, skipping the lunch-room vegetable mix in favor of keeping it all green and white inside with aromatic leeks, crisp green beans, fresh herbs, and chunks of chicken and potato smothered in a creamy sauce, topped with a flaky blanket of phyllo.

Cooking spray

1¼ pounds boneless, skinless chicken breast halves, cut into ½-inch chunks

1 teaspoon salt

½ teaspoon freshly ground black pepper

2 tablespoons olive oil

2 leeks, bottom 4 inches only, trimmed, washed well, and chopped

2 stalks celery, chopped (about ½ cup)

2 medium white potatoes, left unpeeled and cut into ½-inch pieces

½ pound fresh green beans, trimmed and chopped into ½-inch pieces

2 cloves garlic, minced (about 2 teaspoons)

1½ cups nonfat milk

⅓ cup all-purpose flour

2 cups low-sodium chicken broth

1 cup peas, thawed if frozen

2 tablespoons chopped fresh flat-leaf parsley

1 tablespoon chopped fresh thyme

3 sheets frozen phyllo dough, thawed

2 tablespoons freshly grated Parmesan cheese

SERVES 4
SERVING SIZE: 1 POT PIE

PER SERVING
CALORIES: 585;
TOTAL FAT: 13G
 MONO: 7G,
 POLY: 1.5G;
 SAT: 3G,
PROTEIN: 50G;
CARB: 70G;
FIBER: 8G;
CHOL: 88MG;
SODIUM: 960MG

EXCELLENT SOURCE OF
CALCIUM, COPPER, FIBER, FOLATE, IRON, MAGNESIUM, MANGANESE, NIACIN, PANTO-THENIC ACID, PHOSPHORUS, POTASSIUM, PROTEIN, RIBOFLAVIN, SELENIUM, THIAMIN, VITAMIN A, VITAMIN B6, VITAMIN C, VITAMIN K

GOOD SOURCE OF
VITAMIN B12, VITAMIN D, ZINC

Preheat the oven to 350°F. Coat 4 individual-size baking dishes with cooking spray.

Season the chicken with ¼ teaspoon of the salt and ¼ teaspoon of the pepper. In a large nonstick skillet, heat 2 teaspoons of the oil over medium-high heat. Add the chicken and brown, about 2½ minutes per side. Transfer the chicken to a plate.

Add 2 more teaspoons of oil, the leeks, and celery to the pan and cook, stirring a few times, until the vegetables begin to soften, about 3 minutes. Add the potatoes, green beans, garlic, and the remaining ¾ teaspoon salt and ¼ teaspoon pepper and cook for 2 minutes more, stirring to combine everything. Add the milk. Stir the flour into the broth until dissolved and add to the pan. Cook, stirring, until the mixture comes to a boil. Reduce the heat to medium-low, cover, and simmer, stirring occasionally, for 10 minutes.

Stir in the chicken, peas, parsley, and thyme. Spoon the mixture into the baking dishes.

Put the remaining 1⅔ tablespoons oil in a small bowl. Unroll the phyllo dough and cut it into quarters. Place a quarter-sheet on top of each baking dish and brush with the oil. Repeat layering with all three layers. Tuck the edges of the phyllo into the dish rim. Sprinkle the top of each pie with the Parmesan.

Place on a baking sheet and bake until the filling is bubbling, about 30 minutes. Serve hot.

* **EATING WELL TIP**
Phyllo dough is paper-thin sheets of dough that are brushed with oil and layered to form a flaky crust in both sweet and savory dishes. You can use phyllo dough nearly anywhere you would use pastry dough for a lighter, more healthful dish. It can be found in the freezer section at the supermarket, and it usually needs to be thawed overnight before using. When you lay it out to work with it, keep it covered with a moistened towel so it doesn't dry out.

Chicken Cacciatore

Cacciatore, which means "hunter" in Italian, refers to food prepared with mushrooms, onions, tomatoes, and herbs. It is one of those recipes that checks all the boxes: it's easy to make, everyone loves it, and you can prepare it in advance and refrigerate or freeze it so it is ready when you are.

4 skinless bone-in chicken breast halves (about 2½ pounds)
¼ teaspoon salt, plus more to taste
¼ teaspoon freshly ground black pepper, plus more to taste
2 teaspoons olive oil
1 medium onion, cut in half, then thinly sliced into half-moons
1 medium red bell pepper, seeded and cut into thin strips
8 ounces white mushrooms, thinly sliced (about 3 cups)
2 cloves garlic, minced (about 2 teaspoons)
½ cup dry white wine
One 14.5-ounce can no-salt-added diced tomatoes, with their juices
½ teaspoon dried oregano
⅛ teaspoon red pepper flakes, or more to taste

SERVES 4
SERVING SIZE:
1 PIECE CHICKEN
AND ¾ CUP
VEGETABLES
AND SAUCE

PER SERVING
CALORIES: 343;
TOTAL FAT: 5.5G
  MONO: 2.5G,
  POLY: 1G,
  SAT: 1G,
PROTEIN: 56G;
CARB: 11G;
FIBER: 3G;
CHOL: 132MG;
SODIUM:
430MG

EXCELLENT SOURCE OF
MAGNESIUM,
NIACIN,
PANTOTHENIC
ACID,
PHOSPHORUS,
POTASSIUM,
PROTEIN
RIBOFLAVIN,
SELENIUM,
THIAMIN,
VITAMIN A,
VITAMIN B6,
VITAMIN C

GOOD SOURCE OF
COPPER, FIBER,
FOLATE, IRON,
MANGANESE,
VITAMIN B12,
VITAMIN D, ZINC

Rinse the chicken and pat dry with paper towels, then sprinkle with the salt and black pepper. Heat the oil in a large skillet over medium-high heat and brown the chicken on both sides, about 8 minutes total. Transfer the chicken to a plate and set aside.

Reduce the heat under the skillet to medium. Add the onion and bell pepper, cover, and cook, stirring a few times, until the vegetables begin to soften, about 5 minutes. Add the mushrooms and cook, uncovered and stirring occasionally, until the mushrooms begin to brown, about 10 minutes. Add the garlic and cook, stirring, for 30 seconds. Add the wine and cook until reduced by half. Add the tomatoes and their juices, the oregano, and red pepper and simmer, covered, for 10 minutes.

Return the chicken breasts to the pan and simmer, covered, until they are just cooked through, about 20 minutes longer. Taste and adjust the seasonings with salt, black pepper, or red pepper.

Balsamic Chicken with Baby Spinach and Couscous

As a busy mom who is really cranky when she's hungry, I need delicious rush-hour meals I can get on the table fast. This is one of my absolute favorites. The chicken breast is smothered in a balsamic-laced tomato sauce served over garlicky spinach nestled on a bed of warm fluffy couscous. All that and it takes only 15 minutes to make.

3 tablespoons olive oil

4 boneless, skinless chicken breast halves (about 1¼ pounds total),
　pounded between 2 sheets of waxed paper to ½-inch thickness

¼ teaspoon salt, plus more to taste

¼ teaspoon freshly ground black pepper, plus more to taste

3 cloves garlic, chopped (about 1 tablespoon)

8 ounces baby spinach leaves (about 8 cups lightly packed)

2 tablespoons balsamic vinegar

½ cup low-sodium chicken broth

1 cup canned no-salt-added chopped tomatoes, with their juices

2 cups hot cooked whole-wheat couscous (from about ¾ cup uncooked)

SERVES 4

SERVING SIZE: 1 CHICKEN BREAST, 3 TABLESPOONS SAUCE, ⅓ CUP SPINACH, AND ½ CUP COUSCOUS

PER SERVING
CALORIES: 342;
TOTAL FAT: 12G
　MONO: 8G,
　POLY: 1G,
　SAT: 2G,
PROTEIN: 32G;
CARB: 27G;
FIBER: 6G;
CHOL: 66MG;
SODIUM: 336MG

EXCELLENT SOURCE OF
FIBER, IRON, NIACIN, PANTOTHENIC ACID, PHOSPHORUS, PROTEIN, SELENIUM, VITAMIN A, VITAMIN B6, VITAMIN C

GOOD SOURCE OF
POTASSIUM

Heat 1 tablespoon of the oil in a large skillet over medium-high heat. Season the chicken on both sides with the salt and pepper. Add the chicken to the pan and cook until browned and just cooked through, about 4 minutes per side. Remove the chicken to a plate.

　Add the remaining 2 tablespoons oil to the pan, add the garlic, and cook for 1 minute. Add the spinach and cook just until wilted, 1 to 2 minutes. Season with salt and pepper, then transfer the spinach to a bowl and set it aside.

　Add the vinegar, broth, and tomatoes to the pan and stir, scraping any browned bits off the bottom. Bring to a simmer and cook until the sauce is slightly thickened, 3 to 5 minutes.

　Divide the couscous between 4 serving plates. Top with some of the spinach, then a piece of chicken and the balsamic-tomato sauce and serve.

Chicken Chop Suey

My grandma could always get us to her house for dinner by promising to make this dish. My version incorporates more fresh vegetables than she used and gets its crunchy topping from baked wonton skins instead of canned fried noodles. The result is a sumptuous stir-fry of chicken, meaty mushrooms, and tender cabbage melded together in a thickened, mildly flavored sauce that would make Grandma proud. This recipe is a great way to use leftover rotisserie chicken or turkey.

1 tablespoon sesame seeds

1½ teaspoons cornstarch

1 tablespoon dry sherry

Eight 3-inch square wonton skins, separated

1 tablespoon plus 2 teaspoons canola oil

¼ teaspoon salt

2 scallions (white and green parts), thinly sliced

3 cloves garlic, sliced

4 cups cored and thinly sliced napa cabbage

¾ cup thinly sliced celery

One 8-ounce can bamboo shoots, drained and cut into thin strips

2 cups (about 6 ounces) fresh shiitake mushrooms, wiped clean, stems discarded, and caps thinly sliced

¾ teaspoon sugar

1 cup low-sodium chicken broth

1½ tablespoons low-sodium soy sauce

2 tablespoons toasted sesame oil

2 cups cubed or shredded cooked chicken or turkey

2 cups hot cooked brown rice

SERVES 4
SERVING SIZE: ½ CUP BROWN RICE, 1 CUP CHOP SUEY, AND 2 WONTON SKINS

PER SERVING
CALORIES: 470;
TOTAL FAT: 18G
    MONO: 8G,
    POLY: 6G;
    SAT: 2.5G,
PROTEIN: 30G;
CARB: 47G;
FIBER: 6G;
CHOL: 61MG;
SODIUM: 568MG

EXCELLENT SOURCE OF
COPPER, FIBER, MAGNESIUM, MANGANESE, NIACIN, PANTOTHENIC ACID, PHOSPHORUS, PROTEIN, SELENIUM, THIAMIN, VITAMIN A, VITAMIN B6, VITAMIN C, VITAMIN K

GOOD SOURCE OF
FOLATE, IRON, POTASSIUM, RIBOFLAVIN, ZINC

Preheat the oven to 375°F.

Toast the sesame seeds in a small dry skillet over medium-high heat, stirring frequently, until lightly colored, about 2 minutes; set aside. In a small cup, dissolve the cornstarch in the sherry; set aside.

Brush a baking sheet and the wonton skins lightly on both sides with 2 teaspoons of the canola oil. Season with the salt and bake until browned and crisp, 10 to 12 minutes. Transfer to a rack and set aside.

In a large heavy skillet or wok, heat the remaining 1 tablespoon canola oil over medium-high heat. Add the scallions, garlic, cabbage, celery, bamboo shoots, and mushrooms and stir-fry until the cabbage is soft and wilted, 3 to 4 minutes. Add the sugar, ¾ cup of the broth, the soy sauce, and sesame oil and cook for 3 minutes. Add the sherry-cornstarch mixture and, if the mixture is a little dry, the remaining ¼ cup broth. Add the chicken and heat through.

Serve over the cooked brown rice and sprinkle with the sesame seeds and crush the wonton skins on top.

Chicken with Mango Barbecue Sauce

This sauce gets its sweetness from nutrient-rich mango and molasses; it's absolutely free of refined sugars. This recipe may make more than you need for a single sitting, but the leftovers are wonderful sliced up in a sandwich or set over salad greens. If you want, you can make this using only four breast halves. Just use half the barbecue sauce; the extra is wonderful with pork or used as a sandwich slather.

2 tablespoons olive oil
1 small onion, diced (about 1 cup)
1 medium red bell pepper, seeded and diced (about 1 cup)
3 cloves garlic, coarsely chopped (about 1 tablespoon)
1 teaspoon salt
Freshly ground black pepper
½ teaspoon ground allspice
⅓ cup red wine vinegar
3 tablespoons unsulfured molasses
2 tablespoons Worcestershire sauce
2 tablespoon fresh lime juice
¼ cup no-salt-added tomato sauce
1 medium ripe mango, peeled, pitted, and diced (about 1½ cups)
2 to 3 jalapeño peppers, seeded and minced
8 boneless, skinless chicken breast halves (about 2½ pounds),
    pounded between 2 sheets of waxed paper to ½-inch thickness
Cooking spray

SERVES 8
SERVING SIZE: 1 PIECE OF CHICKEN AND 2 TABLESPOONS SAUCE

PER SERVING
CALORIES: 220;
TOTAL FAT: 3G
    MONO: 1.5G,
    POLY: 0.5G;
    SAT: 0.7G;
PROTEIN: 40G;
CARB: 5G;
FIBER: 0.5G;
CHOL: 100MG;
SODIUM: 237MG

EXCELLENT SOURCE OF
NIACIN, PHOSPHORUS, PROTEIN, SELENIUM, VITAMIN B6, VITAMIN C

GOOD SOURCE OF
MAGNESIUM, PANTOTHENIC ACID, POTASSIUM, RIBOFLAVIN, THIAMIN, VITAMIN B12, ZINC

Heat the oil in a medium skillet over medium-high heat. Add the onion and cook, stirring a few times, until translucent, about 3 minutes. Add the bell pepper, garlic, salt, black pepper, and allspice and cook, stirring, for 2 minutes more. Stir in the vinegar, molasses, Worcestershire, lime juice, and tomato sauce and cook for 1 minute more. Transfer the mixture to a blender and add the mango and jalapeños. Blend until smooth.

Put 2 cups of the barbecue sauce in a large sealable plastic bag with the chicken and marinate for 1 hour in the refrigerator. Reserve the rest of the sauce for serving.

Prepare the grill or spray a grill pan with cooking spray and heat over medium-high heat. Remove the chicken from the sauce, discarding the sauce in the bag. Grill the chicken just until cooked all the way through, about 4 minutes per side. Serve the chicken with reserved sauce on the side.

* **DID YOU KNOW?**
Molasses, particularly blackstrap molasses, has a fair amount of essential minerals like copper, manganese, iron, and calcium.

Sesame-Teriyaki Chicken Thighs

When these chicken thighs come out of the oven, fragrant, crackling hot, sticky with caramelized teriyaki sauce, and oozing with juice that can hardly contain itself inside the meat, you will hardly be able to contain yourself. Luckily you just have to hold out until they cool off a bit.

½ cup Teriyaki Sauce (page 197)
8 bone-in chicken thighs (about 2½ pounds), skin removed
1 tablespoon sesame seeds

SERVES 4
SERVING SIZE:
2 PIECES

PER SERVING
CALORIES: 389;
TOTAL FAT: 12G
 MONO: 3.5G,
 POLY: 3G;
 SAT: 3G,
PROTEIN: 57G;
CARB: 8G;
FIBER: 0.5G;
CHOL: 235MG;
SODIUM: 783MG

EXCELLENT SOURCE OF
IRON, NIACIN, PANTOTHENIC ACID, PHOSPHORUS, PROTEIN, RIBOFLAVIN, SELENIUM, VITAMIN B6, ZINC

GOOD SOURCE OF
COPPER, MAGNESIUM, POTASSIUM, THIAMIN, VITAMIN B$_{12}$, VITAMIN K

Pour the sauce into a sealable plastic bag and add the chicken. Seal the bag and marinate the chicken in the refrigerator for at least 30 minutes and up to 4 hours.

Preheat the broiler. Remove the chicken from the marinade and arrange it on a broiler pan skin side down (if the chicken still had skin). Discard the marinade. Broil the chicken until brown and crispy, 8 to 10 minutes, then turn the pieces over and broil until almost cooked through, about 8 minutes longer.

Sprinkle the chicken with the sesame seeds and cook until the seeds turn golden brown and the chicken is done, 1 to 2 minutes longer.

Tuscan Roasted Chicken and Vegetables

This one-pan meal has all the quintessential flavors of the Italian countryside: chicken breast, tomato, fennel, and zucchini all roasted to perfection and accented with garlic, lemon, and rosemary. Its rustic flair means there is not much chopping involved, leaving plenty of time to zip around on a Vespa®. Well, at least one can dream.

6 Roma tomatoes (about 1 pound total)

3 medium zucchini (about ½ pound each)

1 bulb fennel

3 tablespoons olive oil

¾ teaspoon salt

4 bone-in chicken breast halves (about 2½ pounds), skin removed

4 cloves garlic, finely minced (about 4 teaspoons)

1 teaspoon finely grated lemon zest

1 tablespoon fresh lemon juice

Freshly ground black pepper

1 tablespoon chopped fresh rosemary or 1 teaspoon dried, crumbled

SERVES 4

SERVING SIZE: 1 PIECE OF CHICKEN AND 1½ CUPS VEGETABLES

PER SERVING
CALORIES 410;
TOTAL FAT: 13.5G
   MONO: 8.2G,
   POLY: 2G;
   SAT: 2G,
PROTEIN: 56G;
CARB: 15G;
FIBER: 5G;
CHOL: 132MG;
SODIUM: 637MG

EXCELLENT SOURCE OF FIBER, FOLATE, MAGNESIUM, MOLYBDENUM, NIACIN, PANTO-THENIC ACID, PHOSPHORUS, POTASSIUM, PROTEIN, RIBO-FLAVIN, SELE-NIUM, THIAMIN, VITAMIN A, VITAMIN B6, VITAMIN C, VITAMIN K

GOOD SOURCE OF CALCIUM, IRON, VITAMIN B12, VITAMIN E, ZINC

Preheat the oven to 375°F.

Cut the tomatoes lengthwise into quarters and remove the seeds. Trim the zucchini and cut it in half crosswise. Then cut each piece in half lengthwise twice if the piece is thin and three times if it is thicker, so that the pieces are relatively uniform.

Remove the outermost layer of the fennel bulb and discard. Cut the bulb in half so that each half retains part of the stem end. Cut each half into 8 thin wedges so each wedge is held together by a little piece of stem.

Put the vegetables in a large baking dish. Toss them with 2 tablespoons of the oil and ¼ teaspoon of the salt. Arrange the chicken pieces in the pan with the vegetables.

In a small bowl, combine the remaining 1 tablespoon oil and ½ teaspoon salt, the garlic, and lemon zest and juice. Rub the mixture into the chicken in the pan. Season with a few turns of pepper. Roast for 30 minutes, then give the vegetables a stir and add the rosemary. Return to the oven and roast until the chicken is just cooked all the way through and the vegetable are tender and beginning to brown, 20 to 30 minutes more.

Maple-Mustard Chicken Thighs

The grainy mustard and maple syrup form a delectable tangy-sweet crust on these juicy chicken thighs. This recipe may have a small ingredient list, but it has really big flavor!

8 bone-in chicken thighs (about 2½ pounds), skin removed
⅓ cup grainy French mustard
1 clove garlic, minced (about 1 teaspoon)
¾ teaspoon dried marjoram
3 tablespoons pure maple syrup

SERVES 4
SERVING SIZE:
2 PIECES

PER SERVING
CALORIES: 378;
TOTAL FAT: 11G
  MONO: 3.5G,
  POLY: 3G;
  SAT: 3G;
PROTEIN: 56G;
CARB: 10G;
FIBER: 0G;
CHOL: 235MG;
SODIUM: 503MG

EXCELLENT SOURCE OF
MANGANESE, NIACIN, PANTO- THENIC ACID, PHOSPHORUS, POTASSIUM, PROTEIN, RIBO- FLAVIN, SELE- NIUM, VITAMIN B6, ZINC

GOOD SOURCE OF
COPPER, IRON, MAGNESIUM, THIAMIN, VITAMIN B12, VITAMIN K

Preheat the oven to 375°F. Rinse the chicken and pat dry with paper towels.

Combine the mustard, garlic, marjoram, and maple syrup in a small bowl. Spread about 1 tablespoon of the mustard mixture evenly on top of each chicken thigh, being careful to cover as much of the surface as possible to form a "crust." Arrange the chicken in a single layer in a large baking dish. Bake until mustard mixture has formed a crust and is slightly hardened, and the juices run clear when the chicken is pierced in the center, 45 to 50 minutes.

Oven-Fried Chicken

This is definitely finger-lickin' chicken, crispy golden brown on the outside and juicy on the inside. The tangy yogurt coating helps keep the chicken moist and makes the saltine and corn flake crumbs stick. The cayenne pepper gives the chicken a noticeable bite. Use a little less if you prefer it milder.

Cooking spray

½ sleeve (about 20) whole-grain saltine crackers, pulsed in a food processor to fine crumbs (about ½ cup)

2½ cups corn flakes, pulsed in a food processor to fine crumbs (about ½ cup)

2 tablespoons sesame seeds

¾ teaspoon cayenne pepper

½ teaspoon garlic powder

2 large egg whites

1 cup plain nonfat yogurt

1 tablespoon Dijon mustard

½ teaspoon salt

4 skinless bone-in chicken breast halves and 4 skinless bone-in chicken thighs (about 3½ pounds chicken), rinsed and patted dry

SERVES 6
SERVING SIZE: 1 BREAST HALF OR 2 THIGHS

PER SERVING
CALORIES: 270;
TOTAL FAT: 5G
  MONO: 1.5G,
  POLY: 1G;
  SAT: 1G;
PROTEIN: 33G;
CARB: 21G;
FIBER: 1G;
CHOL: 85MG;
SODIUM: 590MG

EXCELLENT SOURCE OF
IRON, NIACIN, PHOSPHORUS, PROTEIN, RIBO-FLAVIN, SELE-NIUM, THIAMIN, VITAMIN B$_6$, VITAMIN B$_{12}$

GOOD SOURCE OF
CALCIUM, FOLATE, MAGNESIUM, MANGANESE, PANTOTHENIC ACID, POTASSIUM, ZINC

Preheat the oven to 375°F. Lightly coat a baking sheet with cooking spray.

Combine the saltine and corn flake crumbs, sesame seeds, cayenne, and garlic powder in a shallow bowl. In a large bowl, combine the egg whites, yogurt, mustard, and salt. Add the chicken pieces and coat thoroughly with the yogurt mixture. Then, one at a time, dip the chicken pieces in the cracker mixture, packing the crumbs evenly onto the chicken. Arrange the chicken on the prepared baking sheet and spray the tops lightly with cooking spray. Bake until the juices run clear when the chicken is pierced with a knife, 45 to 50 minutes.

Jerk Chicken with Cool Pineapple Salsa

This fiery, lively sauce hails from the Caribbean islands and is usually used to marinate meat for up to two days. I turned it into a quick and easy meal so you can have that spicy punch any time. The salsa is the perfect accompaniment, a tropical breeze designed to take down the heat you will surely feel from the sauce.

For the salsa

1 tablespoon honey

1 tablespoon fresh lime juice

1 cup finely diced pineapple, preferably fresh

⅓ cup seeded and finely diced English cucumber

1 tablespoon chopped fresh mint

For the chicken

4 teaspoons olive oil

4 boneless, skinless chicken breast halves (about 1¼ pounds),
    pounded between 2 sheets of wax paper to ½-inch thickness

1 cup chopped scallions (both white and green parts; about 6 scallions)

½ Scotch bonnet or habanero pepper, seeded and finely minced
    (wear gloves when handling and keep your hands away from your eyes)

1 clove garlic, minced (about 1 teaspoon)

1 teaspoon peeled and grated fresh ginger or ¼ teaspoon ground

1 teaspoon ground allspice

1½ teaspoons fresh thyme leaves or ½ teaspoon dried

½ cup low-sodium chicken broth

2 tablespoons low-sodium soy sauce

2 tablespoons fresh lime juice

SERVES 4

SERVING SIZE:
1 CHICKEN
BREAST,
2 TABLESPOONS
SAUCE, AND
⅓ CUP SALSA

PER SERVING
CALORIES: 265;
TOTAL FAT: 7G
    MONO: 4G;
    POLY: 1G;
    SAT: 1G;
PROTEIN: 35G;
CARB: 15G;
FIBER: 2G;
CHOL: 82MG;
SODIUM: 375MG

**EXCELLENT
SOURCE OF**
MANGANESE,
NIACIN,
PHOSPHORUS,
PROTEIN,
SELENIUM,
VITAMIN B6,
VITAMIN C,
VITAMIN K

**GOOD
SOURCE OF**
IRON,
MAGNESIUM,
PANTOTHENIC
ACID, POTASSIUM,
RIBOFLAVIN,
THIAMIN,
VITAMIN B12,
ZINC

To make the salsa, in a small bowl, whisk together the honey and lime juice. Combine the pineapple, cucumber, and mint in a medium bowl, pour the dressing on it, and toss to combine. This can be made up to a day ahead and stored in the refrigerator in an airtight container.

To make the chicken, heat 2 teaspoons of the oil in a large skillet over medium-high heat. Add the chicken breasts and cook until browned and just cooked through, about 4 minutes per side. Transfer the chicken to a plate and cover with aluminum foil to keep warm.

Add the remaining 2 teaspoons oil to the pan. Stir in the scallions, pepper, garlic, ginger, allspice, and thyme and cook for 30 seconds over medium heat. Add the broth and soy sauce and cook until the liquid is reduced by half, about 3 minutes. Stir in the lime juice. Return the chicken to the pan and coat well with the sauce.

Serve the chicken topped with the sauce and the pineapple salsa on the side.

Mom's Turkey Meatloaf

This meatloaf puts me square in the comfort zone with all the homey flavors of Mom's recipe. Only this one is healthier, thanks to a couple of simple substitutions. First, it's made with lean ground turkey. Second, instead of bread crumbs, I use a secret ingredient that binds everything together and keeps the meatloaf wonderfully moist: quick-cooking oats, a healthy whole grain that blends in undetected. All that meaty goodness is covered with tomato sauce and crowned with onion rings that turn golden brown, making for a beautiful presentation.

¾ cup quick-cooking oats

½ cup nonfat milk

1 medium onion, peeled

2 pounds ground turkey breast

½ cup seeded and chopped red bell pepper (½ medium pepper)

2 large eggs, beaten

2 teaspoons Worcestershire sauce

¼ cup ketchup

½ teaspoon salt

Freshly ground black pepper

One 8-ounce can no-salt-added tomato sauce

SERVES 8
SERVING SIZE:
ONE 1-INCH-THICK
SLICE

PER SERVING
CALORIES: 205;
TOTAL FAT: 3.5G
    MONO: 0.5G;
    POLY: 0G;
    SAT: 0.5G,
PROTEIN: 32G;
CARB: 13G;
FIBER: 2G;

CHOL: 98MG;
SODIUM: 490MG

EXCELLENT
SOURCE OF
PROTEIN,
VITAMIN C

GOOD
SOURCE OF
IRON,
VITAMIN A

Preheat the oven to 350°F.

In a small bowl, stir together the oats and milk and allow to soak while you get the rest of the ingredients together, at least 3 minutes.

Thinly slice one-quarter of the onion into rings and set aside. Finely chop the rest of the onion. In a large bowl, combine the turkey, oatmeal mixture, chopped onion, bell pepper, eggs, Worcestershire, ketchup, salt, and a few grinds of pepper. Mix just until well combined.

Transfer the mixture to a 9 x 13-inch baking dish and shape into a loaf about 5 inches wide and 2 inches high. Pour the tomato sauce over the meatloaf and sprinkle with the sliced onions. Bake until an instant-read meat thermometer inserted into the thickest part registers 160°F, about 1 hour.

Remove from the oven and let rest for 10 to 15 minutes before slicing.

Mom's Turkey Meatloaf with
Smashed Potatoes with Sour
Cream and Chives (page 262)

Stuffed Turkey Burgers

There is a delicious element of surprise tucked inside each of these fat, juicy burgers: a luscious ooze of melted mozzarella cheese and sweet smoky red peppers. It's an example of how just a little extra touch can turn ordinary into extraordinary.

1¼ pounds lean ground turkey
½ cup chopped roasted red peppers, drained and rinsed if from a jar
½ cup shredded part-skim mozzarella cheese (2 ounces)
¼ teaspoon salt
Freshly ground black pepper
4 whole-wheat buns

SERVES 4	CHOL: 65MG;
SERVING SIZE:	SODIUM:
1 BURGER	600MG
PER SERVING	**EXCELLENT**
CALORIES: 310;	**SOURCE OF**
TOTAL FAT: 7G	PROTEIN,
MONO: 0.5G,	VITAMIN C
POLY: 1G;	
SAT: 2G,	**GOOD**
PROTEIN: 42G;	**SOURCE OF**
CARB: 24G;	IRON,
FIBER: 3G;	VITAMIN A

Preheat the broiler or prepare the grill. Divide the turkey into 4 equal-sized rounds. Make 2 equal-sized patties out of each round so you have 8 patties total. Sprinkle one side of four of the patties with 2 table-spoons each of roasted red peppers and cheese, and top with remaining patties, working the turkey around the edges to seal the burgers closed. Sprinkle the patties with the salt and a few grinds of pepper. Grill or broil until cooked through, about 5 minutes per side. Serve on the buns.

* ## Does Turkey Make You Tired?

Everyone always blames the poor turkey when they feel like passing out after Thanksgiving dinner. But it's myth-busting time; it's not the turkey's fault.

True, turkey contains tryptophan, an essential amino acid that triggers the production of serotonin, a sleep-inducing brain chemical. But the other amino acids in turkey block trytophan's effect, so it doesn't make you tired after all. A carbohydrate-rich meal with scant protein is more likely to increase tryptophan in the bloodstream and lead to the serotonin sleepies.

There is plenty of evidence that large meals and meals high in fat make you tired, as does drinking alcohol. Hmmm, I wonder if there is any connection there with the Thanksgiving nap.

Herb-Roasted Turkey Breast

A whole turkey breast is a breeze to make and a real crowd pleaser. Prepare this on a weekend any time of the year and have incredible leftovers available to make other recipes in this book during the week, like Poached Eggs with Herb-Roasted Turkey and Sweet Potato Hash (page 33). Using a bone-in turkey breast helps ensure that the meat stays moist.

1 (about 6 pounds) bone-in turkey breast, skin removed
2 tablespoons olive oil
4 cloves garlic, crushed
2 teaspoons finely chopped fresh sage or 1 teaspoon dried, crumbled
2 teaspoons finely chopped fresh thyme or 1 teaspoon dried
2 teaspoons finely chopped fresh rosemary or 1 teaspoon dried, crumbled
1 teaspoon salt
½ teaspoon freshly ground black pepper

SERVES 8
SERVING SIZE:
ABOUT FOUR
½-INCH-THICK
SLICES

PER SERVING
CALORIES: 325;
TOTAL FAT: 4G
    MONO: 2G,
    POLY: 0.5G;
    SAT: 1G,
PROTEIN: 66 G;
CARB: 1G;
FIBER: 0G;
CHOL: 167MG;
SODIUM: 425MG

**EXCELLENT
SOURCE OF**
MAGNESIUM,
NIACIN, PANTO-
THENIC ACID,
PHOSPHORUS,
POTASSIUM,
RIBOFLAVIN,
SELENIUM,
VITAMIN B6,
ZINC

**GOOD
SOURCE OF**
COPPER,
IRON

Preheat the oven to 375°F.

Rinse the turkey breast and pat dry. In a small bowl, combine the oil, garlic, herbs, salt, and pepper and rub the mixture onto the turkey breast.

Transfer the breast to a roasting pan and roast until the juices run clear when pierced with fork and an instant-read meat thermometer inserted into thickest part, away from the bone, registers 165°F, 1 to 1¼ hours. Let rest, covered with aluminum foil, for 10 minutes before carving.

Turkey Roulade with Apple-Cider Gravy

If you really want to wow your guests, here's your ticket. This golden brown turkey breast has a moist pecan-and-cranberry-studded stuffing rolled inside. When you slice it, you can relish in the "oohs" and "aahhs" as you reveal the beautiful spiral intertwining of tender turkey and savory stuffing. Have your butcher do the only hard part—butterflying the turkey breast.

One 2½-pound boneless turkey breast half, skin removed and butterflied

⅓ cup chopped pecans

½ cup unsweetened dried cranberries

2 tablespoons canola oil

1 medium onion, diced (about 1½ cups), plus 1 cup onion
   thinly sliced into half-moons

2 large cloves garlic, minced (about 2 teaspoons)

5 slices day-old whole-wheat bread, crusts removed and cubed (about 2½ cups)

2 tablespoon plus 2 teaspoons chopped fresh sage or
   3 teaspoons dried, crumbled

2½ to 2¾ cups low-sodium chicken broth

½ teaspoon salt, plus more to taste

¼ teaspoon freshly ground black pepper, plus more to taste

Kitchen twine

1 cup apple cider

3 tablespoons cider vinegar

1 teaspoon cornstarch dissolved in 1 tablespoon cold water

SERVES 6

SERVING SIZE:
2 SLICES TURKEY
ROULADE AND
¼ CUP GRAVY

PER SERVING
CALORIES: 400;
TOTAL FAT: 12G
  MONO: 6G,
  POLY: 3.5G;
  SAT: 1.5G;
PROTEIN: 50G;
CARB: 24G;
FIBER: 2G;
CHOL: 117MG;
SODIUM: 371MG

**EXCELLENT
SOURCE OF**
MAGNESIUM,
NIACIN,
PHOSPHORUS,
POTASSIUM,
PROTEIN
SELENIUM,
VITAMIN B6,
ZINC

**GOOD
SOURCE OF**
IRON,
RIBOFLAVIN,
THIAMIN,
VITAMIN B12

Place the turkey breast between two sheets of plastic wrap and pound lightly with a meat mallet to an even thickness of about ¾ inch. Set aside while you prepare the stuffing.

Toast the pecans in a small dry skillet over medium-high heat until fragrant, stirring frequently, about 3 minutes; set aside. Preheat the oven to 375°F.

Place the cranberries in a small saucepan and cover with water. Bring to a boil, cook for 1 minute, then remove from the heat, drain, and set aside.

Heat 1 tablespoon of the oil in a large heavy skillet over medium heat. Add the diced onion and cook, stirring, until golden but not blackened, 12 to 15 minutes. Add the garlic and cook another 2 to 3 minutes. Add the bread, cranberries, pecans, 2 tablespoons of the fresh or 2 teaspoons of the dried sage, and ½ to ¾ cup of the broth, depending upon the consistency of the stuffing (you want the mixture to be moistened, but not too wet, since the turkey will release moisture when cooked). Cook over low heat for 2 to 3 minutes, then remove from the heat.

Sprinkle the salt and pepper over both sides of the turkey breast. Spread the stuffing over one side of the turkey, leaving about 1½ to 2 inches uncovered on all sides. Roll up and secure tightly with kitchen twine, trying to keep all the stuffing intact.

Heat the remaining 1 tablespoon oil in a large Dutch oven or medium roasting pan over medium heat until hot. Sear the stuffed turkey breast on all sides until lightly browned, 3 to 4 minutes per side. Sprinkle the sliced onion around the turkey, pour in 1½ cups of the broth, cover tightly and roast in the oven until an instant-read meat thermometer inserted in the thickest part registers 165°F, 60 to 65 minutes. Remove the turkey breast from the oven, transfer to a cutting board, tent with aluminum foil, and let rest while you make the gravy.

Add the cider, ½ cup of the broth, the vinegar, and the remaining 2 teaspoons fresh or 1 teaspoon dried sage to the roasting pan, bring to a boil, and cook, stirring occasionally, until the liquid is reduced by one-third, about 10 minutes. Slowly add the cornstarch mixture, stirring constantly, and cook for 3 minutes more. The gravy should not be thick, just slightly thicker than a jus. Season with salt and pepper to taste.

Remove the twine from the turkey breast and cut into 1½-inch-thick slices. Serve with the gravy on the side in a gravy boat.

The Dish on Fish

Fish lovers rejoice: Overwhelming research shows that eating fish just two times a week can have a profound impact on your health, lowering your risk of heart disease, stroke, high triglycerides, and high blood pressure.

THE O-3 FACTOR
The main protective factor in fish is omega-3 fat, an essential fat (meaning we need to get it from our diet) that protects the heart by reducing inflammation and helping maintain its rhythm. Omega-3 also may help protect your skin from signs of aging and can help with the pain of arthritis. Fatty fish like salmon, trout, sardines, black cod (sablefish), and herring are the best sources of this valuable fat.

RICH FISH
Besides omega-3, fish is also a great source of protein that's rich in essential vitamins and minerals such as zinc, magnesium, and iron. And when you opt for fish, you are often eating it in place of saturated fat-laden meat.

SOME FISHY CONCERNS
For most people, the benefits of eating fish far outweigh any risks, but unfortunately something to consider when eating seafood are environmental toxins like PCBs and mercury that pollute our waters and our fish. To minimize your exposure:

- Eat a variety of different kinds of fish, especially the types I have included in this book, all of which are known to be lower in contaminants.
- Avoid fish known to be highest in mercury: king mackerel, shark, swordfish, and tilefish.
- Choose wild salmon instead of farmed and light tuna instead of albacore whenever possible.
- Before cooking fish, remove the skin and trim excess fat.
- Women who are pregnant or nursing and children should eat no more than 12 ounces of fish per week.

Poached Salmon with Lemon-Mint Tzatziki

Flaky, cool poached salmon is perfect for a warm-weather dinner party. A large fillet makes an elegant presentation and it can be prepared ahead of time. The tzatziki is the perfect creamy accompaniment,

2 cups dry white wine
4 cups water
2 bay leaves
2 sprigs fresh flat-leaf parsley
2 lemons, thinly sliced
One 2-pound skin-on salmon fillet, any pin bones removed
1 scallion (green part only), thinly sliced
Lemon-Mint Tzatziki (recipe follows)

Put the wine, water, bay leaves, parsley, and one of the sliced lemons in a large skillet and bring to a simmer. Add the salmon, skin side down. Add more water, if necessary, to cover the salmon. Cover the skillet and simmer over low heat until the fish is just cooked through, about 10 minutes per inch thickness. With two large spatulas, transfer the fish to a plate, cover it, and chill it completely in the refrigerator, about 3 hours.

Once cooled, remove the skin from the salmon by uncovering the fish, placing a clean plate or baking sheet on top of it, and flipping the plate over so the fish lands on the plate or baking sheet skin side up. Peel the skin from the fillet and scrape away any brown flesh. Flip the fish again right side up onto a serving plate. Garnish with the scallion greens and the remaining lemon slices. Serve with the tzatziki on the side.

SERVES 6
SERVING SIZE: ONE 2-INCH SLICE AND 2½ TABLESPOONS TZATZIKI

PER SERVING
CALORIES: 310;
TOTAL FAT: 17G
    MONO: 6.5G;
    POLY: 6G;
    SAT: 3.5G;
PROTEIN: 32G;
CARB: 4G;
FIBER: 0G;
CHOL: 90MG;
SODIUM: 113MG

EXCELLENT SOURCE OF
NIACIN, PHOSPHORUS, PROTEIN, SELENIUM, THIAMIN, VITAMIN B_6, VITAMIN B_{12}

GOOD SOURCE OF
FOLATE, MAGNESIUM, POTASSIUM, RIBOFLAVIN, VITAMIN C, VITAMIN K

Lemon-Mint Tzatziki

This lemony cucumber-yogurt sauce makes a lovely dip, as well as a sandwich spread.

1 cup plain nonfat yogurt or ¾ cup plain Greek-style nonfat yogurt
½ large English cucumber, seeded
1 teaspoon olive oil
2 teaspoons fresh lemon juice
¼ teaspoon finely grated lemon zest
½ teaspoon minced garlic
1 tablespoon finely chopped fresh mint
Salt and freshly ground black pepper to taste

SERVES 4
MAKES 1 CUP
SERVING SIZE: ¼ CUP

PER SERVING
CALORIES: 41;
TOTAL FAT: 1G
    MONO: 1G,

POLY: 0G;
SAT: 0G;
PROTEIN: 3G;
CARB: 6G;
FIBER: 0G;
CHOL: 1MG;
SODIUM: 34MG

Continued on page 224

Continued from page 223

If using regular yogurt, spoon it into a strainer lined with paper towels set over a bowl and let drain and thicken for 30 minutes. Coarsely grate the cucumber. Drain it well in another strainer, for a minute or two, pressing out the liquid.

In a medium bowl, stir together the drained or Greek-style yogurt, the grated cucumber, oil, lemon juice and zest, garlic, and mint. Season with salt and pepper. This sauce will keep for 3 days in an airtight container in the refrigerator; stir well before serving.

Roasted Salmon with Shallot-Grapefruit Sauce

This delightfully different champagne-pink sauce has a tangy, sweet, and spicy balance that pairs perfectly with the rich salmon.

4 skinless salmon fillets (5 to 6 ounces each)

¼ teaspoon salt, plus more to taste

2 ruby red grapefruits

2 teaspoons olive oil

1 tablespoon minced shallot

1 teaspoon peeled and grated fresh ginger

2½ teaspoons honey

Pinch of cayenne pepper

2 teaspoons fresh lemon juice

2 tablespoons thinly sliced fresh basil

SERVES 4
SERVING SIZE:
1 SALMON FILLET
AND ABOUT
¼ CUP SAUCE

PER SERVING
CALORIES: 345;
TOTAL FAT: 18G
  MONO: 7.3G;
  POLY: 6G;
  SAT: 3.5G;
PROTEIN: 29G;
CARB: 16G;
FIBER: 1G;
CHOL: 85MG;
SODIUM: 230MG

EXCELLENT SOURCE OF
NIACIN,
PHOSPHORUS,
POTASSIUM,
PROTEIN,
SELENIUM,
THIAMIN,
VITAMIN A,
VITAMIN B$_6$,
VITAMIN B$_{12}$,
VITAMIN C

GOOD SOURCE OF
FOLATE,
MAGNESIUM,
RIBOFLAVIN

Preheat the oven to 350°F. Season the salmon with the salt, place in a baking dish, and roast until just cooked through, about 18 minutes.

While the salmon is cooking, prepare the sauce. Cut one of the grapefruits into sections by cutting off the top and bottom of the fruit, then standing it on one end and cutting down the skin to remove the woolly white pith and peel. Then, with a paring knife, remove each segment of fruit from its membrane and cut the segments in half. Set the segments aside. Juice the other grapefruit and set the juice aside.

In a medium skillet, heat the oil over medium heat. Add the shallot and cook, stirring, until softened, about 2 minutes. Add the ginger, grapefruit juice, honey, and cayenne and bring to simmer. Cook until the sauce is reduced by about half, about 10 minutes. Add the lemon juice and season with salt. Right before serving, toss the grapefruit pieces and basil into the sauce.

Place the salmon on a serving dish, spoon the sauce over it, and serve.

Salmon Cakes with Ginger-Sesame Sauce

These salmon cakes are a modern take on an old family favorite: salmon croquettes. They have a delightful Asian flair, flavored with scallions and cilantro with a subtly sweet crunch from water chestnuts.

6 slices whole-wheat sandwich bread
Two 15-ounce cans salmon, drained and picked over for skin and bones
2 large eggs, lightly beaten
5 scallions (white and green parts)
½ cup canned water chestnuts, drained and finely chopped
¼ cup finely chopped fresh cilantro
½ teaspoon freshly ground black pepper
3 teaspoons olive oil
Ginger-Sesame Sauce (recipe follows)

Remove the crusts from the bread, tear into pieces, and process in a food processor until you get fine bread crumbs. In a large bowl, flake apart the salmon with a fork. Add the eggs and mix well. Finely chop 4 of the scallions and add to the bowl. Add the water chestnuts, cilantro, pepper, and the bread crumbs and mix well. Shape the mixture into 12 patties.

In a large nonstick skillet, heat 1½ teaspoons of the oil over medium heat. Add 6 patties and cook for 5 minutes on each side. Transfer the cooked patties to a plate and cover with aluminum foil to keep warm. Add the remaining 1½ teaspoons oil to the pan and cook the rest of the salmon cakes in the same way.

Chop the remaining scallion. Serve the salmon cakes with the sauce on the side, garnished with the scallion.

SERVES 6
SERVING SIZE:
2 SALMON CAKES
AND ABOUT
1½ TABLESPOONS
SAUCE

PER SERVING
CALORIES: 395;
TOTAL FAT: 20G
   MONO: 8G;
   POLY: 4G;
   SAT: 4G;
PROTEIN: 35G;
CARB: 18G;
FIBER: 3G;
CHOL: 135MG;
SODIUM: 1010MG

EXCELLENT
SOURCE OF
CALCIUM, MAN-
GANESE, NIACIN,
PHOSPHORUS,
POTASSIUM,
PROTEIN, RIBOFLA-
VIN, SELENIUM,
VITAMIN B6,
VITAMIN K

GOOD
SOURCE OF
COPPER, FIBER,
FOLATE, IRON,
MAGNESIUM,
MOLYBDENUM,
PANTOTHENIC
ACID, THIAMIN,
VITAMIN A,
VITAMIN B12, ZINC

Ginger-Sesame Sauce

This makes a fantastic dip for raw vegetables, especially snow peas. It will keep for 3 days in the refrigerator.

½ cup plain nonfat yogurt or 6 tablespoons plain Greek-style nonfat yogurt
2 tablespoons mayonnaise
1½ tablespoons peeled and grated fresh ginger
1 teaspoon toasted sesame oil
1 teaspoon low-sodium soy sauce

If using regular yogurt, place the yogurt in a strainer lined with a paper towel. Set the strainer over a bowl and let drain and thicken for 30 minutes.

Place the drained or Greek-style yogurt in a small bowl. Add the mayonnaise, ginger, sesame oil, and soy sauce and whisk until smooth.

SERVES 7
MAKES ABOUT ⅔ CUP
SERVING SIZE: ABOUT 1½ TABLESPOONS

PER SERVING
CALORIES: 50;

TOTAL FAT: 4.5G
MONO: 0G,
POLY: 0G;
SAT: 0.5G,
PROTEIN: 1G;
CARB: 2G;
FIBER: 0G;
CHOL: 2MG;
SODIUM: 71MG

Salmon with Sweet and Spicy Rub

Tossing a piece of salmon on the grill is one of the quickest routes to a healthful, delicious dinner. But there is no need to settle for plain-Jane grilled fish. This sweet and spicy rub gives the fish a flavor-packed caramelized coating and in seconds transforms it from tame to tantalizing.

Cooking spray
2 tablespoons packed light brown sugar
1 tablespoon chili powder
1 teaspoon ground cumin
⅛ teaspoon salt
⅛ teaspoon freshly ground black pepper
Six 5-ounce salmon fillets, skin and any pin bones removed
1 tablespoon olive oil

Coat your grill or a grill pan with cooking spray and preheat over medium heat. While the grill is heating, combine the brown sugar, chili powder, cumin, salt, and pepper. Brush each salmon fillet with ½ teaspoon of the oil, then rub each fillet with about ½ tablespoon of the spice mixture.

Grill the salmon, flesh side down, until charred, 4 to 5 minutes. Flip the salmon and cook another 5 to 6 minutes for medium doneness. For well-done fish, cook an additional 1 to 2 minutes. Transfer to a platter and serve immediately.

SERVES 6
SERVING SIZE: 1 SALMON FILLET

PER SERVING
CALORIES: 300;
TOTAL FAT: 18G
MONO: 7G,
POLY: 6G;
SAT: 3.5G,
PROTEIN: 28G;
CARB: 5G;
FIBER: 0.5G;
CHOL: 84MG;
SODIUM: 146MG

EXCELLENT SOURCE OF
NIACIN, PANTOTHENIC ACID, PHOSPHO-RUS, PROTEIN, SELENIUM, THIAMIN, VITAMIN B$_6$, VITAMIN B$_{12}$

GOOD SOURCE OF
FOLATE, MAGNESIUM, POTASSIUM, RIBOFLAVIN, VITAMIN A, VITAMIN C

✱ DID YOU KNOW?
Most canned salmon is wild salmon, just like the kind that costs $12 a pound fresh at the store. What a nutritional bargain at less than $3 for a 15-ounce can!

Sea Bass with Tomato, Olives, and Capers

This white, flaky fish is covered in a flavorful tomato sauce studded with briny olives and capers. Fresh spinach adds color and substance. Serve it with some crusty bread and you have a fast and fabulous one-pan meal.

4 teaspoons olive oil

Four 5-ounce skinless sea bass fillets (or other white fish)

1 small onion, diced (about 1 cup)

½ cup dry white wine

1 cup canned no-salt-added diced tomatoes, with their juices

½ cup pitted and chopped calamata olives

2 tablespoons capers, drained

¼ teaspoon red pepper flakes (optional)

2 ounces baby spinach leaves (about 2 lightly packed cups)

Salt and freshly ground black pepper to taste

SERVES 4

SERVING SIZE: 1 FISH FILLET AND ½ CUP TOPPING

PER SERVING
CALORIES: 250;
TOTAL FAT: 9.5G
   MONO: 5.3G;
   POLY: 1.7G;
   SAT: 1.5G;
PROTEIN: 29G;
CARB: 7.5G;
FIBER: 2.5G;
CHOL: 62MG;
SODIUM: 421.5MG

EXCELLENT SOURCE OF
PHOSPHORUS, PROTEIN, SELENIUM, VITAMIN A, VITAMIN B6

GOOD SOURCE OF
FIBER, IRON, MAGNESIUM, MANGANESE, NIACIN, PANTOTHENIC ACID, POTASSIUM, RIBOFLAVIN, THIAMIN, VITAMIN C, VITAMIN E

In a large nonstick skillet, heat 2 teaspoons of the oil over medium-high heat. Add the fish and cook until opaque in the center, about 2½ minutes per side per ½-inch thickness. Transfer the fish to a serving platter and tent with aluminum foil to keep warm.

Heat the remaining 2 teaspoons oil in the same skillet; add the onion and cook, stirring, for 2 minutes. Add the wine and cook until reduced by half, about 2 minutes. Add the tomatoes and let simmer for about 5 minutes. Add the olives, capers, and red pepper, if using, and cook for 1 minute more. Stir in the spinach and cook until it is wilted, about 3 minutes. Season with salt and pepper.

Spoon the topping over the fish and serve.

Fish Tacos with Chipotle Cream

In southern California fish tacos are popular beach fare, served from food trucks by the shore. They are filling and fresh and leave you feeling good in your bathing suit. Here moist, flaky, lime-marinated fish is wrapped in a warm corn tortilla with creamy chipotle sauce and crunchy cabbage and corn.

For the fish

2 tablespoons olive oil

2 tablespoons fresh lime juice

¼ teaspoon salt

Freshly ground black pepper to taste

1 pound white, flaky fish fillets, like tilapia, mahi-mahi, or halibut

For the chipotle cream

½ cup plain nonfat yogurt or ⅓ cup Greek-style nonfat yogurt

2 tablespoons mayonnaise

2 teaspoons finely chopped canned chipotle chile in adobo sauce

For the tacos

Eight 6-inch corn tortillas

1½ cups shredded green cabbage or lettuce

½ cup cooked corn kernels

¼ cup fresh cilantro leaves

Lime wedges

SERVES 4
SERVING SIZE: 2 TACOS

PER SERVING
CALORIES: 405;
TOTAL FAT: 15G
    MONO: 3G;
    POLY: 0G;
    SAT: 3G,
PROTEIN: 34G;
CARB: 36G;
FIBER: 3G;
CHOL: 103MG;
SODIUM: 287MG

EXCELLENT SOURCE OF PROTEIN, VITAMIN C, VITAMIN K

GOOD SOURCE OF FIBER, POTASSIUM, VITAMIN A

To make the fish, in a small bowl, whisk together the oil, lime juice, salt, and pepper. Pour over the fish and let marinate at room temperature for 20 minutes. To make the chipotle cream, if using regular yogurt, put it into a strainer lined with paper towel set over a bowl to drain and thicken for 30 minutes. Preheat a grill or nonstick grill pan over medium-high heat.

Remove the fish from the marinade and grill until cooked thorough, about 3 minutes per side. Set the fish aside on a plate and tent with aluminum foil to keep warm.

In a small bowl combine the drained or Greek-style yogurt, the mayonnaise, and chipotle.

To prepare the tacos, heat the tortillas on the grill or grill pan for 30 seconds on each side.

Flake the fish with a fork. Spread each tortilla with 1 tablespoon of the chipotle cream. Top with the fish, cabbage, corn, and cilantro and serve with lime wedges.

Miso-Glazed Cod with Sesame Stir-Fried Chinese
Greens (page 258) made with baby bok choy

Miso-Glazed Cod

This dish brings home the mouthwatering taste of the haute Japanese restaurant favorite. You need a few specialty ingredients, but I promise they are worth getting because you will make this easy, five-ingredient dish over and over again.

Six 6-ounce black cod (sablefish) or regular cod fillets
⅓ cup low-sodium blond or white miso
¼ cup firmly packed dark brown sugar
1 teaspoon toasted sesame oil
2 tablespoons mirin (Japanese cooking wine)

SERVES 6
SERVING SIZE:
1 FISH FILLET

PER SERVING
CALORIES: 220;
TOTAL FAT: 3G
   MONO: 0.5G;
   POLY: 0.7G;
   SAT: 0.5G,
PROTEIN: 32G;
CARB: 14G;
FIBER: 1G;
CHOL: 73MG;
SODIUM: 745MG

EXCELLENT SOURCE OF
PHOSPHORUS,
POTASSIUM,
PROTEIN,
SELENIUM,
VITAMIN B_6,
VITAMIN B_{12},
VITAMIN D

GOOD SOURCE OF
MAGNESIUM,
NIACIN

Rinse the fish fillets and pat dry with paper towels.

Combine the miso, brown sugar, sesame oil, and mirin in a small bowl until the brown sugar is fully dissolved. Brush about 2 tablespoons of the miso glaze on each fish fillet. Let marinate on a plate in the refrigerator for at least 30 minutes or up to an hour.

Preheat the broiler. Place the fish on a baking sheet, then set under the broiler until their tops are slightly charred and the glaze has caramelized, 3 to 4 minutes. Remove the fish from the oven and brush with the remaining glaze. Reduce the oven temperature to 375°F and cook until the fish is flaky but moist, another 5 to 6 minutes.

* | **DID YOU KNOW?**
Miso, a soybean paste frequently used in Asian cuisine, is rich in protein and important minerals like zinc and copper, though it is high in sodium.

Thai-Style Halibut with Coconut-Curry Broth

Here a flaky, meaty halibut fillet sits on fresh spinach and rice in a slurpingly delicious pool of spicy coconut broth. Flecked with cilantro and scallions and more than a hint of lime, it looks as appealing as it tastes.

2 teaspoons canola oil

2 large shallots, finely chopped (about ¾ cup)

2 teaspoons red curry paste or 2 teaspoons curry powder

2 cups low-sodium chicken broth

½ cup unsweetened light coconut milk

¾ teaspoon salt

Four 5-ounce halibut fillets

5 ounces baby spinach leaves (about 5 cups lightly packed)

2 cups cooked brown rice

½ cup coarsely chopped fresh cilantro

2 scallions (green part only), thinly sliced

2 tablespoons fresh lime juice

Freshly ground black pepper

SERVES 4
SERVING SIZE: 1 HALIBUT FILLET, ½ CUP BROTH, ¼ CUPS SPINACH, AND ½ CUP RICE

PER SERVING
CALORIES: 365;
TOTAL FAT: 9G
  MONO: 3G;
  POLY: 2.5G;
  SAT: 2.5G,
PROTEIN: 37G;
CARB: 36G;
FIBER: 4G;
CHOL: 45MG;
SODIUM: 471MG

EXCELLENT SOURCE OF
IRON, MAGNESIUM, MANGANESE, NIACIN, PHOSPHORUS, POTASSIUM, PROTEIN, SELENIUM, VITAMIN A, VITAMIN B6, VITAMIN B12, VITAMIN C, VITAMIN K

GOOD SOURCE OF
CALCIUM, COPPER, FIBER, FOLATE, RIBOFLAVIN, THIAMIN, ZINC

In a large sauté pan, heat the oil over medium heat. Add the shallots and cook, stirring a few times, until they begin to brown, 3 to 5 minutes. Add the curry paste and cook, stirring, until fragrant, about 30 seconds. Add the broth, coconut milk, and ½ teaspoon of the salt and simmer until reduced to 2 cups, about 5 minutes.

Season the halibut with the remaining ¼ teaspoon salt. Arrange in the pan and gently shake so the fish is coated with the sauce. Cover and cook until the fish flakes easily with a fork, about 7 minutes.

In the meantime, put the spinach in a microwave-safe bowl, cover tightly, and microwave for 2 minutes.

Place ½ cup of the rice and a pile of cooked spinach in the bottom of 4 soup plates. Top with the fish fillets. Stir the cilantro, scallions, and lime juice into the sauce and season to taste with salt and pepper. Ladle the sauce over the fish and serve.

✳ **EATING WELL TIP**
Coconut is the only fruit on my "Rarely" list because it is so high in saturated fat. There is some research that the kind of saturated fat in coconut may not be as unhealthful as other saturated fat, but until the verdict is in, I opt for the light version of coconut milk, which has a wonderful creaminess and island flavor with nearly a quarter of the fat and a third of the calories.

Sole with Vegetables in Foil Packets

The light flavors in this simple recipe bring out the absolute best in the fish, letting its delicate flavor come through. As the sole and vegetables cook in their cozy packets, steeping in white wine and lemon, a delightful, effortless sauce is formed. Serve it over rice to catch every last drop.

Four 5-ounce sole fillets (or other white fish fillets)
½ teaspoon salt
¼ teaspoon freshly ground black pepper
Four 12 x 20-inch pieces aluminum foil
1 medium zucchini (about ½ pound), sliced into thin rounds
1 medium carrot, sliced into thin rounds
1 medium red bell pepper, seeded and cut into a small dice (about 1 cup)
2 medium shallots, thinly sliced (about ⅓ cup)
½ cup dry white wine or water
2 tablespoons olive oil
1 lemon, thinly sliced
2 tablespoons chopped fresh chives

SERVES 4
SERVING SIZE:
1 PACKET

PER SERVING
CALORIES: 245;
TOTAL FAT: 9G
    MONO: 6G,
    POLY: 1G;
    SAT FAT: 1G,
PROTEIN: 26G;
CARB: 11G;
FIBER: 1.5G;
CHOL: 67MG;
SODIUM: 411MG

EXCELLENT SOURCE OF
MAGNESIUM,
PHOSPHORUS,
PROTEIN,
SELENIUM,
VITAMIN A,
VITAMIN B$_6$,
VITAMIN B$_{12}$,
VITAMIN C

GOOD SOURCE OF
MANGANESE,
MOLYBDENUM,
NIACIN,
POTASSIUM,
RIBOFLAVIN,
VITAMIN K

Preheat the oven to 425°F.

Season the fish fillets with the salt and pepper. Place one fish fillet at the center of each piece of foil. Evenly distribute the zucchini, carrot, bell pepper, and shallots among the 4 packets. Sprinkle each fillet with 2 tablespoons of the wine and ½ tablespoon of the oil. Top each fillet with 3 lemon slices. Seal the packets securely, leaving a little room to allow the fish to steam. Transfer the packets to a baking sheet and bake for 15 minutes.

Remove from the oven and carefully open the packets. Remove the lemon slices. Serve the fish topped with the vegetables and garnished with the chives.

Baked Shrimp with Tomatoes and Feta

Succulent shrimp tucked into a rich tomato sauce fragrant with fresh dill, topped with feta cheese, and baked until bubbling—it's a meal you'll make over and over. Serve this over cooked rice or orzo.

1 tablespoon olive oil
1 medium onion, diced (about 1½ cups)
2 cloves garlic, minced (about 2 teaspoons)
Two 14.5-ounce cans no-salt-added diced tomatoes, with their juices
¼ cup finely minced fresh flat-leaf parsley
1 tablespoon finely minced fresh dill
1¼ pounds medium shrimp, peeled and deveined
¼ teaspoon salt, plus more to taste
¼ teaspoon freshly ground black pepper, plus more to taste
⅔ cup crumbled feta cheese (about 3 ounces)

Preheat the oven to 425°F.

Heat the oil in an ovenproof skillet over medium-high heat. Add the onion and cook, stirring, until softened, about 3 minutes, then add the garlic and cook for 1 minute. Add the tomatoes and bring to a boil. Reduce the heat to medium-low and let simmer for about 5 minutes, until the tomato juices thicken.

Remove from the heat. Stir in the parsley, dill, and shrimp and season with salt and pepper. Sprinkle the feta over the top. Bake until the shrimp are cooked though and the cheese melts, about 12 minutes.

SERVES 4
SERVING SIZE: 1½ CUPS

PER SERVING
CALORIES: 295;
TOTAL FAT: 10.5G
  MONO: 4G,
  POLY: 1G;
  SAT: 4G,
PROTEIN: 34G;
CARB: 12G;
FIBER: 2G;
CHOL: 235MG;
SODIUM: 645MG

EXCELLENT SOURCE OF
CALCIUM, COPPER, IRON, NIACIN, PHOSPHORUS, PROTEIN, SELENIUM, VITAMIN A, VITAMIN B12, VITAMIN C, VITAMIN D, VITAMIN K

GOOD SOURCE OF
MAGNESIUM, POTASSIUM, RIBOFLAVIN, VITAMIN B6, ZINC

* ## Shellfish and Cholesterol

There is good news for shellfish lovers: You don't need to avoid it because of its cholesterol. Shrimp, crab, lobsters, and the like are relatively high in cholesterol, but it turns out that the cholesterol you eat isn't the biggest determinant of your blood cholesterol—the amount of saturated fat and trans fat you eat is. And these delicacies from the sea are incredibly low in fat. Plus they are rich in important minerals like zinc as well as protein. So go ahead, enjoy those succulent crab legs, juicy shrimp, and sweet lobster: just keep portions moderate and hold the butter!

Jambalaya with Shrimp and Ham

Jambalaya is a belly-satisfying Creole rice dish that has as many variations as there are cooks. Mine tends toward the traditional, only better for you: long-grain white rice (brown rice just doesn't cut it here!) stewed with tomatoes, onion, peppers, and spices and chock-full of smoky ham and succulent shrimp. It is feel-good food that's loaded with flavor and stick-to-your-ribs heartiness.

1 tablespoon olive oil

1 large onion, diced (about 2 cups)

1 medium red bell pepper, seeded and diced (about 1 cup)

1 medium green bell pepper, seeded and diced (about 1 cup)

2 cloves garlic, minced (about 2 teaspoons)

½ teaspoon salt, plus more to taste

¼ teaspoon freshly ground black pepper, plus more to taste

1 teaspoon paprika

½ teaspoon dried oregano

½ teaspoon dried thyme

1 bay leaf

¼ teaspoon cayenne pepper

1 tablespoon tomato paste

6 ounces smoked ham, diced

2½ cups low-sodium chicken broth

One 14.5-ounce can no-salt-added diced tomatoes, with their juices

1 cup uncooked long-grain white rice

1 pound medium shrimp, peeled and deveined

Hot pepper sauce

SERVES 4
SERVING SIZE: 2 CUPS

PER SERVING
CALORIES: 440;
TOTAL FAT: 9G
   MONO: 3.5G,
   POLY: 1.4G;
   SAT: 2G,
PROTEIN: 38G;
CARB: 50G;
FIBER: 3G;
CHOL: 190MG;
SODIUM: 1040MG

EXCELLENT SOURCE OF
IRON, NIACIN, PHOSPHORUS, PROTEIN, SELENIUM, VITAMIN A, VITAMIN B6, VITAMIN B12, VITAMIN C, VITAMIN D

GOOD SOURCE OF
FIBER, MAGNESIUM, MANGANESE, POTASSIUM, VITAMIN E, ZINC

Heat the oil in a large Dutch oven over medium heat. Add the onion, bell peppers, and garlic and cook, stirring occasionally, until softened, about 10 minutes. Add in everything else but the rice, shrimp, and hot sauce and bring to a boil. Stir in the rice, cover, reduce the heat to low, and simmer until the rice is done and most of the liquid is absorbed, about 20 minutes.

   Add the shrimp and cook, covered, until the shrimp is cooked through, about another 5 minutes. Season with salt and pepper. Serve with hot pepper sauce on the side.

Shrimp Scampi with Artichokes

The intoxicating taste and aroma of this dish make it perfectly clear why shrimp and garlic are paired so often. The softly pungent garlic brings out a richness in the shrimp, transforming it into something truly decadent. Here meaty artichoke hearts add color and texture, and white wine and lemon juice brighten it all without subtracting any depth. The result is a dish that magically manages to be light and hearty at the same time.

2 tablespoons olive oil

4 large cloves garlic, minced (about 4 teaspoons)

2 medium shallots, thinly sliced (about ⅓ cup)

1¼ pounds large shrimp, peeled and deveined

One 11-ounce package frozen artichoke hearts, thawed,
    or one 14-ounce can artichoke hearts, rinsed, drained, and quartered

⅓ cup dry white wine

2 tablespoons fresh lemon juice

2 tablespoons chopped fresh flat-leaf parsley, plus more for garnish

½ teaspoon salt

¼ teaspoon freshly ground black pepper

SERVES 4
SERVING SIZE:
2 CUPS

PER SERVING
CALORIES: 285;
TOTAL FAT: 10G,
    MONO: 6G,
    POLY: 1.5G;
    SAT: 1.5G,
PROTEIN: 32G;
CARB: 14G;
FIBER: 5G;
CHOL: 215MG;
SODIUM: 540MG

EXCELLENT SOURCE OF
COPPER, FIBER, FOLATE, IRON, MAGNESIUM, NIACIN, PROTEIN, PHOSPHORUS, SELENIUM, VITAMIN B12, VITAMIN C, VITAMIN D, VITAMIN K

GOOD SOURCE OF
CALCIUM, MANGANESE, POTASSIUM, RIBOFLAVIN, VITAMIN A, VITAMIN B6, ZINC

Heat the oil in a large skillet over medium heat. Add the garlic and shallots and cook, stirring, until softened but not browned, 2 to 3 minutes. Add the shrimp, artichoke hearts, wine, and lemon juice and cook until the shrimp are cooked through, 3 to 4 minutes. Stir in the parsley, salt, and pepper. Divide among 4 plates, garnish with additional parsley, and serve.

✳   **EATING WELL TIP**
Frozen and jarred artichokes are processed with an acid to protect their color. Be sure to drain and rinse them well before using so your food doesn't wind up with an overly acidic flavor.

Scallops with Succotash and Parsley Drizzle

Every summer my family spends a week in Montauk, a low-key beach town at the very end of Long Island. This supper is one of the easy, fresh meals I usually whip up for dinner there. I just mosey over to the local farmstand and fill my basket with the season's bounty: sweet corn, luscious tomatoes, tender zucchini, and intoxicatingly aromatic basil. Nature's done most the work. All I do it sauté it together, top with some fresh grilled scallops and a drizzle of lemony parsley sauce, then kick back and enjoy.

4 ears corn or 2½ cups frozen corn kernels, thawed
2 teaspoons olive oil
1 small onion, diced (about 1 cup)
2 cloves garlic, minced (about 2 teaspoons)
One 10-ounce package frozen lima beans, thawed
1 medium zucchini (about ½ pound),
    quartered lengthwise and thinly sliced across
1 pint grape tomatoes, cut in half
Cooking spray
1¼ pounds large sea scallops (about 16)
¼ teaspoon salt, plus more to taste
¼ teaspoon freshly ground black pepper, plus more to taste
1 tablespoon cider vinegar
¼ cup chopped fresh basil
Parsley Drizzle (recipe follows)

SERVES 4
SERVING SIZE:
1 CUP SUCCOTASH,
4 SCALLOPS, AND
1 TABLESPOON
PARSLEY DRIZZLE

PER SERVING
CALORIES: 435;
TOTAL FAT: 12G
    MONO: 7.5G,
    POLY: 2G;
    SAT: 2G,
 PROTEIN: 34G;
 CARB: 51G;
 FIBER: 9G;
CHOL: 47MG;
SODIUM: 480MG

**EXCELLENT
SOURCE OF**
FIBER, FOLATE,
IRON, MAGNE-
SIUM, MANGA-
NESE, NIACIN,
PHOSPHORUS,
POTASSIUM,
PROTEIN, RIBOFLA-
VIN, SELENIUM,
VITAMIN A,
VITAMIN B6,
VITAMIN B12,
VITAMIN C,
VITAMIN K, ZINC

**GOOD
SOURCE OF**
CALCIUM, COPPER,
MOLYBDENUM,
THIAMIN

If using ears of corn, cut the kernels off and set aside. Discard the cobs.
　Heat the oil in a large skillet over medium heat. Add the onion and cook, stirring a few times, until softened, about 2 minutes. Add the garlic and cook for 1 minute. Stir in the corn, lima beans, zucchini, and tomatoes and cook, stirring occasionally, until the vegetables are tender, about 7 minutes.
　Coat a large nonstick skillet or grill pan with cooking spray and preheat it over medium-high heat.
　In the meantime, prepare the scallops. Pat them dry and sprinkle with the salt and pepper. Set the scallops in the hot pan and cook until the insides are opaque, 5 to 6 minutes, turning once.
　Stir the vinegar and basil into the succotash, season with salt and pepper and serve topped with the grilled scallops and the Parsley Drizzle.

Parsley Drizzle

This simple lemony grassy drizzle is lovely atop grilled or poached fish as well as grilled or steamed vegetables.

1 cup lightly packed fresh flat-leaf parsley
2 tablespoons olive oil
1 tablespoon fresh lemon juice
2 tablespoons water

Combine all the ingredients in a blender and purée.

SERVES 4
MAKES ¼ CUP
SERVING SIZE:
1 TABLESPOON

PER SERVING
CALORIES: 68;
TOTAL FAT: 7G
   MONO: 5.5G,
   POLY: 0.5G;
   SAT: 1G;
PROTEIN: 0G;
CARB: 1G;

FIBER: 0G;
CHOL: 0MG;
SODIUM: 6MG

**EXCELLENT
SOURCE OF**
VITAMIN C,
VITAMIN K

**GOOD
SOURCE OF**
VITAMIN A

Crab Cakes with Smarter Tartar

Unlike the fried crab-flavored bread crumb patties you get at most restaurants, these crab cakes are almost entirely succulent crabmeat, with just enough bread crumbs to hold them together. They are flavored with all the classic crab cake tastes, then baked so they are crisp outside and moist inside. Served with a dollop of Smarter Tartar Sauce, they are truly heavenly.

Cooking spray
1 large egg, lightly beaten
2 teaspoons Dijon mustard
1 teaspoon Worcestershire sauce
1 tablespoon fresh lemon juice
Dash of hot sauce
½ teaspoon Old Bay seasoning
½ cup finely chopped red bell pepper
1 scallion (white and green parts), finely chopped
1 pound lump crabmeat, picked over for shells and cartilage
¾ cup plain dry bread crumbs
¼ teaspoon salt
Pinch of freshly ground black pepper
½ cup Smarter Tartar Sauce (recipe follows)

SERVES 4
SERVING SIZE: 2 CRAB CAKES AND 2 TABLE-SPOONS SMARTER TARTAR

PER SERVING
CALORIES: 255
TOTAL FAT: 8G
    MONO: 1G,
    POLY: 1G;
    SAT: 1G,
PROTEIN: 26G;
CARB: 18G;
FIBER: 1G;
CHOL: 145MG;
SODIUM: 826MG

EXCELLENT SOURCE OF COPPER, PHOSPHORUS, PROTEIN, SELENIUM, VITAMIN B$_{12}$, VITAMIN C, VITAMIN K, ZINC

GOOD SOURCE OF CALCIUM, FOLATE, IRON, MAGNESIUM, MANGANESE, NIACIN, POTASSIUM, VITAMIN A, VITAMIN B$_6$

Preheat the oven to 400°F. Coat a baking sheet with cooking spray.

In a medium bowl, mix together the egg, mustard, Worcestershire, lemon juice, hot sauce, and Old Bay. Stir in the bell pepper and scallion. Gently fold in the crab, ¼ cup of the bread crumbs, salt, and pepper. Put the remaining ½ cup bread crumbs in a shallow dish.

Divide the crab mixture into 8 mounds. Shape each mound into a round and coat evenly in bread crumbs. Transfer to the prepared baking sheet and flatten the crab cake to form a patty about 1 inch high. Spray each crab cake with a little cooking spray.

Bake until golden on the bottom, about 10 minutes. Gently flip the crab cakes and cook until the second side is golden, 5 to 10 minutes longer. Serve hot with Smarter Tartar Sauce.

✳ DID YOU KNOW?
My creamy, delicious Smarter Tartar has about one-quarter the fat and calories of traditional tartar sauce.

Smarter Tartar Sauce

This fantastic tarter sauce goes beautifully with grilled or baked fish fillets.

⅓ cup plain nonfat yogurt or ¼ cup plain Greek-style nonfat yogurt
2 tablespoons mayonnaise
1 scallion (white and green parts), finely chopped
¼ cup finely chopped sour pickles
1 tablespoon chopped capers

If using regular yogurt, spoon it into a strainer lined with paper towels set over a bowl and let drain and thicken for 30 minutes.

In a small bowl combine the drained or Greek-style yogurt, the mayonnaise, scallion, pickles, and capers. Stir to combine. This sauce will keep for 3 days in an airtight container in the refrigerator.

SERVES 6
MAKES ¾ CUP
SERVING SIZE:
2 TABLESPOONS

PER SERVING
CALORIES: 41;
TOTAL FAT: 4G
  MONO: 0G,
  POLY: 0G;
  SAT: 0.5G,

PROTEIN: 0.5G;
CARB: 1.5G;
FIBER: 0G;
CHOL: 2MG;
SODIUM: 81MG

sides

Jewel Roasted Vegetables

My sister Rachelle makes a version of this family favorite every Thanksgiving. I call it Jewel Roasted Vegetables because the chunky colors look like gems on the plate: ruby red beets, deep orange carrots, and emerald Brussels sprouts. The sweet-savory, deeply flavored taste combination is a royal flush as well.

4 medium beets
3 tablespoons olive oil
1½ pounds carrots
1½ pounds Brussels sprouts
8 large cloves garlic, left unpeeled
½ teaspoon salt, plus more to taste
¼ teaspoon freshly ground black pepper, plus more to taste
1 tablespoon chopped fresh thyme

SERVES 6
SERVING SIZE:
1⅓ CUPS

PER SERVING
CALORIES: 190;
TOTAL FAT: 7.5G
  MONO: 5.5G,
  POLY: 1G;
  SAT: 1G,
PROTEIN: 6G;
CARB: 28G;
FIBER: 9G;
CHOL: 0MG;
SODIUM: 345MG

EXCELLENT SOURCE OF
FIBER, FOLATE, MANGANESE, POTASSIUM, VITAMIN A, VITAMIN B6, VITAMIN C, VITAMIN K

GOOD SOURCE OF
CALCIUM, IRON, MAGNESIUM, NIACIN, PHOSPHORUS, PROTEIN, RIBOFLAVIN, THIAMIN, VITAMIN E

Preheat the oven to 375°F.

Put the beets into a small baking dish and rub them with 1 tablespoon of the oil. Cover the dish with aluminum foil and roast for 30 minutes.

While the beets are roasting, peel and cut the carrots into 1-inch-thick rounds, and trim the Brussels sprouts and cut them in half lengthwise. Put the carrots, sprouts, and garlic cloves in a large baking dish and toss with the remaining 2 tablespoons oil. Sprinkle with salt and pepper.

After the beets have been cooking for 30 minutes, add the large pan of vegetables to the oven separately, and cook everything for 1 hour more, stirring the vegetable mixture once or twice.

Remove the beets from the oven and transfer them to a cutting board to cool. Stir the thyme into the carrot and Brussels sprout mixture and let it continue to cook for another 10 minutes while the beets are cooled and cut.

When the beets are cool enough to handle, after about 5 minutes, peel, then cut them into 1-inch chunks. Remove the other vegetables from the oven, toss with the beets, season with salt and pepper, and serve.

Green Beans with Mushrooms and Shallots

This simple trio of soft, meaty mushrooms, snappy green beans, and aromatic shallots tastes like much more than the sum of its parts. Each vegetable elevates the others, turning the mundane into the magical.

1 pound fresh green beans, trimmed and cut into 1-inch pieces
1 tablespoon water
2 tablespoons olive oil
⅓ cup sliced shallots (about 2 medium)
¾ pound assorted fresh mushrooms (i.e., button, baby bella, shiitake, oyster, chanterelle), sliced
Salt and freshly ground black pepper to taste

Put the green beans in a microwave-safe bowl with the water. Cover tightly and microwave on high for 4 minutes. Carefully remove the cover, drain it in a colander, shaking off any excess water, and set aside.

While the beans are cooking, heat the oil over medium-high heat in a large nonstick skillet. Add the shallots and cook, stirring, until softened slightly, about 2 minutes. Add the mushrooms and cook, stirring occasionally, until the water they release has evaporated and they begin to brown, about 10 minutes. Add the green beans and stir to combine and rewarm. Season with salt and pepper and serve.

SERVES 4
SERVING SIZE: ¾ CUP

PER SERVING
CALORIES: 143;
TOTAL FAT: 7G
MONO: 5.5G,
POLY: 1G;
SAT: 1G,
PROTEIN: 5.5G;
CARB: 18G;
FIBER: 4G;
CHOL: 0MG;
SODIUM: 12MG

EXCELLENT SOURCE OF
COPPER, NIACIN, RIBOFLAVIN, SELENIUM, VITAMIN C, VITAMIN K

GOOD SOURCE OF
FIBER, FOLATE, IRON, MANGANESE, PANTOTHENIC ACID, PHOSPHORUS, POTASSIUM, PROTEIN, THIAMIN, VITAMIN A

Ranch Beans

This chunky bean dish is hearty campfire food that's packed with flavor from smoky ancho chile, onions, and fresh cilantro. It's a natural with Steak Tacos with Cucumber-Avacodo Dressing (page 184).

1 tablespoon olive oil
1 medium onion, diced (about 1½ cups)
1 medium green bell pepper, seeded and diced (about 1 cup)
1 tablespoon ground ancho chile or regular chili powder
Two 15-ounce cans pinto beans, preferably low-sodium, drained and rinsed
¼ cup low-sodium chicken broth, plus more if needed
2 tablespoons chopped fresh cilantro
Salt and freshly ground black pepper to taste

SERVES 8
SERVING SIZE: ½ CUP

PER SERVING
CALORIES: 120;
TOTAL FAT: 3G
MONO: 1G,
POLY: 1G;
SAT: 0G,
PROTEIN: 6G;
CARB: 17G;
FIBER: 6.5G;
CHOL: 0MG;
SODIUM: 218MG

EXCELLENT SOURCE OF
FIBER, VITAMIN C

GOOD SOURCE OF
PROTEIN

Heat the oil in a large skillet over medium heat. Add the onion and bell pepper and cook, stirring, until softened, about 3 minutes. Stir in the ancho and cook for 1 minute more. Stir in the beans and broth and cook until the beans are warmed through, about 5 minutes. Stir in the cilantro. Mash the beans coarsely with the back of a wooden spoon, adding more broth to moisten if needed. Season with salt and black pepper and serve.

Sugar Snap Peas with Miso Sauce

Crisp green sugar snap peas are tossed in a luxuriously savory-sweet miso sauce. It is perfect served alongside grilled salmon spritzed with lemon.

1 pound sugar snap peas or snow peas, trimmed

1 tablespoon water

2 teaspoons canola oil

3 scallions (white and green parts), thinly sliced

1 tablespoon peeled and minced fresh ginger

¼ cup orange juice

½ cup low-sodium chicken broth

1 tablespoon rice vinegar

2 tablespoons reduced-sodium white miso paste

1 teaspoon toasted sesame oil

SERVES 6
SERVING SIZE:
½ CUP

PER SERVING
CALORIES: 75;
TOTAL FAT: 3G
MONO: 1G,
POLY: 1G;
SAT: 0G,
PROTEIN: 3G;
CARB: 9G;
FIBER: 2G;

CHOL: 0MG;
SODIUM: 255MG

EXCELLENT
SOURCE OF
VITAMIN C,
VITAMIN K

GOOD
SOURCE OF
FIBER

Place the snap peas in a microwave-safe bowl with the water. Cover tightly and microwave on high for 2 minutes. Carefully remove the cover, drain the snap peas in a colander, shaking off any excess water, and set aside.

While the peas are cooking, heat the oil in a medium saucepan over medium-high heat. Add the scallions and ginger and cook, stirring, for 2 minutes. Add the orange juice, broth, and vinegar and cook for 5 minutes. Turn the heat to low and stir in the miso paste and sesame oil. Stir until the miso paste is dissolved, about 1 minute. Pour the sauce over the snap peas, toss to coat, and serve.

Broccoli with Toasted Garlic

This recipe is a perfect example of how little effort it takes to make vegetables truly crave-able. Cooking thinly sliced garlic in olive oil does double duty: first, it infuses the oil with garlic flavor, and second, it makes crispy bits of toasted garlic to sprinkle on top of the broccoli.

1 bunch broccoli (about 1¼ pounds)
1 tablespoon water
2 tablespoons olive oil
3 cloves garlic, thinly sliced
Salt and freshly ground black pepper to taste

SERVES 4
SERVING SIZE:
1 CUP

PER SERVING
CALORIES: 115;
TOTAL FAT: 7.5G
MONO: 5G,
POLY: 1G;
SAT: 1G,
PROTEIN: 4G;
CARB: 10G;
FIBER: 4G;
CHOL: 0MG;
SODIUM: 47MG

EXCELLENT SOURCE OF
FOLATE,
VITAMIN C,
VITAMIN K

GOOD SOURCE OF
FIBER,
MANGANESE,
MOLYBDENUM,
PHOSPHORUS,
POTASSIUM,
RIBOFLAVIN,
VITAMIN A,
VITAMIN B6

Cut the broccoli into spears and put into a large microwave-safe bowl with the water. Cover tightly and microwave on high for 4 minutes.

While the broccoli is cooking, heat the oil in a large skillet over medium heat and add the garlic. Cook the garlic, stirring frequently, until it is golden, about 3 minutes. Take care not to overcook the garlic or it will become bitter. Using a slotted spoon, transfer the toasted garlic to a small dish.

Remove the bowl of broccoli from the microwave, carefully uncover it, and drain it in a colander, shaking off any excess water. Transfer the broccoli to the skillet with the oil and cook over medium heat, stirring a few times, for 3 minutes. Sprinkle with the toasted garlic, season with salt and pepper, and serve.

✱   **EATING WELL TIP**
Cooking firm vegetables like broccoli briefly before sautéing or stir-frying them enhances their taste and texture. Traditionally chefs accomplish this by blanching the vegetable—cooking it briefly in boiling water. Microwaving or steaming gives the effect of blanching without leaching as many nutrients.

"Dirty" Broccoli

Golden brown bread crumbs flavored with oregano and garlic are what make this broccoli "dirty" and delectable. You can use store-bought crumbs or substitute ½ cup fresh bread crumbs made from 1 slice of whole-wheat bread processed into fine crumbs.

1 bunch broccoli (about 1¼ pounds)
1 tablespoon water
2 tablespoons olive oil
2 cloves garlic, minced
¼ cup plain dry bread crumbs, preferably whole-wheat
¼ teaspoon dried oregano
¼ teaspoon salt
Pinch of freshly ground black pepper

SERVES 4
SERVING SIZE:
1 CUP

PER SERVING
CALORIES: 130;
TOTAL FAT: 8G
    MONO: 5.5G,
    POLY: 1 G;
    SAT: 1G,
PROTEIN: 5G;
CARB: 13G;
FIBER: 4G;
CHOL: 0MG;
SODIUM: 230MG

EXCELLENT
SOURCE OF
FOLATE,
MANGANESE,
VITAMIN A,
VITAMIN C,
VITAMIN K

GOOD
SOURCE OF
FIBER,
MAGNESIUM,
MOLYBDENUM,
PHOSPHORUS,
POTASSIUM,
PROTEIN,
RIBOFLAVIN,
SELENIUM,
VITAMIN B6

Cut the broccoli into spears and put in a large microwave-safe bowl with the water. Cover tightly and microwave on high for 5 minutes. Carefully remove the cover, drain the broccoli well, and set aside.

While the broccoli is cooking, heat the oil in a large skillet over medium-high heat. Add the garlic and cook for 1 minute. Add the bread crumbs, oregano, salt, and pepper and cook, stirring, cook until the crumbs are toasted and golden brown, about 2 minutes. Add the broccoli, toss to coat with bread crumbs, and serve.

Roasted Nutmeg Cauliflower

I have turned around numerous self-proclaimed cauliflower haters with this dish. It comes out of the oven golden brown, tender, subtly sweet, and more flavorful than you ever imagined cauliflower could be.

1 head cauliflower (about 2 pounds), cut into florets
2 tablespoons extra-virgin olive oil
¼ teaspoon ground nutmeg
¼ teaspoon salt

Preheat the oven to 350°F.

Place the cauliflower in a 9 x 13-inch baking dish, toss with the oil, and sprinkle with the nutmeg and salt. Cover the dish and roast for 30 minutes.

Remove the cover, stir, and cook for another 30 to 45 minutes, until the cauliflower is tender and nicely browned, stirring occasionally.

SERVES 4
SERVING SIZE:
1 CUP

PER SERVING
CALORIES: 99;
TOTAL FAT: 7G
  MONO: 5.5G;
  POLY: 1G;
  SAT: 1G;
PROTEIN: 3G;
CARB: 8G;
FIBER: 3.5G;
CHOL: 0MG;
SODIUM: 189MG

EXCELLENT SOURCE OF
FOLATE,
VITAMIN C,
VITAMIN K

GOOD SOURCE OF
FIBER,
MANGANESE,
MOLYBDENUM,
POTASSIUM,
VITAMIN B6

Zucchini Parmesan Crisps

These thin zucchini slices are coated in Parmesan cheese and crisped in the oven until they have the snap of freshly made chips. I bet you can't eat just one.

Cooking spray
1 pound zucchini (about 2 medium)
1 tablespoon olive oil
¼ cup freshly grated Parmesan cheese
¼ cup plain dry bread crumbs
⅛ teaspoon salt
Freshly ground black pepper

SERVES 4
SERVING SIZE:
½ CUP

PER SERVING
CALORIES: 105;
TOTAL FAT: 6G
  MONO: 2G;
  POLY: 0G;
  SAT: 2G;
PROTEIN: 5G;
CARB: 8.5G;
FIBER: 1.5G;
CHOL: 1MG;
SODIUM: 222MG

EXCELLENT SOURCE OF
MOLYBDENUM,
VITAMIN C

GOOD SOURCE OF
CALCIUM,
MANGANESE,
PROTEIN,
VITAMIN B6

Preheat the oven to 450°F. Coat a baking sheet with cooking spray.

Slice the zucchini into ¼-inch-thick rounds. In a medium bowl, toss the zucchini with the oil. In a small bowl, combine the Parmesan, bread crumbs, salt, and a few turns of pepper. Dip each round into the Parmesan mixture, coating it evenly on both sides, and place in a single layer on the prepared baking sheet.

Bake the zucchini rounds until browned and crisp, 25 to 30 minutes. Serve immediately.

Asparagus with Lemon and Tarragon

This dish just sings of spring, when asparagus is at its peak and fresh herbs start to become plentiful. The bright accent of lemon and subtle anise flavor of the tarragon balance the deep flavor of the vegetable. This makes a lovely accompaniment for roasted meat at a spring holiday dinner.

1 bunch asparagus (about 1¼ pounds), woody bottoms removed
   and cut diagonally into 2-inch pieces
1 tablespoon water
1 tablespoon olive oil
½ teaspoon finely grated lemon zest
2 teaspoons fresh lemon juice
¼ teaspoon salt
Pinch of freshly ground black pepper
1 teaspoon chopped fresh tarragon

SERVES 4
SERVING SIZE:
½ CUP

PER SERVING
CALORIES: 60;
TOTAL FAT: 4G
   MONO: 2.5G;
   POLY: 0 G;
   SAT: 0.5G,
PROTEIN: 3G;
CARB: 6G;
FIBER: 3G;
CHOL: 0MG;
SODIUM: 148MG

EXCELLENT SOURCE OF
FOLATE,
VITAMIN A,
VITAMIN K

GOOD SOURCE OF
COPPER,
FIBER, IRON,
MANGANESE,
MOLYBDENUM,
RIBOFLAVIN,
THIAMIN,
VITAMIN C

Place the asparagus in a microwave-safe bowl with the water, cover tightly, and microwave on high for 2 minutes. Drain well.

While the asparagus is cooking, whisk together the oil, lemon zest and juice, salt, and pepper in a small bowl. Pour the dressing over the asparagus, add the tarragon, toss, and serve.

Lovin' Leftovers

For me, there is no richer treasure chest than a fridge full of leftovers. It means I can eat really well, effortlessly. That's why I often double a recipe just to have some to wrap up for another day. Some leftovers are delicious right out of the refrigerator, like Mom's Turkey Meatloaf (page 216), which makes incredible cold sandwiches, and Asparagus with Mimosa Topping (page 255), which does wonders for a boxed lunch. Others, like Chicken Cacciatore (page 204), just need to be gently reheated, and are just as good (if not better!) than the first time around.

Here are some guidelines for using your refrigerator and freezer to get two (or more) meals out of one.

SEAL AND COOL
Wrap leftovers and chill them as soon as possible. There is no need to wait for them to cool at room temperature. Just put them in shallow, covered containers and refrigerate immediately. Leftovers should never be left out on the counter for more than 2 hours, or 1 hour in hot weather. Meat, poultry, and vegetable dishes will keep refrigerated for about 3 days and seafood dishes for 2 days.

FREEZING FUNDAMENTALS
Stews, soups, chilis, and sauces freeze especially well. Consider freezing in individual portions in microwave-safe containers for convenient thawing and reheating. Meat dishes will last 2 to 3 months in the freezer, poultry 3 to 6 months, and seafood about 1 month. Label containers with the date and contents so you can keep track of what you have.

THAW AND HEAT RIGHT
Never thaw food at room temperature. That is just the right environment for bacteria to grow, and no one wants that. Instead, defrost in the refrigerator or, for quicker options, submerge the container in cold water, changing the water every half hour, or microwave on the low or defrost setting. When reheating, make sure you warm the food thoroughly, cooking it until it is bubbling hot throughout. When reheating in the microwave, stir and allow the food to sit after cooking so the heat can distribute evenly.

Asparagus with Mimosa Topping

A mimosa is not just a champagne cocktail; it is also the name of a classic French topping of crumbled egg, because its yellow color resembles the mimosa flower. This version is made with egg, toasted bread crumbs, and freshly grated Parmesan cheese. It's a flavorful sprinkle that turns simple steamed asparagus into something spectacular. This recipe makes a lot of asparagus, but the leftovers are very tasty and can be used as an ingredient in other recipes, like a frittata. It's best to store the asparagus and the topping in separate containers.

2 slices whole-wheat bread, crusts removed
Cooking spray
1 hard-boiled egg
3 tablespoons chopped fresh flat-leaf parsley
¼ cup freshly grated Parmesan cheese
¼ teaspoon salt
Pinch of freshly ground black pepper
2 bunches asparagus (about 2½ pounds), woody bottoms removed
1 tablespoon water

SERVES 8
SERVING SIZE: ABOUT 6 ASPARAGUS AND 3 TABLESPOONS TOPPING

EXCELLENT SOURCE OF
FOLATE, MANGANESE, VITAMIN A, VITAMIN K

PER SERVING
CALORIES 66;
TOTAL FAT: 2G,
   MONO: 0G,
   POLY: 0G;
   SAT: 1G,
PROTEIN: 6G;
CARB: 9G;
FIBER: 3.5G;
CHOL: 27MG;
SODIUM: 151MG

GOOD SOURCE OF
COPPER, FIBER, IRON, MOLYBDENUM, PHOSPHORUS, PROTEIN, RIBOFLAVIN, SELENIUM, THIAMIN, VITAMIN C

Pulse the bread in a food processor until it becomes fine crumbs. Coat a medium nonstick skillet with cooking spray and heat the pan over medium-high heat until hot. Lower the heat to medium, add the bread crumbs, and toast, tossing often, until they are golden brown and toasted, 5 to 6 minutes. Remove from the heat and let cool completely.

Peel, then grate the egg, using the medium holes of a box grater or on a medium rasp grater. Combine the egg, bread crumbs, parsley, Parmesan, salt, and pepper in a medium bowl and toss to combine.

Place the asparagus in a large microwave-safe bowl with the water. Cover tightly and microwave on high for 3 minutes. Drain well.

Arrange the asparagus on a serving platter and sprinkle evenly with the topping.

Shortcut Collard Greens

My version of this Southern comfort favorite is loaded with flavor—smoky meatiness from Canadian bacon, a spicy kick from red pepper flakes, and a touch of sweetness from maple syrup. The greens are simmered until nice and tender but take a fraction of the time of the traditional recipe, thanks to a quick start in the microwave.

1¼ pounds collard greens
1 tablespoon water
2 slices Canadian bacon (2 ounces)
1 tablespoon olive oil
1 small onion, chopped (about 1 cup)
1 tablespoon cider vinegar
1 tablespoon pure maple syrup
⅛ teaspoon red pepper flakes
¾ cup low-sodium chicken broth
Salt to taste

SERVES 4
SERVING SIZE:
½ CUP

PER SERVING
CALORIES: 138;
TOTAL FAT: 6G
  MONO: 3.6G,
  POLY: 1G;
  SAT: 1.2G,
PROTEIN: 9G;
CARB: 15G;
FIBER: 5G;
CHOL: 14MG;
SODIUM: 327MG

EXCELLENT
SOURCE OF
CALCIUM,
FIBER, FOLATE,
MANGANESE,
VITAMIN A,
VITAMIN C,
VITAMIN K

**GOOD
SOURCE OF**
MOLYBDENUM,
POTASSIUM,
PROTEIN,
RIBOFLAVIN,
VITAMIN B6

Remove the stems and center ribs from the collard greens and discard. Cut the leaves across into ½-inch-wide strips. Place the greens in a large, microwave-safe bowl with the water and cover tightly. Microwave on high for 5 minutes. Drain in a colander, shaking off any excess water.

   While the collards are cooking, heat a large skillet over medium-high heat and cook the bacon for 2 minutes on each side. Remove the bacon from the pan, chop, and set aside. Add the oil and onion to the pan and cook, stirring, until softened, about 3 minutes. Add the microwaved collard greens and stir in the vinegar, maple syrup, red pepper, and broth. Bring to a simmer and cook, covered, over low heat for 30 minutes.

   Add the chopped bacon to the pan, season with salt, and serve.

Getting the Most from Your Vegetables

BUY RIGHT

Vegetables begin to lose nutrients as soon as they are picked, so:

- **Look for local.** Locally grown produce doesn't have to travel as far from farm to table, so it will likely have retained more of its nutrients.
- **Don't buy too much.** It might seem like a bargain to buy three heads of that fresh broccoli on sale, but unless you are going to feed a crowd you are better off buying a smaller amount. Most fresh produce stays at peak quality only for a few days—keep in mind that the average head of broccoli travels more than 1,800 miles before it even gets to the store. Buy just what you plan to use that week.

STORE SMART

The way you store produce affects its taste and nutrition, so make sure you store it right.

- **Not everything goes in the fridge.** For optimal taste and texture, tomatoes should be kept at room temperature. Store potatoes, onions, and garlic in a dark, cool, well-ventilated place. Keep avocados at room temperature until ripe, then they can be refrigerated.
- **Paper or plastic?** Most other vegetables are best stored in the refrigerator in plastic bags, except mushrooms and chile peppers; store those in paper for better ventilation. Greens are best stored, unwashed, in perforated plastic bags. Herbs store well with their stems in a cup of water, then covered with a plastic bag secured with a rubber band.

COOK WITH CARE

How you prep and cook vegetables can make a huge difference nutritionally.

- **Wait to wash and cut.** Cutting and washing vegetables speeds their deterioration. To maximize nutrients, prep veggies just before you plan to cook or eat them.
- **Leave the peel.** A vegetable's peel contains a lot of nutrients and fiber, so leave it on whenever possible, like with cucumbers, potatoes, and summer squash. Just be sure to scrub well under cold water, and/or buy organic to minimize pesticide residues.
- **Cook in little water** Cooking inevitably destroys some nutrients, but it also releases others from the vegetable's cells. Minimize nutrient loss by cooking vegetables in as little water as possible (unless you'll be drinking the water, as in a soup) because water-soluble vitamins leach into the cooking liquid. Microwaving, steaming, and stir-frying are the best cooking methods for preserving nutrients.

Sesame Stir-Fried Chinese Greens

Chinese cabbage is a delicacy to me—mild yet flavorful, tender yet nicely crisp. The distinctively rich toasted sesame oil and a finishing sprinkle of sesame seeds give it a luxurious touch.

1 tablespoon sesame seeds
2 teaspoons canola oil
2 pounds bok choy or napa cabbage, cut across into 1-inch wide strips
2 tablespoons low-sodium soy sauce
1 tablespoon rice wine vinegar
2 teaspoons toasted sesame oil

Toast the sesame seeds in a small dry skillet over medium-high heat until golden, about 2 minutes, stirring frequently; set aside.

In a wok or large skillet, heat the oil over high heat until very hot but not smoking. Add the bok choy or cabbage and stir-fry until it begins to soften slightly, 1 to 2 minutes. Add the soy sauce, vinegar, and sesame oil and cook until just done, 1 to 2 minutes longer. Sprinkle with the sesame seeds and serve immediately.

SERVES 6
SERVING SIZE:
¾ CUP

PER SERVING
CALORIES: 61;
TOTAL FAT: 4G
  MONO: 1.5G,
  POLY: 1.3G;
  SAT: 0.4G;
PROTEIN: 3G;
CARB: 4G;
FIBER: 2G;
CHOL: 0MG;
SODIUM: 276MG

EXCELLENT SOURCE OF
FOLATE, IRON,
VITAMIN A,
VITAMIN C,
VITAMIN K

GOOD SOURCE OF
CALCIUM,
MANGANESE,
POTASSIUM,
VITAMIN B6

Grilled Romaine Hearts

If you want to really surprise your guests, toss some lettuce on the grill. Yes, lettuce. Grilling romaine until it wilts slightly but still retains its shape and underlying crispness intensifies and transforms its flavor. It tastes as delightful as it looks.

2 hearts of romaine lettuce
2 tablespoons olive oil
Salt and freshly ground black pepper to taste

Preheat your grill or a grill pan over medium-high heat.

Cut the romaine hearts in half lengthwise, leaving the end intact so each half holds together. Cut off the tops if they're bruised at all. Brush the hearts with the oil and grill over medium heat until they char and wilt slightly, about 6 minutes, turning a few times. Season with salt and pepper and serve immediately.

SERVES 4
SERVING SIZE:
1 ROMAINE HALF

PER SERVING
CALORIES: 85;
TOTAL FAT: 7G
  MONO: 5G,
  POLY: 0.5G;
  SAT: 1G;
PROTEIN: 1G;

CARB: 4G;
FIBER: 1G;
CHOL: 0MG;
SODIUM: 7MG

EXCELLENT SOURCE OF
VITAMIN A,
VITAMIN C

Go Organic

Organic food is produced without the application of chemical pesticides, growth hormones, or antibiotics. That means that organic farming and husbandry doesn't pollute the land, it is more humane for the farm animals, and it could be better for your health. Also, packaged organic foods are made without the addition of trans fat or artificial ingredients. They also tend to contain less sodium.

IS ORGANIC BETTER FOR YOU?

Eating organic food can significantly reduce your intake of pesticides and artificial additives. No one knows the health effect of consuming these chemicals over a lifetime, but experts agree that the less you are exposed to them, the better. Plus, there is emerging evidence that organic produce may contain higher levels of some antioxidants than conventionally grown produce.

IS ORGANIC WORTH THE EXTRA COST?

Organic foods can be more expensive than nonorganic, so going organic is a decision based on what is important to you and what you can afford. You can take comfort in knowing the benefits of eating fruits and vegetables, grains, lowfat dairy, and lean meat, even if they are not organic, far outweigh any downsides. But when you consider all that organic food provides, you'll probably be convinced of its value.

START SMALL

You don't have to commit to organic 100% in order to reap the benefits. Generally, the most important fruits and vegetables to buy organic are those with soft skins that you don't peel. So as a starting point, get organic grapes, but stick to conventional bananas. Another way to approach it is to look at the foods you and your family eat most often, and make those staples organic.

Tomato Stuffed Peppers

In this stunning dish, red pepper halves make little boats that hold tomato, garlic, and cured olives. All the juices collect in them as the vegetables soften and their flavors mellow and meld. Enjoy this with some crusty bread for sopping up every last drop.

Cooking spray
4 large red bell peppers
2 cloves garlic, thinly sliced
3 tablespoons chopped calamata olives
4 medium ripe tomatoes
2 tablespoons olive oil
Freshly ground black pepper

SERVES 4
SERVING SIZE:
1 PEPPER

EXCELLENT SOURCE OF
VITAMIN A,
VITAMIN C

PER SERVING
CALORIES: 150;
TOTAL FAT: 9G
  MONO: 6.5G,
  POLY: 1G;
  SAT: 1G,
PROTEIN: 2.5G;
CARB: 15G;
FIBER: 3G;
CHOL: 0MG;
SODIUM: 100MG

GOOD SOURCE OF
FIBER,
POTASSIUM,
VITAMIN B6,
VITAMIN E

Preheat the oven to 375°F. Coat a large, shallow baking dish with cooking spray.

Cut the peppers in half lengthwise, removing the seeds but leaving the stem. Although the stem is not edible, it looks good in this dish and helps the pepper retain its shape. Place the peppers cut side up in the baking dish.

Divide the sliced garlic and olives evenly among the peppers. Cut each tomato into 8 wedges and put 4 wedges into each pepper half. Drizzle each stuffed pepper with a little oil and season with a few grinds of pepper.

Roast the peppers until they are tender and beginning to brown around the edges, about 50 minutes. Serve immediately.

✳ DID YOU KNOW?
One red pepper has three times the vitamin C of an orange!

Smashed Potatoes with Sour Cream and Chives

These mashed potatoes are true home-style comfort, smashed so they have a rustic chunkiness and mixed with familiar mashed potato flavors—tangy sour cream and chives.

1¼ pounds Yukon Gold potatoes (about 4 medium), left unpeeled
    and cut into 1-inch pieces
¼ cup low-sodium chicken broth, warmed
¼ cup reduced-fat sour cream
1½ tablespoons chopped fresh chives
Salt and freshly ground black pepper to taste

Place the potatoes in a steamer basket fitted over a large pot of boiling water. Cover and steam until the potatoes are knife-tender, 12 to 15 minutes.

Drain the potatoes and return them to their pot. Add the warm broth and coarsely mash. Stir in the sour cream and chives, season with salt and pepper, and serve.

SERVES 4
SERVING SIZE:
¾ CUP

PER SERVING
CALORIES: 130;
TOTAL FAT: 2G
    MONO: 0G,
    POLY: 0G;
    SAT: 1G,
PROTEIN: 4G;
CARB: 24G;
FIBER: 2.5G;
CHOL: 8MG;
SODIUM: 22MG

**EXCELLENT
SOURCE OF**
POTASSIUM,
    VITAMIN C

**GOOD
SOURCE OF**
FIBER,
MANGANESE,
NIACIN,
PHOSPHORUS,
VITAMIN B6

Parmesan Mashed Potatoes

These buttery-tasting mashed potatoes owe their velvety texture to naturally creamy Yukon Gold potatoes and rich, tangy buttermilk. Parmesan pumps up the flavor further.

1¼ pounds Yukon Gold potatoes (about 4 medium),
    left unpeeled and cut into 1-inch pieces
¼ cup low-fat buttermilk
¼ cup nonfat milk
2 tablespoons freshly grated Parmesan cheese
Salt to taste
2 teaspoons unsalted butter (optional), cut into 4 pieces

SERVES 4
SERVING SIZE:
¾ CUP

PER SERVING
CALORIES: 209;
TOTAL FAT: 7G
    MONO: 0G,
    POLY: 0G;
    SAT: 1.5G,

PROTEIN: 5.5G;
CARB: 32G;
FIBER: 3G;
CHOL: 2.5MG;
SODIUM: 518MG

**GOOD
SOURCE OF**
FIBER

Place the potatoes in a steamer basket fitted over a large pot of boiling water. Cover and steam until the potatoes are knife-tender, 12 to 15 minutes.

While the potatoes are cooking, combine the buttermilk and regular milk in a small saucepan and cook over the lowest possible heat until just warm. Be careful not to let it boil or the milk will curdle.

Dairy Done Right

Just like with cheese (see Cheese Rules! on page 171), the kind of milk, yogurt, and cream you buy can make or break a dish, health-wise and taste-wise. Here are a few simple guidelines to help you navigate the dairy aisle.

GO LOW WITH MILK AND YOGURT

Milk and yogurt are the most wholesome of foods, packed with protein, calcium, and B vitamins. But most people don't realize that a glass of regular milk or cup of regular yogurt has nearly the same amount of fat as two pats of butter. When milk and yogurt are skimmed, you wind up with a great nutritional bargain. Fat is taken out but no additives are put in. I find nonfat (skim) or lowfat milk, yogurt, and buttermilk work well in most recipes. If you really need the extra body, try evaporated lowfat milk or just go for full-fat.

LESS (FAT) IS MORE

With some dairy, going nonfat does compromise taste and texture, but reduced fat is a great alternative—examples are ice cream, frozen yogurt, and sour cream. There are many wonderful light ice creams and frozen yogurts on the market that are less rich but just as coolly satisfying as full-fat versions. I always look for those with all-natural ingredients so I don't get stuck eating a bowlful of additives. Same goes for sour cream—reduced fat is the way to go.

A LITTLE OF THE REAL THING

Some foods, like whipped cream, just cannot be duplicated with less fat. To me, nonfat or lower fat whipped toppings and creamers taste just like the chemicals they are made of. In the case of whipped cream or a dash of cream added to a sauce, use the real thing, just don't overindulge.

Drain the potatoes, return them to their pot, add the warmed milk, and mash together to the consistency you prefer. Stir in the Parmesan and season with salt. If desired, serve with a dab of butter on top.

EATING WELL TIP

Putting a pat of butter on top of the mashed potatoes gives you maximum sensory impact. It satisfies you by announcing visually that something rich and creamy is coming.

Garlic "Fries"

I have to confess, french fries are one of my favorite foods. I can't resist them, whether they are from a fast-food drive-through or a fine restaurant. Luckily, these garlic-laced "fries" satisfy my cravings in a more healthful way. They come out golden brown, tender on the inside and crisp outside. A final toss with chopped parsley gives them that real French bistro feel.

3 cloves garlic, minced (about 1 tablespoon)
2 tablespoons canola oil
3 large baking potatoes
½ teaspoon salt, plus more to taste
Cooking spray
1 tablespoon finely chopped fresh flat-leaf parsley

SERVES 4
SERVING SIZE:
¾ CUP

PER SERVING
CALORIES: 270;
TOTAL FAT: 7G
  MONO: 4G,
  POLY: 2G;
  SAT: 0.6G;
PROTEIN: 6G;
CARB: 47G;
FIBER: 3.5G;
CHOL: 0MG;
SODIUM:
304MG

EXCELLENT SOURCE OF
MANGANESE,
POTASSIUM,
VITAMIN B6,
VITAMIN C,
VITAMIN K

GOOD SOURCE OF
COPPER, FIBER,
FOLATE, IRON,
MAGNESIUM,
NIACIN,
PHOSPHORUS,
PROTEIN,
THIAMIN

Preheat the oven to 450°F.

Heat the garlic and oil together in a small saucepan over medium heat for 2 minutes. Strain the garlic from the oil with a small mesh strainer. Set both garlic and oil aside.

Cut the potatoes into ¼-inch-thick matchsticks. In a large bowl, toss together the oil, potatoes, and salt. Coat a baking sheet with cooking spray and spread the potatoes on it in a single layer. Bake until golden and crisp, about 35 minutes.

Remove the potatoes from the baking sheet with a metal spatula. In a serving bowl, toss them with the parsley, reserved garlic, and salt to taste. Serve immediately.

Mashed Sweet Potatoes with Orange Essence

Zesty orange is just the thing to enliven the rich, deep flavor of sweet potato. It adds an unexpected brightness and an almost refreshing quality to this mash. Serve it at your next holiday dinner and you'll never go back to marshmallows again.

2 large sweet potatoes (about 1½ pounds), peeled and cut into 1-inch pieces
¼ cup lowfat buttermilk
2 tablespoons fresh orange juice
1 teaspoon finely grated orange zest
Pinch of ground nutmeg
1 teaspoon light brown sugar (optional)
Salt to taste
2 teaspoons unsalted butter (optional), cut into 4 pieces

SERVES 4
SERVING SIZE: ⅔ CUP

PER SERVING
CALORIES: 157;
TOTAL FAT: 0G;
PROTEIN: 3G;
CARB: 36G;
FIBER: 5G;
CHOL: 0.5MG;
SODIUM: 110MG

EXCELLENT SOURCE OF
FIBER,
MANGANESE,
THIAMIN,
VITAMIN A

GOOD SOURCE OF
COPPER,
MAGNESIUM,
MOLYBDENUM,
PANTOTHENIC
ACID, PHOS
PHORUS,
POTASSIUM,
VITAMIN B6,
VITAMIN C

Place the sweet potatoes in a steamer basket fitted over a large pot of boiling water. Cover and steam until the potatoes are knife-tender, 12 to 15 minutes.

While potatoes are cooking, place the buttermilk into a small saucepan and cook over the lowest possible heat until just warm. Be careful not to let it boil or it will curdle.

Drain the potatoes and return them to their pot. Add the warm buttermilk and orange juice and mash until smooth. Stir in the orange zest, nutmeg, and brown sugar, if using. Season with salt. Serve the potatoes topped with the butter, if desired.

Honey-Roasted Sweet Potatoes

Roasting sweet potatoes concentrates their flavor and leaves them caramelized outside and tender inside. Coating them with a touch of lemon and honey before cooking makes them all the more flavorful.

3 large sweet potatoes (about 2 pounds), peeled and cut into 1-inch pieces
2 tablespoons olive oil
2 tablespoons honey
1 teaspoon fresh lemon juice
½ teaspoon salt, plus more to taste

SERVES 6
SERVING SIZE:
¾ CUP

PER SERVING
CALORIES: 170;
TOTAL FAT: 5G
 MONO: 3G,
 POLY: 0.5G;
 SAT: 0.5G;
PROTEIN: 2G;
CARB: 30G;
FIBER: 4G;
CHOL: 0MG;
SODIUM: 237MG

**EXCELLENT
SOURCE OF**
MANGANESE,
VITAMIN A,
VITAMIN C

**GOOD
SOURCE OF**
COPPER, FIBER,
PANTOTHENIC
ACID, POTASSIUM,
VITAMIN B6

Preheat the oven to 350°F.

Place the potatoes in a 9 x 13-inch baking dish. In a small bowl, whisk together the oil, honey, and lemon juice. Pour the mixture over the potatoes and toss to coat. Sprinkle with the salt, and bake, stirring occasionally, until the potatoes are tender, about 1 hour. Season with more salt to taste and serve.

✳ DID YOU KNOW?
Citrus zest packs more than a flavor punch. It contains a compound called D-limonine, which could help prevent skin cancer.

Oven-Baked Onion Rings

Tangy buttermilk and crushed baked potato chips make a flavorful coating for these big sweet onion rings that brown into a beautifully crunchy shell in the oven.

Canola oil spray
4 cups baked potato chips
½ teaspoon cayenne pepper
1 cup low-fat buttermilk
½ cup plus 2 tablespoons all-purpose flour
½ teaspoon salt, plus more to taste
¼ teaspoon freshly ground black pepper
1 to 2 large Vidalia onions, peeled

SERVES 4
SERVING SIZE: 3 TO 4 ONION RINGS

PER SERVING
CALORIES: 205;
TOTAL FAT: 3.5G
MONO: 0G,
POLY: 0G;
SAT: 0G,
PROTEIN: 5G;
CARB: 40G;
FIBER: 2G;

CHOL: 1MG;
SODIUM: 530MG

EXCELLENT SOURCE OF VITAMIN C

GOOD SOURCE OF CALCIUM, FOLATE, PROTEIN

Preheat the oven to 450°F. Coat a baking sheet lightly with cooking spray and set aside.

Place the potato chips in a food processor and process into fine crumbs, about 20 seconds. Transfer to a shallow bowl, stir in the cayenne, and set aside. In another bowl, combine the buttermilk, 2 tablespoons of the flour, the salt, and pepper and set aside.

Slice the onions into ½-inch-thick rounds and separate into rings, keeping only the large, whole rings (reserve the rest of the onion for other uses). You should have 12 to 14 rings.

Place the remaining ½ cup flour in a sealable plastic bag, then add the onions and shake to coat. One at a time, dip the onion rings into the buttermilk mixture, then dip into the potato chip crumbs, coating each ring evenly, and place on the baking sheet. Coat the surface of the rings lightly with canola oil spray and bake until the coating is crisp, about 20 minutes. Season with salt and serve immediately.

Grilled Scallion Skewers

Grilling brings out the natural sugars in the scallions, giving them a succulent sweetness. These skewers look gorgeous and taste fantastic alongside any kind of grilled kebab or meat.

4 wooden skewers, soaked in water for 20 minutes
20 scallions
2 teaspoons olive oil

SERVES 4	CHOL: 0MG;
SERVING SIZE:	SODIUM: 12MG
1 SKEWER	
	EXCELLENT
PER SERVING	**SOURCE OF**
CALORIES: 45;	VITAMIN C
TOTAL FAT: 2.5G	VITAMIN K
MONO: 2G,	
POLY: 0G;	**GOOD**
SAT: 0G,	**SOURCE OF**
PROTEIN: 1G;	FOLATE,
CARB: 6G;	VITAMIN A
FIBER: 2G;	

Preheat the grill or a grill pan over medium-high heat.

Cut the roots and tops off of the scallions so you have the bulb plus 1 inch of the green left. Reserve the scallion tops for another use.

Make a few slices into the green part of the scallion so it splays out a little. Thread 5 scallions onto each of the skewers, brush with the oil, and grill over medium heat until they are softened and develop char marks, about 10 minutes, turning once or twice.

Herbed Couscous Timbale with Dried Fruits and Nuts

This colorful couscous dish is studded with enticing tastes and textures: chewy, sweet dried fruit; crunchy, buttery toasted nuts; and aromatic fresh basil. The extra step of molding it in ramekins turns it from simple to sophisticated.

3 tablespoons pine nuts
1 cup low-sodium chicken broth
1 cup couscous, preferably whole-wheat
¼ cup dried currants
⅓ cup chopped dried apricots (about 8 apricots)
¼ cup fresh basil ribbons
1 teaspoon finely grated lemon zest
½ cup seeded and finely diced red bell pepper

SERVES 6	CHOL: 0MG;
SERVING SIZE:	SODIUM: 22MG
½ CUP	
	EXCELLENT
PER SERVING	**SOURCE OF**
CALORIES: 165;	VITAMIN C,
TOTAL FAT: 5G	VITAMIN K
MONO: 1.5G,	
POLY: 2G;	**GOOD**
SAT: 1G,	**SOURCE OF**
PROTEIN: 5G;	FIBER, IRON,
CARB: 27G;	PROTEIN,
FIBER: 4G;	VITAMIN A

Toast the pine nuts in a small dry skillet over medium-high heat until golden, about 2 minutes, stirring frequently; set aside.

In a medium saucepan, bring the broth to a boil. Remove from the heat. Stir in the couscous, cover, and let stand for 5 minutes.

Uncover and fluff with a fork. Stir in the currants, apricots, 2 tablespoons of the pine nuts, most of the basil, the lemon zest, and all but 2 tablespoons of the red pepper. Pack the couscous into a 4-inch ramekin, a ½-cup measure, or a cookie cutter and invert onto each serving plate. Top with a sprinkle of the remaining red pepper, pine nuts, and basil and serve.

Garden Risotto

Don't let risotto intimidate you, it's really quite easy. The key is to use Arborio rice, an Italian short-grain rice that gives the dish its decadent, creamy texture. This risotto had a field day in the garden and returned as two side dishes in one—vegetable and grain.

½ pound asparagus, woody bottoms removed
6 cups low-sodium chicken broth
2 teaspoons olive oil
1 medium onion, chopped (about 1½ cups)
1½ cups Arborio rice
½ cup dry white wine
¾ teaspoon salt
Freshly ground black pepper
3 ounces baby spinach leaves (about 3 cups lightly packed)
1 cup frozen peas
¼ cup freshly grated Parmesan cheese

SERVES 6
SERVING SIZE:
1 CUP

PER SERVING
CALORIES: 205;
TOTAL FAT: 4G
  MONO: 2G,
  POLY: 0.5G;
  SAT: 1.5G,
PROTEIN: 10.5G;
CARB: 30G;
FIBER: 3.5G;
CHOL: 1MG;
SODIUM: 466MG

EXCELLENT SOURCE OF
NIACIN, PROTEIN,
VITAMIN A,
VITAMIN C,
VITAMIN K

GOOD SOURCE OF
FIBER, FOLATE,
IRON,
PHOSPHORUS,
POTASSIUM,
RIBOFLAVIN,
THIAMIN

Microwave the asparagus in a tightly covered microwave-safe bowl with 1 teaspoon water for 90 seconds, and cut into ¾-inch pieces; set aside.

Bring the broth to a simmer in a medium saucepan. Heat the oil in a large heavy saucepan over medium-low heat and cook the onion, stirring a few times, until softened, 3 to 5 minutes. Add the rice and cook, stirring constantly, for 1 minute. Add the wine and simmer, stirring constantly, until absorbed, about 1 minute. Add ¾ cup of the hot broth, the salt, and a few grinds of pepper and simmer, stirring constantly, until the broth is absorbed. Continue simmering and adding hot broth, about ¾ cup at a time, stirring frequently and allowing the broth to be absorbed before adding more, until the rice is almost tender and creamy looking, about 18 minutes.

Stir in the spinach and peas and cook until the spinach is wilted. Add the asparagus and cook just until the vegetables are hot. Stir in the Parmesan and a little more broth if the risotto seems too thick. Serve in soup plates.

desserts

Banana Cream Pie

Fragrant vanilla pudding cradled in a graham cracker crumb crust, topped with bananas and real whipped cream—no wonder this pie is the reigning favorite at my in-laws' house!

Cooking spray
14 graham cracker squares (7 full sheets)
2 tablespoons unsalted butter, softened
1 tablespoon water
1½ teaspoons unflavored gelatin
3 tablespoons boiling water
⅓ cup plus ½ teaspoon sugar
3 tablespoons all-purpose flour
1½ cups low-fat milk
2 large egg yolks
1 teaspoon vanilla extract
2 cups ¼-inch-thick banana slices (3 medium bananas)
¼ cup well-chilled heavy cream

SERVES 8
MAKES ONE
9-INCH PIE;
SERVING SIZE:
1 SLICE

PROTEIN: 4G;
CARB: 33G;
FIBER: 1.5G;
CHOL: 72MG;
SODIUM: 102MG

PER SERVING
CALORIES: 218;
TOTAL FAT: 8G
  MONO: 2G;
  POLY: 1G;
  SAT: 4G,

**GOOD
SOURCE OF**
MANGANESE,
VITAMIN B6

Preheat the oven to 350°F. Coat a 9-inch pie plate with cooking spray.

To make the crust, in a food processor, process the graham crackers until finely ground. Add the butter and water and process until the crumbs clump together. Press the mixture into the bottom of the pie plate and about 1 inch up the sides. Bake for 10 minutes, then let cool.

Meanwhile, make the filling. Put the gelatin in a small bowl; add the boiling water and stir until the gelatin is dissolved. In a medium saucepan, whisk together ⅓ cup of the sugar and the flour. In a medium bowl, lightly beat the milk and egg yolks together. Add the egg-and-milk mixture to the saucepan and whisk so the flour and sugar dissolve. Cook over medium heat, stirring constantly, until the mixture comes to a boil and has thickened. Stir in the vanilla and gelatin slurry. Set aside to cool slightly.

Arrange the sliced banana in the crust and pour the pudding on top. Place in the refrigerator until the pudding has set, about 3 hours.

Whip the cream in a medium bowl with an electric mixer. When it is about halfway to soft peaks, add the remaining ½ teaspoon sugar, then continue whipping until it barely holds a soft peak. Put the whipped cream in a plastic bag, concentrating it in one corner of the bag. Snip that corner off the bag and squeeze the whipped cream out of the bag in a decorative pattern around the pie. The pie will keep in the refrigerator for 1 to 2 days.

✳ **DID YOU KNOW?**
Graham flour is a whole-wheat flour that is ground coarser than other flours. All graham crackers contain at least some graham flour, but ideally look for 100% whole-wheat graham crackers.

Plum Tart with Almond Pastry Crust

This tart is a true showcase for nature's best, so it is as good as the fruit you use. If you can't find great plums, go for perfectly ripe peaches or pears in season.

6 ripe but firm plums (about 1½ pounds)

5 tablespoons sugar, plus more to taste

¼ teaspoon plus ⅛ teaspoon ground cinnamon

½ teaspoon fresh lemon juice

Heaping ⅓ cup unsalted blanched almonds

1 cup whole-wheat pastry flour or regular whole-wheat flour

¼ teaspoon salt

⅛ teaspoon ground nutmeg

2 tablespoons chilled unsalted butter, cubed

2 tablespoons canola oil

1 large egg white

1 tablespoon seedless raspberry or strawberry preserves,
   mixed with 2 teaspoons water

SERVES 8
MAKES ONE
9-INCH TART;
SERVING SIZE:
1 SLICE

PER SERVING
CALORIES: 185
TOTAL FAT: 10G
   MONO: 4G,
   POLY: 1G;
   SAT: 2G,
PROTEIN: 4G;
CARB: 25G;

FIBER: 1.5G;
CHOL: 7.5 MG;
SODIUM: 80MG

**EXCELLENT
SOURCE OF**
THIAMIN

**GOOD
SOURCE OF**
FIBER,
VITAMIN K

To prepare the filling, fill a large stockpot halfway with water and bring to a boil. While water is coming to a boil, take a paring knife and cut a half-inch "x" on the bottom of each plum. Set aside. Fill a large bowl with ice and water and set aside. When the water is boiling, gently drop the plums into the water until their skins begin to separate from the flesh, 30 to 45 seconds. Remove with a slotted spoon and immediately submerge in the ice water for 2 minutes. Remove from the water. Over a medium bowl, remove the skins from the plums—they should slip off fairly easily. Slice the plums in half and remove the pits. Toss with 1 tablespoon of the sugar, ¼ teaspoon of the cinnamon, and the lemon juice. Add one or two more teaspoons of sugar to taste if necessary, to adjust for variations in the natural sweetness of the fruit. Set aside.

To make the crust, preheat the oven to 375°F. Grind the almonds into fine crumbs in a food processor. Add the flour, salt, nutmeg, and the remaining 4 tablespoons sugar and ⅛ teaspoon cinnamon and pulse five times to incorporate. Add the butter and oil and process for about 20 seconds, until the mixture is moistened. Add the egg white and pulse another 20 times. The dough will be crumbly and slightly sticky. Evenly press the dough into the bottom and up the sides a 9-inch tart pan with a detachable bottom.
Bake until the surface of the crust is no longer shiny, 8 to 10 minutes. Remove from the oven and let cool.

Place the tart shell, still in the tart pan, on a cookie sheet. Arrange the plum halves, cut side down, in the tart shell, crowding as many plums as you can into the tart. Bake until the fruit is slightly tender but still firm, 15 to 20 minutes. Remove from the oven and let cool.

Heat the preserves and water over low heat in a small saucepan until melted. Brush over the plums. Remove the tart from the pan and place on a serving plate. Store in the refrigerator for up to 1 day.

Double Chocolate Pudding Pie

Growing up, a holiday at my house just wasn't a holiday without my grandma's chocolate pudding pie. I still make it at holiday time, but have lightened it up while intensifying the chocolate flavor.

Cooking spray
14 graham cracker squares (7 full sheets)
2 tablespoons unsalted butter, softened
1 tablespoon water
1 tablespoon unflavored gelatin
⅓ cup boiling water
⅔ cup plus ½ teaspoon sugar
⅓ cup unsweetened cocoa powder
¼ cup cornstarch
⅛ teaspoon salt
3 cups lowfat milk
2 ounces bittersweet chocolate, chopped
2 teaspoons vanilla extract
¼ cup well-chilled heavy cream

SERVES 8
MAKES ONE
9-INCH PIE;
SERVING SIZE :
1 SLICE

PROTEIN: 7G;
CARB: 35G;
FIBER: 2G;
CHOL: 23MG;
SODIUM: 165MG

PER SERVING
CALORIES: 255;
TOTAL FAT: 11G
  MONO: 2.5G,
  POLY: 0.7G;
  SAT: 5.7G,

GOOD SOURCE OF
CALCIUM,
PROTEIN,
VITAMIN D

Preheat the oven to 350°F. Coat a 9-inch pie plate with cooking spray.

To make the crust, in a food processor, process the graham crackers until finely ground. Add the butter and water, and process until the crumbs clump together. Press the mixture into the bottom of the pie plate and about 1 inch up the sides. Bake for 10 minutes, then let cool.

Meanwhile, make the filling. Put the gelatin in a small bowl, add the boiling water and stir until dissolved. Set aside.

In a medium saucepan, mix ⅔ cup of the sugar, the cocoa powder, cornstarch, and salt. Gradually add half of the milk, whisking until the mixture is smooth. Whisk in the rest of the milk. Turn the heat to medium and cook, whisking constantly, until the mixture thickens and comes to a boil, about 10 minutes. Remove from the heat. Add the bittersweet chocolate and stir until it is melted. Stir in the vanilla and the gelatin slurry. Pour the mixture into the pie crust and let set for 3 hours in the refrigerator.

Whip the cream in a medium bowl with an electric mixer. When it is about halfway to soft peaks, add the remaining ½ teaspoon sugar, then continue whipping until it barely holds a soft peak. Put the whipped cream in a plastic bag, concentrating it in one corner of the bag. Snip that corner off the bag and squeeze the whipped cream out of the bag in a decorative pattern around the pie. The pie should be stored in the refrigerator, where it will keep for 2 to 3 days.

Ricotta Cheesecake with Fresh Raspberries

This luxuriously creamy cheesecake is a dessert triple-treat. It tastes incredible, looks gorgeous, and it's easy to make. As it bakes, it forms its own golden brown "crust," and it is absolutely stunning crowned with ruby-red raspberries.

Cooking spray
One 15-ounce container part-skim ricotta cheese
½ cup reduced-fat sour cream
4 ounces Neufchâtel cheese (reduced-fat cream cheese), softened
3 large eggs
¾ cup sugar
¼ cup all-purpose flour
1 teaspoon vanilla extract
1 teaspoon finely grated orange zest
¼ teaspoon salt
¼ cup all-fruit seedless raspberry jam
1 tablespoon orange liqueur or water
Two 6-ounce containers fresh raspberries

SERVES 8
MAKES ONE 9-INCH CHEESECAKE; SERVING SIZE: 1 SLICE

PER SERVING
CALORIES: 295;
TOTAL FAT: 13G
MONO: 1G
POLY: 0G;
SAT: 8G,

PROTEIN: 10G;
CARB: 36G;
FIBER: 3G;
CHOL: 127MG;
SODIUM: 375MG

GOOD SOURCE OF
CALCIUM, FIBER, PROTEIN, VITAMIN A, VITAMIN C

Preheat the oven to 325°F. Coat a 9-inch springform pan with cooking spray.

Place the ricotta in a food processor and process until smooth and creamy. Add the sour cream, Neufchâtel, eggs, sugar, flour, vanilla, orange zest, and salt and process until well blended. Pour into the prepared pan and bake until the center is just set, 50 to 55 minutes.

Transfer to a wire rack to cool, then cover and chill in the refrigerator for at least 3 hours before removing it from the pan. The cheesecake will be about 2 inches high.

In a small saucepan, bring the jam and liqueur to a boil over low heat, stirring constantly until smooth. Brush the cheesecake with the jam mixture and top with raspberries, flat side down. The cake should be stored in the refrigerator, where it will keep for 2 to 3 days.

Mocha Cake with Mocha Cream Cheese Frosting

A shot of espresso makes this dense chocolate cake even moister and gives it a tantalizing java jolt. It's topped with a decadent, yet not overly sweet, cream cheese frosting spiked with coffee to echo the flavor in the cake. It's your childhood favorite chocolate cake, all grown up.

For the cake

Cooking spray
¾ cup whole-wheat pastry flour or regular whole-wheat flour
½ cup all-purpose flour
½ cup unsweetened cocoa powder, preferably Dutch-processed
¼ teaspoon salt
1 teaspoon baking soda
1 teaspoon baking powder
2 tablespoons unsalted butter, melted
2 tablespoons canola oil
2 large eggs
2 large egg whites
1½ cups plain nonfat yogurt
2 teaspoons vanilla extract
¾ cup granulated sugar
1 tablespoon instant espresso powder, dissolved in 1 tablespoon hot water
2 ounces good-quality dark chocolate (60–70% cocoa solids)

For the frosting

One 8-ounce package Neufchâtel cheese (reduced-fat cream cheese), softened
⅓ cup confectioners' sugar
1 teaspoon instant espresso powder, dissolved in 1 teaspoon hot water
1 teaspoon coffee liqueur or vanilla extract

For garnish

1 small square (¹⁄₁₆ ounce) good-quality dark chocolate (60–70% cocoa solids)

SERVES 16
SERVING SIZE: ONE 2¼ X 3¼-INCH SQUARE

PROTEIN: 5G;
CARB: 24G;
FIBER: 1G;
CHOL: 41MG;
SODIUM: 238MG

PER SERVING
CALORIES: 191;
TOTAL FAT: 10.5G
    MONO: 2G,
    POLY: 1G;
    SAT: 4G,

GOOD
SOURCE OF
PROTEIN,
THIAMIN

Arrange a rack in the center of the oven and preheat the oven to 350°F. Coat a 9 x 13-inch cake pan with cooking spray and set aside.

Whisk together both flours, the cocoa, salt, baking soda, and baking powder in a medium bowl.

In a large bowl, whisk together the melted butter and oil. Add the whole eggs and egg whites and whisk to incorporate. Fold in the yogurt, vanilla, granulated sugar, and dissolved espresso powder. Melt the chocolate in a small microwave-safe bowl in the microwave for 90 seconds on high or over simmering water in a double

boiler. Fold the melted chocolate into the batter. Gradually add the dry ingredients and stir until just incorporated; do not overbeat. Pour the batter into the prepared pan. Bake until the cake has risen nicely and a toothpick inserted into the center comes out clean, 25 to 30 minutes. Let cool completely on a rack.

While the cake is cooling, make the frosting. Combine all the frosting ingredients in a medium bowl and beat with an electric mixer until soft and creamy. Spread the frosting evenly over the cooled cake in the pan and cut into squares. Finely grate the square of chocolate on the small holes of a box grater or using a rasp grater. Sprinkle the chocolate shavings over the cake. The cake should be stored in the refrigerator, where it will keep for about 3 days.

Carrot Cake Cupcakes with Lemony Cream Cheese Frosting

These cupcakes are moist, studded with nuts, fragrant with nutmeg and cinnamon, and topped with a velvety cream cheese frosting. Whenever I make them, I half expect a line to start forming outside my door!

For the cupcakes
¾ cup whole-wheat pastry flour or regular whole-wheat flour
½ cup all-purpose flour
1 teaspoon baking soda
¼ teaspoon salt
½ teaspoon ground cinnamon
¼ teaspoon ground nutmeg
¼ cup canola oil
¾ cup firmly packed light brown sugar
2 large eggs
½ cup natural unsweetened applesauce
½ teaspoon vanilla extract
1½ cups finely shredded carrots (about 2 carrots)
¼ cup finely chopped walnuts

For the frosting
4 ounces Neufchâtel cheese (reduced-fat cream cheese), softened
¾ cup confectioners' sugar
½ teaspoon finely grated lemon zest

For garnish
2 tablespoons finely chopped walnuts

SERVES 12
SERVING SIZE: 1 CUPCAKE

CHOL: 42MG;
SODIUM: 220MG

PER SERVING
CALORIES: 230;
TOTAL FAT: 10G
MONO: 3.5G,
POLY: 3G;
SAT: 2G,
PROTEIN: 4G;
CARB: 32G;
FIBER: 1.5G;

EXCELLENT SOURCE OF VITAMIN A

GOOD SOURCE OF MANGANESE, VITAMIN K

Preheat the oven to 350°F. Line 12 muffin cups with paper liners.

In a medium bowl, sift together both flours, the baking soda, salt, and spices. In a large bowl, whisk together the oil, brown sugar, and eggs until well combined. Whisk in the applesauce, vanilla, and carrots. Add the dry ingredients and mix until just combined. Stir in the walnuts.

Divide the batter between the muffin cups. Bake until a toothpick inserted in a cupcake comes out clean, about 20 minutes. Transfer to a wire rack to cool completely.

To make the frosting, with an electric mixer, beat together the cream cheese, confectioners' sugar, and lemon zest until smooth and creamy. Frost the cooled cupcakes and sprinkle with the walnuts. The cupcakes should be stored in the refrigerator, where they will keep for about 3 days.

Grilled Bananas with Chai Syrup

Exotically spiced chai tea and honey make a memorably sumptuous syrup to bathe intensely sweet grilled bananas. It's different and exciting but somehow feels like a familiar comfort food. The syrup also works well on grilled peaches or pineapple.

For the chai syrup
½ cup water
1 chai tea bag
¾ cup honey
5 black peppercorns
1 cinnamon stick
1 whole star anise
2 cardamom pods
2 whole cloves
One 1-inch piece fresh ginger, peeled

For the grilled bananas
Cooking spray
4 ripe, firm bananas

SERVES 4
SERVING SIZE:
2 BANANA
HALVES AND
2 TABLESPOONS
SYRUP

**EXCELLENT
SOURCE OF**
MANGANESE,
VITAMIN B6,
VITAMIN C

PER SERVING
CALORIES: 300;
TOTAL FAT: 0G;
PROTEIN: 2G;
CARB: 79G;
FIBER: 3G;
CHOL: 0MG;
SODIUM: 20MG

**GOOD
SOURCE OF**
FIBER,
POTASSIUM,
RIBOFLAVIN

To make the syrup, in a small saucepan, boil the water. Turn off the heat, add the tea bag, and brew the tea, leaving the bag in the water until cool and the tea is very dark. Remove the tea bag, squeezing out the excess tea. Add the honey, spices, and ginger. Bring to a boil, then reduce the heat to a simmer and simmer until the liquid has reduced to 1 cup, 5 to 7 minutes. Remove from the heat and let cool for 30 minutes. Using a fine-mesh strainer or tea brewer, strain out the whole spices and ginger. The syrup should be thinner than honey, but still have body.

To grill the bananas, coat the grate of an outdoor grill or a grill pan with cooking spray and preheat over medium-high heat. Peel, then slice the bananas in half lengthwise. Grill the fruit until slightly softened and light grill marks form, 2 to 3 minutes per side.

Place 2 banana halves on a dessert plate, drizzle with 2 tablespoons syrup, and serve.

Pear-Ginger Crumble

Here tender, sweet pears are spiked with zingy ginger and baked under a sweet crumb topping. It is a wonderful dessert, especially when it is served warm à la mode. I have to admit I have been known to indulge in the leftovers for breakfast the morning after with a dollop of yogurt.

For the topping

¼ cup oat flour or whole-wheat flour

⅔ cup old-fashioned rolled oats

½ cup firmly packed light brown sugar

1 teaspoon ground cinnamon

⅛ teaspoon salt

¼ cup canola oil

For the filling

3 pounds firm but ripe pears, peeled, cored, and cut into ¼-inch-thick slices

1 tablespoon fresh lemon juice

1 tablespoon peeled and grated fresh ginger

2 tablespoons granulated sugar

1½ tablespoons all-purpose flour

For the assembly

Cooking spray

2 cups light vanilla ice cream or frozen vanilla yogurt (optional)

SERVES 8
SERVING SIZE: ¾ CUP

PER SERVING
CALORIES: 265;
TOTAL FAT: 8G,
  MONO: 4G,
  POLY: 2G;
  SAT: 0.6G,
PROTEIN: 2G;
CARB: 50G;
FIBER: 6.5G;

CHOL: 0MG;
SODIUM: 39MG

EXCELLENT
SOURCE OF
FIBER,
VITAMIN K

GOOD
SOURCE OF
VITAMIN C

Preheat the oven to 375°F.

Combine the topping ingredients in a medium bowl and work them together with a fork or your fingertips until uniformly moistened.

To make the filling, combine the pears slices, lemon juice, and ginger in a large bowl. Add the granulated sugar and flour and toss to blend.

To assemble, coat an 8-inch square baking dish with cooking spray. Transfer the pear mixture to the dish. Sprinkle the topping evenly over the pears. Bake the crumble until the pears are fork-tender and the topping is golden brown, about 40 minutes. Let cool for 10 minutes before serving. (The crumble may also be stored in the refrigerator for 2 to 3 days.)

Serve the crumble warm or at room temperature, with a scoop of ice cream, if desired.

Raspberry Fool

Puréed and strained raspberries give this luxurious whipped dessert a gorgeous, bright pink color and a lovely tanginess to balance the sweet yogurt-cream base. It is the definition of elegance, served in cocktail glasses with crisp ladyfinger cookies.

1½ cups vanilla nonfat yogurt
One 10-ounce package frozen unsweetened raspberries, thawed
⅓ cup confectioners' sugar
¼ cup well-chilled heavy cream
4 ladyfinger cookies

SERVES 4
SERVING SIZE:
½ CUP

CHOL: 62MG;
SODIUM: 85MG

EXCELLENT
SOURCE OF
VITAMIN C

PER SERVING
CALORIES: 240;
TOTAL FAT: 7G
  MONO: 2G,
  POLY: 0.4G;
  SAT: 4G,
PROTEIN: 7G;
CARB: 40G;
FIBER: 1G;

**GOOD
SOURCE OF**
CALCIUM,
PHOSPHORUS,
PROTEIN,
RIBOFLAVIN,
VITAMIN B12

Place the yogurt in a strainer lined with a paper towel and let it drain and thicken in the refrigerator for at least 4 hours and up to 1 day. Discard the liquid and set the thickened yogurt aside.

Process half the raspberries in a food processor until smooth. Transfer the purée to a fine mesh strainer and strain it into a large bowl, pressing the liquid out with a rubber spatula. Discard the seeds. Whisk in the confectioners' sugar. Stir in the remaining raspberries.

In a chilled medium bowl, whip the cream with an electric mixer until soft peaks are formed. Gently fold in the yogurt. Fold in the raspberry mixture.

Spoon the fool into cocktail glasses and chill, covered with plastic wrap, for at least 1 hour and up to one day. Serve with ladyfinger cookies.

---

*   **EATING WELL TIP**
Well-chilled cream whips more easily and gives you more volume than room-temperature cream, which means a bigger dollop for the same amount of calories. So keep your cream refrigerated for at least 12 hours before using it and take it out just before whipping. It also helps to chill the bowl and beaters, too. You can whip cream several hours in advance and store it, covered, in the fridge until you are ready to use it.

Peaches with Balsamic Cherries

This recipe takes two summer favorites—peaches and cherries—and combines them in a fabulously unique dessert. Balsamic vinegar is the secret ingredient, transforming the cherries into a warm sauce that, when tossed with the peaches, softens them ever so slightly.

½ pound fresh sweet cherries, cut in half and pitted
2 tablespoons sugar, plus more to taste
2 tablespoons balsamic vinegar
1 pound ripe peaches, cut in half, pitted, and sliced

SERVES 4
SERVING SIZE:
1 CUP

EXCELLENT
SOURCE OF
VITAMIN C

PER SERVING
CALORIES: 100;
TOTAL FAT: 0G;
PROTEIN: 2G;
CARB: 25G;
FIBER: 3G;
CHOL: 0MG;
SODIUM: 2.5MG

GOOD
SOURCE OF
FIBER, NIACIN,
POTASSIUM,
VITAMIN A,
VITAMIN K

In a medium saucepan, stir together the cherries, 2 tablespoons of the sugar, and the vinegar, and place over medium heat. Bring to a boil and continue to cook for 5 minutes, stirring a few times. In a medium bowl, toss the warm cherries and their syrup with the peaches; taste and add more sugar if necessary. Serve warm.

Chocolate-Covered Banana Pops

These frozen bananas are fun to eat and feel like a real indulgence.

4 medium ripe but firm bananas
8 wooden craft sticks
3 tablespoons finely chopped lightly salted peanuts
6 ounces good-quality dark chocolate (60–70% cocoa solids), chopped

Peel, then cut each banana in half crosswise and insert a craft stick into each half. Place on a tray, cover with plastic wrap, and place in the freezer until frozen, about 3 hours.

   Place the peanuts in a shallow dish or on a plate. Melt the chocolate in the top of a double boiler over slightly simmering water, over the lowest possible heat, stirring frequently. Make sure the water is not touching the bottom of the top pan. Pour the melted chocolate into a tall glass. Dip each frozen banana into the chocolate, turning it to coat, and immediately roll in the peanuts. Place on a tray covered in waxed paper. Serve immediately or wrap individually in plastic wrap or waxed paper and freeze for up to 2 weeks.

SERVES 8
MAKES 8 BANANA POPS; SERVING SIZE: 1 POP

PER SERVING
CALORIES: 185;
TOTAL FAT: 11G
   MONO: 0G,
   POLY: 0G;
   SAT: 5G,

PROTEIN: 3G;
CARB: 25G;
FIBER: 3G;
CHOL: 0MG;
SODIUM: 23MG

GOOD SOURCE OF FIBER, VITAMIN A

* Chocolate Love

Chocolate contains substances that impart a sense of well-being which mimics the feeling of being in love. But you have another reason to feel good about eating chocolate: It may have serious health benefits. The cocoa bean is rich in flavonoids, powerful antioxidants that could help improve your skin and circulation and prevent heart disease. The antioxidant power in chocolate is in its cocoa solids, which also determine the darkness of the chocolate. When it comes to health, the darker (the higher the percentage of cocoa solids) the better. But 100% cocoa solids would be incredibly bitter. For the optimal balance of deliciousness and health, go for 60% (bittersweet) to 70% (extra bittersweet) dark chocolate. Cocoa powder and baking chocolate also have loads of antioxidant power. Milk chocolate has very little and white chocolate has virtually none. Spend a little extra to get the really good stuff and eat it sparingly to make it last—my rule of thumb is to keep it to one ounce a day, about the span and thickness of your three middle fingers.

Spiced Red Wine–Poached Pears

This elegant dessert puts pears on the pedestal they deserve. They come out sweet and juicy, colored a stunning shade of purple from the wine. The pear juices mingled with wine, orange, cinnamon, cloves, and a touch of sugar make a glorious syrup to drizzle on them.

2 cups dry red wine, such as Cabernet or Merlot
¼ cup plus 1 tablespoon sugar
Juice of 1 orange (about ½ cup)
One 1 x 3-inch strip orange zest
1 cinnamon stick
2 whole cloves
4 firm, ripe pears

SERVES 4
SERVING SIZE:
1 PEAR AND
2 TABLESPOONS
SYRUP

EXCELLENT SOURCE OF
MANGANESE,
VITAMIN C

GOOD SOURCE OF
FIBER,
POTASSIUM,
VITAMIN K

PER SERVING
CALORIES: 260;
TOTAL FAT: 0G;
PROTEIN: 1G;
CARB: 47G;
FIBER: 2.5G;
CHOL: 0MG;
SODIUM: 8MG

In a 4-quart saucepan, combine the wine, sugar, orange juice and zest, cinnamon stick, and cloves. Bring to a boil, reduce the heat to medium-low, and simmer for 5 minutes.

While the liquid is simmering, peel the pears, leaving the stem intact and being careful not to blemish the flesh of the pears. Slice ½ inch off the bottom of the pears to create a flat bottom they can stand on. Gently lay the pears down in the poaching liquid, cover, and simmer, turning them every 5 minutes to ensure even color, until they are cooked but still firm, 15 to 20 minutes.

Gently transfer the pears to a serving dish, keeping them upright. Let them cool to room temperature.

Meanwhile, with a slotted spoon, remove the orange zest, cloves, and cinnamon stick from the poaching liquid. Turn the heat up to medium-high and reduce the liquid until it is thick and slightly syrupy, about 15 minutes.

Drizzle each pear with 2 tablespoons of the warm syrup and serve. The pears and sauce may also be stored in the refrigerator for 1 to 2 days and served cold or at room temperature.

Apple-Cranberry Turnovers

Flaky phyllo dough makes a perfect golden brown wrapper for tender apple pie filling studded with cranberries. Crushed ladyfinger cookies layered with the dough make it extra crisp and lend a lovely sweetness.

4 Granny Smith apples (about 1½ pounds), peeled, cored, and cut into ¼-inch-thick slices
⅓ cup unsweetened dried cranberries
⅓ cup firmly packed light brown sugar
½ teaspoon ground cinnamon
Pinch of ground nutmeg
1 teaspoon cornstarch dissolved in 1 tablespoon cold water
6 sheets frozen phyllo dough, thawed
3 tablespoons canola oil
4 ladyfinger cookies, crushed
Cooking spray

SERVES 8
SERVING SIZE:
1 TURNOVER

PER SERVING
CALORIES: 200;
TOTAL FAT: 6.5G;
  MONO: 3.5G,
  POLY: 2G;
  SAT: 1G,

PROTEIN: 2G;
CARB: 35G;
FIBER: 2G;
CHOL: 20MG;
SODIUM: 82MG

**GOOD
SOURCE OF**
FIBER

Preheat the oven to 350°F.

In a large nonstick skillet, combine the apples, cranberries, brown sugar, cinnamon, and nutmeg and cook over medium heat, stirring occasionally, until the fruit is tender, about 10 minutes. Stir in the cornstarch slurry and cook until the juices in the skillet thicken, another 2 to 3 minutes. Set aside to cool.

Lay a sheet of phyllo on a large cutting board and brush with the oil. Top with a second sheet and brush with the oil. Sprinkle half of the crushed cookies on top. Add another sheet of phyllo and brush with the oil. Cut the layered phyllo into 4 long strips. Put a small mound of the apple mixture about an inch from the bottom of one strip and fold the phyllo over the mixture into a triangle-shaped pocket. Continue to fold the strip up in the way to maintain the triangle shape so a turnover is formed. Repeat with the other three strips. Repeat the whole process again with the remaining three sheets of phyllo so that you wind up with 8 turnovers. Be sure to reserve a little oil to brush the top of each turnover.

Coat a baking sheet with cooking spray, place the turnovers on the sheet, brush the tops with the remaining oil, and bake until nicely browned, 20 to 25 minutes. Serve warm.

✳ **EATING WELL TIP**
Puff pastry dough is a regular on the party circuit, used to blanket sausages, create turnovers, and make cups to hold sweet and savory fillings. But beware: It is loaded with the worst kinds of fat—trans fat and saturated fat. Fortunately, there are much-better-for-you crispy, flaky options. Baked wonton wrappers (used in Crab Salad in Crisp Wonton Cups on page 59) make lovely crunchy cups, and they contain very little fat. They also make lovely bite-size parcels. The same goes for phyllo dough, which you can brush with healthful olive oil, layer, and bake to produce exceptionally flaky cups or little pie crusts.

Rainbow Fruit Skewers with Chocolate-Dipped Strawberries

The full spectrum of fruit is represented all in a row, with a big, juicy chocolate-dipped strawberry payoff at the end. This is a delightful treat for kids and grown-ups alike. Just make sure you break off the pointy tip of the skewer for the little ones.

1 kiwi, peeled
1 large orange, peeled
½ cup large fresh blueberries, picked over for stems
1 cup pineapple chunks
12 Chocolate-Dipped Strawberries (recipe follows)

Cut the kiwi and orange crosswise into 4 rounds, then cut each round into 3 pieces, so you end up with 12 pieces of each fruit.

To prepare the skewers, work 2 blueberries about a third of the way down the skewer, add a piece of kiwi, a pineapple chunk, a piece of orange, and top with a chocolate-dipped strawberry. Serve immediately or refrigerate and serve within a few hours.

SERVES 12
SERVING SIZE:
2 SKEWERS

PER SERVING
CALORIES: 100;
TOTAL FAT: 3G
  MONO: 0G,
  POLY: 0G,
  SAT: 1.5G,
PROTEIN: 1G;
CARB: 19G;
FIBER: 3G;

CHOL: 2MG;
SODIUM: 1MG

EXCELLENT
SOURCE OF
MANGANESE,
VITAMIN C

GOOD
SOURCE OF
FIBER

Chocolate-Dipped Strawberries

Succulent strawberries luxuriously coated in smooth dark chocolate is the ultimate healthy indulgence.

2½ ounces good-quality dark chocolate (60–70% cocoa solids)
One 16-ounce container strawberries, washed, hulled, and patted dry

Line a tray with waxed paper. Break up the chocolate into small pieces and place about two-thirds of it in the top of a double boiler set over barely simmering water. Make sure that the bottom of the bowl does not touch the water. Stir occasionally, very gently, until the chocolate has melted, about 1 minute. Remove from the double boiler and add the rest of the chocolate, stirring gently until it has melted.

Dip the strawberries in the chocolate, place on the waxed paper, and chill in the refrigerator until the chocolate has set, about 15 minutes or up to several hours.

SERVES 6
SERVING SIZE:
3 MEDIUM
STRAWBERRIES

PER SERVING
CALORIES: 88;
TOTAL FAT: 4G
  MONO: 0G,
  POLY: 0G,
  SAT: 2.5G,
PROTEIN: 1G;
CARB: 13G;

FIBER: 2.5G;
CHOL: 1MG;
SODIUM: 1MG

EXCELLENT
SOURCE OF
VITAMIN C

GOOD
SOURCE OF
FIBER,
MANGANESE

Pumpkin Pie Flan

Pie-spiced pumpkin turns this classic caramel-covered Spanish custard into a Thanksgiving-worthy dessert.

Cooking spray
2/3 cup sugar
1/2 cup whole milk
1/4 cup evaporated milk
4 cups water
2 large eggs
2 large egg yolks
1 teaspoon vanilla extract
1/2 teaspoon ground nutmeg
1 teaspoon ground cinnamon
3/4 cup canned solid-pack pumpkin

SERVES 8
MAKES 8
INDIVIDUAL-SIZE
FLANS
SERVING SIZE:
1 FLAN

PER SERVING
CALORIES: 100;
TOTAL FAT: 3.5G
MONO: 1.2G,
POLY: 0.5G;
SAT: 1.5G,

PROTEIN: 3.5G;
CARB: 16G;
FIBER: 1G;
CHOL: 110MG;
SODIUM: 35MG

EXCELLENT
SOURCE OF
VITAMIN A

GOOD
SOURCE OF
SELENIUM

Arrange eight 4-ounce ramekins in a 9 x 13-inch baking pan. Coat the ramekins lightly with cooking spray.

In a small saucepan, heat 1/3 cup of the sugar over medium heat, stirring constantly, until it melts and forms medium-brown caramel, about 7 minutes. Working quickly, transfer 2 teaspoons of the caramel to each ramekin, swirling as soon as you spoon in the caramel (it will harden quickly). Set aside.

Combine the whole milk and evaporated milk in a medium saucepan over medium heat until warm. Reduce the heat to a low simmer and keep warm.

Meanwhile, bring the water to a boil and keep hot.

Whisk together the whole eggs, egg yolks, the remaining 1/3 cup sugar, the vanilla, nutmeg, and cinnamon in a medium bowl. Fold in the pumpkin, then fold the pumpkin mixture into the warm milk mixture. Divide the filling among the ramekins, then place the baking pan in the oven. Pour the hot water into the baking pan until it reaches halfway up the sides of the ramekins. Bake until the flans are just set, 35 to 40 minutes. Let cool completely.

Place a dessert plate on top of each ramekin and invert; the flan should slide out and syrup should flow onto the sides of the dish. The flans may be plated several hours ahead, covered with plastic wrap, and refrigerated.

Watermelon, Lime, and Mint Granita

This icy pleasure is the very essence of watermelon, but even more refreshing. Bright pink with flecks of green mint, it is as beautiful to look at as it is to eat. And it will definitely cool you off on the hottest summer days.

9 cups (about 4 pounds with the rind) seeded and cubed watermelon
1 cup fresh mint leaves, finely chopped, plus more for garnish
⅓ cup fresh lime juice
⅓ cup sugar

SERVES 8-10
SERVING SIZE:
1 CUP

FIBER: 0G;
CHOL: 0MG;
SODIUM: 4MG

PER SERVING
CALORIES: 70;
TOTAL FAT: 0G;
PROTEIN: 1G;
CARB: 18G;

**EXCELLENT
SOURCE OF**
VITAMIN A,
VITAMIN C

Working in two batches, purée the watermelon in a food processor. Strain the purée through a fine mesh sieve, forcing the liquid out with a wooden spoon. Discard the solids.

Combine the watermelon purée, mint, lime juice, and sugar in a 9 x 13-inch metal pan. Place the mixture in the freezer, scraping it thoroughly with a fork every 20 to 30 minutes for about 2½ hours, until the granita resembles coarse crystals. Scrape one last time and spoon into parfait glasses or bowls. Top with a mint sprig.

* ## Mindful Eating

One of the cornerstones of my approach to food is eating mindfully, enjoying each bite thoroughly and extracting every drop of pleasure from it. This is especially relevant when it comes to dessert, which people often gobble guiltily as if they are trying to get rid of it before someone catches them with it. Whether you are eating one of the better-for-you desserts here or an outrageous dessert at a restaurant, make sure you savor it slowly, relishing each bite without judging yourself. You'll likely end up eating less and enjoying it more.

Very Vanilla Rice Pudding

This pudding is intoxicatingly fragrant and flavorful, offering a big dose of comforting deliciousness. Arborio rice, the same kind used in risotto, lends a thick creaminess to this pudding without the addition of any cream, while the vanilla soy milk imparts a richer flavor and texture than regular milk.

2 cups water

1 cup Arborio rice

3 cups vanilla soy milk

¼ cup sugar

Pinch of salt

1 cinnamon stick

½ teaspoon vanilla extract

¼ teaspoon ground cinnamon, plus more for dusting

¼ teaspoon ground nutmeg, plus more for dusting

SERVES 8
SERVING SIZE: ⅔ CUP

PER SERVING
CALORIES: 154;
TOTAL FAT: 2G
  MONO: 0G,
  POLY: 0G;
  SAT: 0.5G,

PROTEIN: 5G;
CARB: 36G;
FIBER: 0.7G;
CHOL: 1.7MG;
SODIUM: 59MG

**GOOD
SOURCE OF**
PROTEIN

Preheat the oven to 375°F.

Bring the water to a boil in a medium, heavy, ovenproof saucepan. Add the rice, cover, reduce the heat to low, and simmer until the rice is nearly cooked, about 20 minutes.

In a large bowl, whisk together the soy milk, sugar, and salt. When the rice is cooked and still hot, add the soy milk mixture and cinnamon stick. Cover, place in the oven, and cook for 45 minutes.

Remove from the oven, uncover, and remove the cinnamon stick. Stir in the vanilla, ground cinnamon, and nutmeg. The pudding will be slightly liquidy; the liquid will continue to absorb into the rice and thicken as the pudding cools. Distribute among 8 bowls. Dust with more cinnamon and nutmeg. Serve warm or at room temperature. The pudding will keep in the refrigerator in an airtight container for about 3 days.

Dark Chocolate Mousse

This is a real chocolate lover's mousse, deep, dark, and rich. Its smooth, creamy base is silken tofu, which is essentially flavorless on its own, so the chocolate can really take over. For a thick mousse, use the silken tofu labeled "firm" in the shelf-stable box. The kind you find in the refrigerator section will yield a slightly thinner, but equally decadent dessert.

One 12.3-ounce package silken tofu, drained
3 ounces good-quality dark chocolate (60–70% cocoa solids), finely chopped
¼ cup unsweetened cocoa powder, preferably Dutch-processed
¼ cup water
1 tablespoon brandy
½ cup plus ½ teaspoon confectioners' sugar
¼ cup well-chilled heavy cream
1½ teaspoons shaved chocolate (use a vegetable peeler to do this)

SERVES 6
SERVING SIZE:
⅓ CUP MOUSSE,
1 HEAPING TABLE-
SPOON WHIPPED
CREAM, AND
¼ TEASPOON
SHAVED
CHOCOLATE

PER SERVING
CALORIES: 235;
TOTAL FAT: 11.5G
MONO: 2G,

POLY: 1G;
SAT: 6G,
PROTEIN: 5G;
CARB: 29G;
FIBER: 1G;
CHOL: 16MG;
SODIUM: 13MG

GOOD
SOURCE OF
PROTEIN

In a blender or food processor, process the tofu until it is very smooth.

Combine the chopped chocolate, cocoa, water, and brandy in a small saucepan or heatproof bowl fitted over a pot containing 1 inch of barely simmering water. Stir frequently until melted and smooth. Remove from the heat. Mix in ½ cup of the confectioners' sugar, a little at a time, until smooth. Add the chocolate mixture to the tofu and process until smooth and well blended. Spoon the mousse into small ramekins or champagne glasses, cover with plastic wrap, and refrigerate for at least 1 hour and up to 3 days.

Whip the cream in a medium bowl with an electric mixer until the cream is about halfway to soft peaks, then add the remaining ½ teaspoon confectioners' sugar and finish whipping until it barely holds a soft peak. Top each serving with a dollop of whipped cream and a sprinkle of chocolate shavings and serve.

Chocolate Cherry-Almond Biscotti

Chunks of dark chocolate, nutty almonds, and fruity cherries are a flavor trio that makes these biscotti really stand out. Dip them in coffee for an ultrasatisfying afternoon pick-me-up.

1¼ cups all-purpose flour
1¼ cups whole-wheat pastry flour or regular whole-wheat flour
1½ teaspoons baking powder
½ teaspoon salt
½ cup sugar
2 large eggs
¼ cup olive oil
1 teaspoon finely grated orange zest
1 teaspoon vanilla extract
½ cup dried tart cherries, finely chopped
½ cup raw almonds, finely chopped
2 ounces good-quality dark chocolate (60–70% cocoa solids), finely chopped

SERVES 12
SERVING SIZE:
1 BISCOTTI

PER SERVING
CALORIES: 228;
TOTAL FAT: 10G
  MONO: 6G,
  POLY: 1G;
  SAT: 2G,
PROTEIN: 5G;
CARB: 31G;

FIBER: 2G;
CHOL: 35MG;
SODIUM: 178MG

EXCELLENT SOURCE OF
THIAMIN

GOOD SOURCE OF
PROTEIN
RIBOFLAVIN

Preheat the oven to 350°F.

In a medium bowl, whisk together the flours, baking powder, and salt. In a large bowl, beat together the sugar, eggs, oil, orange zest, and vanilla until well combined. In batches, add the flour mixture until the mixture forms a dough. Stir in the cherries, almonds, and chocolate.

Transfer the dough to a floured work surface and knead several times. Shape into a log about 10 inches long and 3 inches wide. Transfer to a parchment lined baking sheet and bake for 25 minutes. Transfer to a wire rack and let cool for 15 minutes.

With a serrated knife, cut the log across at a diagonal into ½-inch-thick slices. Arrange on the baking sheet, cut side down, and bake for 10 minutes. Turn the cookies over and bake until golden, 5 to 10 minutes longer. Transfer to a wire rack to cool. Keep the biscotti stored at room temperature in an airtight container, where they will keep for about a week.

Triple Chocolate Cookies

You'd never think by tasting these sinful-seeming treats that they are actually better for you than most cookies. With their powerful chocolate chunk flavor and soft texture, all you'll be able to think is "yummmm."

¼ cup (½ stick) unsalted butter, softened
½ cup firmly packed dark brown sugar
¼ cup granulated sugar
¼ cup canola oil
1 large egg
1 teaspoon vanilla extract
½ cup all-purpose flour
½ cup whole-wheat pastry flour or regular whole-wheat flour
¼ cup unsweetened natural cocoa powder
¼ teaspoon salt (optional)
2 ounces good-quality dark chocolate (60–70% cocoa solids), coarsely chopped
2 ounces milk chocolate, coarsely chopped
⅔ cup chopped pecans (optional)

SERVES 24
SERVING SIZE :
1 COOKIE

PER SERVING
CALORIES: 110;
TOTAL FAT: 6G
  MONO: 2G,
  POLY: 1G;
  SAT: 2.5G,

PROTEIN: 1G;
CARB: 13G;
FIBER: 1G;
CHOL: 15MG;
SODIUM: 7MG

Preheat the oven to 350°F.

In a large bowl, mash together the butter and sugars with a fork until well combined. Add the oil and egg and beat until creamy. Mix in the vanilla.

In a medium bowl, whisk together the flours, cocoa, and salt, if using. Add the flour mixture to the butter mixture and mix well. Stir in both chocolates and, if desired, the pecans, and mix well. Using a tablespoon, scoop the batter onto an ungreased cookie sheet. Bake until the cookies are just set, about 12 minutes. Transfer the cookies to a rack to cool. Store the cookies at room temperature in an airtight container, where they will keep for up to 4 days.

* DID YOU KNOW?
Cocoa powder is low in fat and loaded with antioxidants. It can be used to replace some of the flour in baked goods.

Vanilla Hot Cocoa

The cozy factor of this drink is off the charts, thanks to vanilla's aromatic calming effect.

1 cup nonfat milk
1 cinnamon stick
2 teaspoons unsweetened cocoa powder
2 teaspoons sugar
2 teaspoons water
¼ teaspoon vanilla extract
¼ teaspoon shaved dark chocolate

SERVES 1
MAKES ONE
8-OUNCE MUG

PER SERVING
CALORIES: 155;
TOTAL FAT: 4G
  MONO: 1G,
  POLY: 0G;
  SAT: 2G,
PROTEIN: 9G;
CARB: 22G;
FIBER: 1G;

CHOL: 14MG;
SODIUM: 119MG

**EXCELLENT
SOURCE OF**
CALCIUM,
VITAMIN D

**GOOD
SOURCE OF**
PROTEIN,
VITAMIN A

In a small saucepan, heat the milk and cinnamon stick over medium-low heat until scalding hot (little bubbles will start forming around the edge of the pan), about 4 minutes. While the milk is warming, put the cocoa and sugar in a mug. Add the water to the mug and stir until it has the consistency of a paste. Remove the cinnamon stick from the milk, add the cocoa mixture and vanilla to the milk, and whisk until slightly frothy. Pour into the mug, top with the chocolate shavings, and enjoy.

Ginger Spiced Hot Cocoa

One of my favorite new-fashioned additions to chocolate is ginger, which adds a tingly excitement to the deep chocolate flavor. It works especially well in this warming hot cocoa.

1 cup nonfat milk
One ¼-inch-thick slice fresh ginger, peeled and sliced into 2 rounds
2 teaspoons unsweetened cocoa powder
2 teaspoons sugar
2 teaspoons water
¼ teaspoon dark chocolate shavings

SERVES 1
MAKES ONE
8-OUNCE MUG

PER SERVING
CALORIES: 165;
TOTAL FAT: 4G
  MONO: 1G,
  POLY: 0G;
  SAT: 2G,
PROTEIN: 9G;
CARB: 24G;
FIBER: 1G;

CHOL: 14MG;
SODIUM: 120MG

**EXCELLENT
SOURCE OF**
CALCIUM,
VITAMIN D

**GOOD
SOURCE OF**
PROTEIN,
VITAMIN A

In a small saucepan, heat the milk and ginger together over medium-low heat until scalding hot (little bubbles will start forming around the edge of the pan), about 4 minutes.

While the milk is warming, put the cocoa and sugar into a mug. Add the water to the mug and stir until the mixture has the consistency of a paste.

Remove the ginger from the warmed milk. Add the cocoa mixture to the milk and whisk until slightly frothy. Pour the hot chocolate into the mug, top with the chocolate shavings, and enjoy.

Chocolate Egg Cream

An egg cream is a frothy, indulgent drink that tastes similar to an ice cream soda. My dad made them for me all the time when I was a kid, and he showed me the right way to maximize the glorious foam head and was clear that you need a pretzel rod as an edible stirrer. I make my own simple chocolate syrup instead of using the traditional store-bought one.

1 tablespoon unsweetened cocoa powder
2½ tablespoons sugar
1 tablespoon boiling water
½ cup very cold nonfat milk
1½ cups seltzer water (not club soda)
1 pretzel rod

SERVES 1
MAKES ONE
16-OUNCE GLASS

PER SERVING
CALORIES: 230;
TOTAL FAT: 2G
  MONO: 0.5G,
  POLY: 0G;
  SAT: 1G,
PROTEIN: 6.5G;

CARB: 50G;
FIBER: 1G;
CHOL: 7.5MG;
SODIUM: 190MG

**GOOD
SOURCE OF**
CALCIUM,
PROTEIN,
VITAMIN D

In a small cup, mix together the cocoa and sugar. Add the water and stir well until a paste is formed. Put the milk in a tall fountain glass. Slowly add the seltzer water. Stir gently. Drizzle the chocolate syrup in slowly, being careful to disturb the foam as little as possible. Stir gently with a tall spoon. Your drink should be two-toned, chocolate brown on the bottom with white foam on top. Serve with a pretzel rod.

Equivalent Charts

LIQUID/DRY MEASURES	
U.S.	**METRIC**
¼ teaspoon	1.25 milliliters
½ teaspoon	2.5 milliliters
1 teaspoon	5 milliliters
1 tablespoon (3 teaspoons)	15 milliliters
1 fluid ounce (2 tablespoons)	30 milliliters
¼ cup	60 milliliters
⅓ cup	80 milliliters
½ cup	120 milliliters
1 cup	240 milliliters
1 pint (2 cups)	480 milliliters
1 quart (4 cups; 32 ounces)	960 milliliters
1 gallon (4 quarts)	3.84 liters
1 ounce (by weight)	28 grams
1 pound	454 grams
2.2 pounds	1 kilogram

OVEN TEMPERATURES		
°F	**GAS MARK**	**°C**
250	½	120
275	1	140
300	2	150
325	3	165
350	4	180
375	5	190
400	6	200
425	7	220
450	8	230
475	9	240
500	10	260
550	Broil	290

Index